M. K. Gandhi

NON-VIOLENT RESISTANCE

(Satyagraha)

SCHOCKEN BOOKS • NEW YORK

First SCHOCKEN edition 1961

10   83 84 85

This edition is published by arrangement
with the Navajivan Trust, Ahmedabad

Library of Congress Catalog Card No. 61-16650

Printed in the United States of America

ISBN 0-8052-0017-7

EDITOR'S NOTE

Satyagraha means literally 'clinging to truth', and as Truth for Gandhiji was God, Satyagraha in the general sense of the word means the way of life of one who holds steadfastly to God and dedicates his life to Him. The true Satyagrahi is, accordingly, a man of God.

Such an individual in this world finds himself up against evil, which he cannot but resist. He comes across injustice, cruelty, exploitation and oppression. These he has to oppose with all the resources at his command. In his crusade his reliance is on Truth or God; and since the greatest truth is the unity of all life, Truth can be attained only by loving service of all, i.e. by non-violence. The weapon of the Satyagrahi is therefore non-violence. Satyagraha, in the narrower sense in which it is ordinarily understood, accordingly means resisting evil through soul-force or non-violence.

For the required soul-force the individual has to discipline himself in self-control, simplicity of life, suffering without fear or hatred, recognition of the unity of all living beings, and whole-hearted and disinterested service of one's neighbours. The vows which Gandhiji elaborated for members of his Satyagraha Ashram at Sabarmati are of interest from this point of view. They were truth, non-violence, *brahmacharya*, fearlessness, control of the palate, non-possession, non-stealing, bread-labour, equality of religions, anti-untouchability and *swadeshi*.

Gandhiji derived his doctrine of Satyagraha from many sources. It can be traced essentially to the *Gita* ideal of the *karmayogin*, and also to Jesus' Sermon on the Mount; and recently to the writings of Thoreau, Ruskin and more especially Tolstoy. But his practical application of it in the social and political spheres was entirely his own.

Satyagraha, in the narrower sense, takes many forms. Primarily it is a case of appealing to the reason and conscience of the opponent by inviting suffering on oneself. The motive is to convert the opponent and make him one's willing ally and friend. It is based on the idea that the moral appeal to the heart and conscience is, in the case of human beings, more effective than an appeal based on threat of bodily pain or violence. Indeed violence, according to Gandhiji, does not ever overcome evil; it suppresses it for the time being to rise later with redoubled vigour. Non-violence, on the other hand, puts an end to evil, for it converts the evil-doer.

But the non-violence which thus overcomes evil is not the passive resistance of the weak. The non-violence of a Satyagrahi is unflinching. It is the non-violence of the brave. It will lead the Satyagrahi to die with a smile on his lips and with no trace of hatred in his heart.

iii

It presupposes a disciplined character, selflessness and unswerving devotion to duty. The passive resister, or the one who adopts non-violence as policy, on the other hand, is really not non-violent, for he would be violent if he could, and is nonviolent only because he does not for the time being have the means or the capacity for violence. It is a far cry, therefore, from passive resistance to Satyagraha.

Satyagraha may take the form of non-cooperation. When it does, it is not non-cooperation with the evil-doer but with his evil deed. This is an important distinction. The Satyagrahi cooperates with the evil-doer in what is good, for he has no hatred for him. On the contrary, he has nothing but friendship for him. Through cooperating with him in what is not evil, the Satyagrahi wins him over from evil.

Satyagraha may at times take the form of fasting. When it does, there is to be no trace of self in the motive. The fast should be prompted by the highest devotion to duty and love for the opponent. It should aim at purifying oneself, for lack of capacity to convince the opponent shows defect in oneself. It should seek to influence the opponent by converting him, not by coercing him to do something against his conviction. Fasting should be undertaken, according to Gandhiji, only when one is thoroughly convinced of the rightness of one's stand, when all other methods have failed, and as a last resort, and never for personal gain. It should be in the nature of prayer for purity and strength and power from God.

Satyagraha in the political sphere assumes the form of Civil Disobedience. It is for this form of Satyagraha that Gandhiji came to be most reputed. It means mass resistance on a non-violent basis against the Government when negotiations and constitutional methods have failed. It is called 'civil' because it is non-violent resistance by people who are ordinarily law-abiding citizens; also because the laws which they choose to disobey are not moral laws but only such as are harmful to the people. It is civil also in the sense that those who break the law are to observe the greatest courtesy and gentleness in regard to those who enforce the law. They are even to seek not to embarrass the opponent if possible.

Gandhiji organized such Satyagraha for the first time in South Africa against humiliating laws enforced by the South African Government on Indians in that country. With the experience so gained, he organized successfully peasant Satyagraha in Champaran, Kheda, and Bardoli to remove specific local grievances.

But Satyagraha can also be on a nation-wide scale to resist an entire Government when that Government is corrupt and demoralizes the people. It may then take the form of non-cooperation with the Government, as it did in Gandhiji's Civil Disobedience movements of 1920-22, 1930-34 and 1940-44 in India. Non-cooperation may express itself in giving up titles and honours bestowed by the Government, resignation from Government service, withdrawal from the police and military, non-payment of taxes, boycott of courts, schools and legislatures, and running parallel institutions to perform these functions. Gandhiji, however, was very cautious in regard to some of these forms of non-cooperation, as they were likely to bring down on the people the wrath of an indignant Government, and he did not want the people to suffer more than was necessary from Government repression.

Such Civil Disobedience demands on the part of the people disciplined group action, infinite capacity for suffering without retaliation, and strict obedience to leaders. As this discipline and obedience are not, as in the case of the military, based on force, the leaders have to be men of character and public service, whom the people respect and willingly obey. This implies that the leaders are men who generally carry on various forms of constructive service for the people. Gandhiji, therefore, emphasized working of his Constructive Programme as essential for Satyagraha; and not only for this reason, but also because discipline and group action need to be built up steadily among the people. They have to be taught, for example, cooperation, communal unity, fearlessness, consideration for the social good, self-help and resourcefulness, and have to have physical, mental and moral strength. All this can be done only through various forms of constructive endeavour advocated by Gandhiji, such as working for economic self-sufficiency in villages; education, abolition of drink and untouchability, communal concord, uplift of women, sanitation, hygiene, improved diet, child welfare, and so on. Satyagraha in the political sphere is not, therefore, a plan of action adopted merely for a time, wound up thereafter, and requiring no further effort; it presupposes day to day non-political constructive work aiming at the all-around development of the individual from the cradle to the grave.

In this respect Satyagraha or non-violent resistance, as conceived by Gandhiji, has an important lesson for pacifists and war-resisters of the West. Western pacifists have so far proved ineffective because they have thought that war can be resisted by mere propaganda, conscientious objection, and organization for settling disputes. Gandhiji showed that non-violence to be effective requires constructive effort in every sphere of life, individual, social, economic and political. These spheres have to be organized and refashioned in such a way that the people will have learnt to be non-violent in their daily lives, manage their affairs on a cooperative and non-violent basis, and thus have acquired sufficient strength and resourcefulness to be able to offer non-violent resistance against organized violence. The practice of non-violence in the political sphere is not, therefore, a mere matter of preaching or even of establishing arbitration courts or Leagues of Nations, but involves building up brick by brick with patience and industry a new non-violent social and economic order. It depends ultimately on banishing violence from the heart of the individual, and making of him a transformed disciplined person. Gandhiji's contribution lay in evolving the necessary technique and showing by example how all this can be done.

There can be no doubt that in developing Satyagraha in its various forms as a practical means of overcoming violence, more especially in group life, Gandhiji established a new mile-stone in the history of the human race in its march towards peace on earth and goodwill among men. He himself did not claim finality for his methods, as after all he was a pioneer in the field and a humble experimenter. The science of Satyagraha is therefore still in the making. But his teachings and experience are invaluable for all future students and makers of this science. The purpose of this volume is to help in the process by making available for the reader Gandhiji's findings in his own words and in as comprehensive a form as possible.

Bombay, August, 1950   BHARATAN KUMARAPPA

From my introductory note to Section Eighth the impression is created that the *Harijan* after its suspension in November 1940 was permitted to be published again only in February, 1946. This is wrong. As a matter of fact it was restarted in January, 1942, after a lapse of about 14 months. It was published in three separate languages (English, Gujarati and Hindi) by the Navajivan Press from Ahmedabad till August of that year when the press was confiscated by the Government after the arrest of Gandhiji and other leaders. Since that time the press remained in the custody of the Government and the publication of the *Harijan* weeklies could be resumed only in February, 1946.

NON-ENGLISH WORDS WITH THEIR MEANINGS

Abkari : a tax on spirituous liquors and narcotics

Anand : bliss

Abhyasa : repetition, study

Ahimsa : non-violence

Bhajan : a religious song

Bhang : an intoxicant drink made from a kind of hemp

Brahmachari : a celibate

Brahmacharya : celibacy, continence

Bhakti : devotion

Brahma : the Divine Reality

Brahmavidya : knowledge of the Divine Reality, the Upanishads

Charkha : a spinning wheel

Chit : knowledge

Diva-dandi : a light-house

Dhurana : mode of extorting compliance to any demand

Dukkha : misery

Duragraha : foolish obstinacy

Ganja : a kind of hemp

Goonda : a ruffian

Goondaism : reign of ruffians

Gumasta : a shop-assistant

Guru : a teacher

Hai Hai : shame, shame

Harijans : literally, the people of Hari, i.e. God; the name which Gandhiji gave to untouchables

Harijan, Harijanbandhu, Harijansevak : names of weekly journals in English Gujarati and Hindi respectively, conducted by Mahatma Gandhi

Hartal : cessation of work; a strike

Hathayoga : a rigorous mode of religious meditation

Hijrat : exodus or going away from one's native land

Himsa : violence

Jam-i-Jam : universal provider

Kalpadruma : a tree supposed to grant all desires

Khaddar, Khadi : hand-spun and hand-woven cloth

Lathi : a long stick

Lotaful : potful (*lota*, a metal pot)

Mahajan : a trade guild, elders of a trade guild

Mahatma : a high-souled man

Mahayajna : a great sacrifice

Mantra : a sacred incantation meant for recitation and meditation

Mukti : emancipation

Navajivan : literally new life; name of a weekly journal in Gujarati edited by Mahatma Gandhi

Neti, Neti : not this, not this

Nirvana : extinction

Panchama : a fifth-caste man, an outcaste

Pan : a kind of leaf chewed with lime and betel nut

Pardanashin : sitting behind a purdah (veil), veiled

Purna Swaraj : complete independence

Raj : a kingdom

Rishi : a seer

Salaam : a salute

Sanatani : orthodox

Sangha : a commune, an association

Sarkari : governmental

Sat, Satya : Truth

Satyagraha : clinging to truth; civil or non-violent disobedience or resistance

Satyagrahashram : Ashram founded by Gandhi at Ahmedabad in 1915

Satyagrahi : a follower of Satyagraha

Savarna : belonging to one of the four castes

Sena : an army

Shastra : a scripture

Shethia : a merchant, a wealthy man

Shraddha : ceremony in honour of departed spirits of dead relatives

Swadeshi : of indigenous or native make; the principle of using goods made locally or in one's own country

Swaraj : self-government, home-rule

Tahsil : a district

Takli : a wooden or metal device for spinning

Talati : a village revenue officer

Tapa, Tapasya : penance, religious austerity

Thana : a police station

Tonga : horse-carriage

Vairagya : aversion or indifference to worldly interests, desirelessness

Varnashrama : the four castes and stages in life

Yajna : a sacrifice

Young India : name of a weekly journal in English edited by Gandhi

Zoolum : oppression

CONTENTS

SECTION THIRD : NON-CO-OPERATION AND
CIVIL DISOBEDIENCE

III. Satyagraha in Social Reform

SECTION TENTH : QUESTIONS AND ANSWERS

SECTION ELEVENTH : CONCLUSION

SATYAGRAHA

SECTION FIRST : WHAT SATYAGRAHA IS

1

SATYAGRAHA, CIVIL DISOBEDIENCE
PASSIVE RESISTANCE, NON-CO-OPERATION

Satyagraha is literally holding on to Truth and it means, therefore, Truth-force. Truth is soul or spirit. It is, therefore, known as soul-force. It excludes the use of violence because man is not capable of knowing the absolute truth and, therefore, not competent to punish. The word was coined in South Africa to distinguish the non-violent resistance of the Indians of South Africa from the contemporary ' passive resistance ' of the suffragettes and others. It is not conceived as a weapon of the weak.

Passive resistance is used in the orthodox English sense and covers the suffragette movement as well as the resistance of the Non-conformists. Passive resistance has been conceived and is regarded as a weapon of the weak. Whilst it avoids violence, being not open to the weak, it does not exclude its use if, in the opinion of a passive resister, the occasion demands it. However, it has always been distinguished from armed resistance and its application was at one time confined to Christian martyrs.

Civil Disobedience is civil breach of unmoral statutory enactments. The expression was, so far as I am aware, coined by Thoreau to signify his own resistance to the laws of a slave State. He has left a masterly treatise on the duty of Civil Disobedience. But Thoreau was not perhaps an out and out champion of non-violence. Probably, also, Thoreau limited his breach of statutory laws to the revenue law, i.e. payment of taxes. Whereas the

term Civil Disobedience as practised in 1919 covered a
breach of any statutory and unmoral law. It signified the
resister's outlawry in a civil, i.e., non-violent manner. He
invoked the sanctions of the law and cheerfully suffered
imprisonment. It is a branch of Satyagraha.

Non-co-operation predominantly implies withdrawing
of co-operation from the State that in the non-co-operator's
view has become corrupt and excludes Civil Disobedience
of the fierce type described above. By its very nature,
non-co-operation is even open to children of understanding
and can be safely practised by the masses. Civil Disobedience presupposes the habit of willing obedience to laws
without fear of their sanctions. It can, therefore, be practised only as a last resort and by a select few in the first
instance at any rate. Non-co-operation, too, like Civil
Disobedience is a branch of Satyagraha which includes all
non-violent resistance for the vindication of Truth.

Young India, 23-3-'21

2

DOMESTIC SATYAGRAHA

I had read in some books on vegetarianism that salt
was not a necessary article of diet for man, that on the
contrary saltless diet was better for health. I had deduced
that a *brahmachari* benefited by a saltless diet. I had
read and realized that the weak-bodied should avoid
pulses. I was very fond of them. Now it happened that
Kasturba,* who had a brief respite after that operation,
had again begun getting hemorrhage and the malady
seemed to be obstinate. Hydropathic treatment by itself
did not answer. Kasturba had not much faith in my
remedies though she did not resist them. She certainly
did not ask for outside help. So when all my remedies
had failed, I entreated her to give up salt and pulses. She
would not agree, however much I pleaded with her,

---
* Gandhiji's wife.

supporting myself with authorities. At last she challenged me saying that even I could not give up these articles if I was advised to do so. I was pained and equally delighted, — delighted in that I got an opportunity to shower my love on her. I said to her : " You are mistaken. If I was ailing and the doctor advised me to give up these or any other articles I should unhesitatingly do so. But there ! Without any medical advice, I give up salt and pulses for one year, whether you do so or not."

She was rudely shocked and exclaimed in deep sorrow : " Pray forgive me. Knowing you, I should not have provoked you. I promise to abstain from these things, but for heaven's sake take back your vow. This is too hard on me."

" It is very good for you to give up these articles. I have not the slightest doubt that you will be all the better without them. As for me, I cannot retract a vow seriously taken. And it is sure to benefit me, for all restraint, whatever prompts it, is wholesome for man. You will therefore leave me alone. It will be a test for me, and a moral support to you in carrying out your resolve."

So she gave me up. " You are too obstinate. You will listen to none," she said, and sought relief in tears.

I would like to count this incident as an instance of Satyagraha and as one of the sweetest recollections of my life.

Medically there may be two opinions as to the value of a saltless and pulseless diet, but morally I have no doubt that all self-denial is good for the soul. The diet of a man of self-restraint must be different from that of a man of pleasure just as their ways of life are different.

The Story of My Experiments with Truth, Part IV — Chapter XXIX

3

SATYAGRAHA *

For the past thirty years I have been preaching and practising Satyagraha. The principles of Satyagraha, as I know it today, constitute a gradual evolution.

Satyagraha differs from Passive Resistance as the North Pole from the South. The latter has been conceived as a weapon of the weak and does not exclude the use of physical force or violence for the purpose of gaining one's end, whereas the former has been conceived as a weapon of the strongest and excludes the use of violence in any shape or form.

The term *Satyagraha* was coined by me in South Africa to express the force that the Indians there used for full eight years and it was coined in order to distinguish it from the movement then going on in the United Kingdom and South Africa under the name of Passive Resistance.

Its root meaning is holding on to truth, hence truth-force. I have also called it Love-force or Soul-force. In the application of Satyagraha I discovered in the earliest stages that pursuit of truth did not admit of violence being inflicted on one's opponent but that he must be weaned from error by patience and sympathy. For what appears to be truth to the one may appear to be error to the other. And patience means self-suffering. So the doctrine came to mean vindication of truth not by infliction of suffering on the opponent but on one's self.

But on the political field the struggle on behalf of the people mostly consists in opposing error in the shape of unjust laws. When you have failed to bring the error home to the lawgiver by way of petitions and the like, the only remedy open to you, if you do not wish to submit to error, is to compel him by physical force to yield to you or by suffering in your own person by inviting the penalty for the breach of the law. Hence Satyagraha largely

---

* Extract from a Statement by Gandhiji to the Hunter Committee.

appears to the public as Civil Disobedience or Civil Resistance. It is civil in the sense that it is not criminal.

The lawbreaker breaks the law surreptitiously and tries to avoid the penalty, not so the civil resister. He ever obeys the laws of the State to which he belongs, not out of fear of the sanctions but because he considers them to be good for the welfare of society. But there come occasions, generally rare, when he considers certain laws to be so unjust as to render obedience to them a dishonour. He then openly and civilly breaks them and quietly suffers the penalty for their breach. And in order to register his protest against the action of the law givers, it is open to him to withdraw his co-operation from the State by disobeying such other laws whose breach does not involve moral turpitude.

In my opinion, the beauty and efficacy of Satyagraha are so great and the doctrine so simple that it can be preached even to children. It was preached by me to thousands of men, women and children commonly called indentured Indians with excellent results.

Rowlatt Bills *

When the Rowlatt Bills were published I felt that they were so restrictive of human liberty that they must be resisted to the utmost. I observed too that the opposition to them was universal among Indians. I submit that no State however despotic has the right to enact laws which are repugnant to the whole body of the people, much less a Government guided by constitutional usage and precedent such as the Indian Government. I felt too that the oncoming agitation needed a definite direction if it was neither to collapse nor to run into violent channels.

The Sixth April

I ventured therefore to present Satyagraha to the country emphasizing its civil-resistance aspect. And as

---

* For information about the Rowlatt Act see Editor's introductory notes to III Non-co-operation and Civil Disobedience, at the commencement of Chapter 43 below.

it is purely an inward and purifying movement I suggested the observance of fast, prayer and suspension of all work for one day — the 6th of April. There was a magnificent response throughout the length and breadth of India even in little villages although there was no organization and no great previous preparation. The idea was given to the public as soon as it was conceived. On the 6th April there was no violence used by the people and no collision with the police worth naming. The *hartal* was purely voluntary and spontaneous. I attach hereto the letter in which the idea was announced.

My Arrest

The observance of the 6th April was to be followed by Civil Disobedience. For the purpose the committee of the Satyagraha Sabha had selected certain political laws for disobedience. And we commenced the distribution of prohibited literature of a perfectly healthy type, e.g., a pamphlet written by me on Home Rule, a translation of Ruskin's *Unto This Last*, *The Defence and Death of Socrates*, etc.

Disorder

But there is no doubt that the 6th of April found India vitalized as never before. The people who were fear-stricken ceased to fear authority. Moreover, hitherto the masses had lain inert. The leaders had not really acted upon them. They were undisciplined. They had found a new force but they did not know what it was and how to use it.

At Delhi the leaders found it difficult to restrain the very large number of people who had remained unmoved before. At Amritsar, Dr Satyapal was anxious that I should go there and show to the people the peaceful nature of Satyagraha. Swami Shraddhanandji from Delhi and Dr Satyapal from Amritsar wrote to me asking me to go to their respective places for pacifying the people and for explaining to them the nature of Satyagraha. I had never been to Amritsar and for that matter to the Punjab before. These two messages were sent by the authorities and they knew that I was invited to both the places for peaceful purposes.

I left Bombay for Delhi and the Punjab on the 8th April and had telegraphed to Dr Satyapal whom I had never met before to meet me at Delhi. But after passing Mathura I was served with an order prohibiting me from entering the Province of Delhi. I felt that I was bound to disregard this order and I proceeded on my journey. At Palwal I was served with an order prohibiting me from entering the Punjab and confining me to the Bombay Presidency. And I was arrested by a party of Police and taken off the train at that station. The Superintendent of the Police who arrested me acted with every courtesy. I was taken to Mathura by the first available train and thence by goods train early in the morning to Siwai Madhupur, where I joined the Bombay Mail from Peshawar and was taken charge of by Superintendent Bowring. I was discharged at Bombay on the 10th April.

But the people of Ahmedabad and Viramgam and in Gujarat generally had heard of my arrest. They became furious, shops were closed, crowds gathered and murder, arson, pillage, wire-cutting and attempts at derailment followed.

Young India, 14-1-'20

4

MEANS AND ENDS

Reader : Why should we not obtain our goal, which is good, by any means whatsoever, even by using violence ? Shall I think of the means when I have to deal with a thief in the house ? My duty is to drive him out anyhow. You seem to admit that we have received nothing, and that we shall receive nothing by petitioning. Why, then, may we not do so by using brute force ? And, to retain what we may receive we shall keep up the fear by using the same force to the extent that it may be necessary. You will not find fault with a continuance of force to prevent a child from thrusting its foot into fire? Somehow or other we have to gain our end.

Editor : Your reasoning is plausible. It has deluded many. I have used similar arguments before now. But I think I know better now, and I shall endeavour to undeceive you. Let us first take the argument that we are justified in gaining our end by using brute force because the English gained theirs by using similar means. It is perfectly true that they used brute force and that it is possible for us to do likewise, but by using similar means we can get only the same thing that they got. You will admit that we do not want that. Your belief that there is no connection between the means and the end is a great mistake. Through that mistake even men who have been considered religious have committed grievous crimes. Your reasoning is the same as saying that we can get a rose through planting a noxious weed. If I want to cross the ocean, I can do so only by means of a vessel ; if I were to use a cart for that purpose, both the cart and I would soon find the bottom. " As is the God, so is the votary ", is a maxim worth considering. Its meaning has been distorted and men have gone astray. The means may be likened to a seed, the end to a tree ; and there is just the same inviolable connection between the means and the end as there is between the seed and the tree. I am not likely to obtain the result flowing from the worship of God by laying myself prostrate before Satan. If, therefore, any one were to say : " I want to worship God ; it does not matter that I do so by means of Satan," it would be set down as ignorant folly. We reap exactly as we sow. The English in 1833 obtained greater voting power by violence. Did they by using brute force better appreciate their duty ? They wanted the right of voting, which they obtained by using physical force. But real rights are a result of performance of duty ; these rights they have not obtained. We, therefore, have before us in England the force of everybody wanting and insisting on his rights, nobody thinking of his duty. And, where everybody wants rights, who shall give them to whom ? I do not wish to imply that they do no duties. They don't perform the duties corresponding to those rights ; and as they do not perform that particular duty, namely, acquire fitness, their rights have proved a burden to them. In other words, what they have obtained is an exact result of the means they adopted. They used the means corresponding to the end. If I want to deprive you of your watch, I shall certainly have to fight for it ; if I want to buy your watch, I shall have to pay for it ; and if I want a gift, I shall have to plead for it ; and, according to the means I employ, the watch is stolen property, my own property, or a donation. Thus we see three different results from three different means. Will you still say that means do not matter ?

Now we shall take the example given by you of the thief to be driven out. I do not agree with you that the thief may be driven out by any means. If it is my father who has come to steal I shall use one kind of means. If it is an acquaintance I shall use another ; and in the case of a perfect stranger I shall use a third. If it is a white man, you will perhaps say you will use means different from those you will adopt with an Indian thief. If it is a weakling, the means will be different from those to be adopted for dealing with an equal in physical strength ; and if the thief is armed from top to toe, I shall simply remain quiet. Thus we have a variety of means between the father and the armed man. Again, I fancy that I should pretend to be sleeping whether the thief was my father or that strong armed man. The reason for this is that my father would also be armed and I should succumb to the strength possessed by either and allow my things to be stolen. The strength of my father would make me weep with pity ; the strength of the armed man would rouse in me anger and we should become enemies. Such is the curious situation. From these examples we may not be able to agree as to the means to be adopted in each case. I myself seem clearly to see what should be done in all these cases, but the remedy may frighten you. I therefore hesitate to place it before you. For the time being I will leave you to guess it, and if you cannot, it is clear you will have to adopt different means in each case. You will also have seen that any means will not avail to drive away the thief. You will have to adopt means to fit each case. Hence it follows that your duty is not to drive away the thief by any means you like.

Let us proceed a little further. That well-armed man has stolen your property ; you have harboured the thought of his act ; you are filled with anger ; you argue that you want to punish that rogue, not for your own sake, but for the good of your neighbours ; you have collected a number of armed men, you want to take his house by assault ; he is duly informed of it, he runs away ; he too is incensed. He collects his brother robbers, and sends you a defiant message that he will commit robbery in broad daylight. You are strong, you do not fear him, you are prepared to receive him. Meanwhile, the robber pesters your neighbours. They complain before you. You reply that you are doing all for their sake, you do not mind that your own goods have been stolen. Your neighbours reply that the robber never pestered them before, and that he commenced his depredations only after you declared hostilities against him. You are between Scylla and Charybdis. You are full of pity for the poor men. What they say is true. What are you to do ? You will be disgraced if you now leave the robber alone. You, therefore, tell the poor men : " Never mind. Come, my wealth is yours, I will give you 'arms, I will teach you how to use them ; you should belabour the rogue ; don't you leave him alone." And so the battle grows ; the robbers increase in numbers ; your neighbours have deliberately put themselves to inconvenience. Thus the result of wanting to take revenge upon the robber is that you have disturbed your own peace ; you are in perpetual fear of being robbed and assaulted ; your courage has given place to cowardice. If you will patiently examine the argument, you will see that I have not overdrawn the picture. This is one of the means. Now let us examine the other. You set this armed robber down as an ignorant

brother ; you intend to reason with him at a suitable
opportunity ; you argue that he is, after all, a fellow man ;
you do not know what prompted him to steal. You, therefore, decide that, when you can, you will destroy the man's
motive for stealing. Whilst you are thus reasoning with
yourself, the man comes again to steal. Instead of being
angry with him you take pity on him. You think that this
stealing habit must be a disease with him. Henceforth,
you, therefore, keep your doors and windows open, you
change your sleeping-place, and you keep your things in
a manner most accessible to him. The robber comes again
and is confused as all this is new to him ; nevertheless, he
takes away your things. But his mind is agitated. He
inquires about you in the village, he comes to learn about
your broad and loving heart, he repents, he begs your
pardon, returns you your things, and leaves off the stealing
habit. He becomes your servant, and you will find for him
honourable employment. This is the second method. Thus,
you see, different means have brought about totally different results. I do not wish to deduce from this that robbers
will act in the above manner or that all will have the
same pity and love like you, but I only wish to show
that fair means alone can produce fair results, and that,
at least in the majority of cases, if not indeed in all, the
force of love and pity is infinitely greater than the force
of arms. There is harm in the exercise of brute force, never
in that of pity.

Now we will take the question of petitioning. It is a
fact beyond dispute that a petition, without the backing
of force, is useless. However, the late Justice Ranade
used to say that petitions served a useful purpose because
they were a means of educating people. They give the
latter an idea of their condition and warn the rulers.
From this point of view, they are not altogether useless.
A petition of an equal is a sign of courtesy ; a petition
from a slave is a symbol of his slavery. A petition backed
by force is a petition from an equal and, when he trans-
mits his demand in the form of a petition, it testifies to
his nobility. Two kinds of force can back petitions. " We

shall hurt you if you do not give this," is one kind of force ; it is the force of arms, whose evil results we have already examined. The second kind of force can thus be stated : " If you do not concede our demand, we shall be no longer your petitioners. You can govern us only so long as we remain the governed ; we shall no longer have any dealings with you." The force implied in this may be described as love-force, soul-force, or, more popularly but less accurately, passive resistance.* This force is indestructible. He who uses it perfectly understands his position. We have an ancient proverb which literally means : " One negative cures thirty-six diseases." The force of arms is powerless when matched against the force of love or the soul.

Now we shall take your last illustration, that of the child thrusting its foot into fire. It will not avail you. What do you really do to the child ? Supposing that it can exert so much physical force that it renders you powerless and rushes into fire, then you cannot prevent it. There are only two remedies open to you — either you must kill it in order to prevent it from perishing in the flames, or you must give your own life because you do not wish to see it perish before your very eyes. You will not kill it. If your heart is not quite full of pity, it is possible that you will not surrender yourself by preceding the child and going into the fire yourself. You, therefore, helplessly allow it to go to the flames. Thus, at any rate, you are not using physical force. I hope you will not consider that it is still physical force, though of a low order, when you would forcibly prevent the child from rushing towards the fire if you could. That force is of a different order and we have to understand what it is.

Remember that, in thus preventing the child, you are minding entirely its own interest, you are exercising authority for its sole benefit. Your example does not apply to the English. In using brute force against the English

---

* Finding the word misleading Gandhiji later called the same force Satyagraha or non-violent resistance.   — Ed.

you consult entirely your own, that is the national, interest. There is no question here either of pity or of love.
If you say that the actions of the English, being evil,
represent fire, and that they proceed to their actions
through ignorance, and that therefore they occupy the
position of a child and that you want to protect such a
child, then you will have to overtake every evil action of
that kind by whomsoever committed and, as in the case
of the evil child, you will have to sacrifice yourself. If
you are capable of such immeasurable pity, I wish you
well in its exercise.

Hind Swaraj or Indian Home Rule, chap. xvi

5

SATYAGRAHA OR PASSIVE RESISTANCE

Reader :   Is there any historical evidence as to the
success of what you have called soul-force or truth-force ?
No instance seems to have happened of any nation having
risen through soul-force. I still think that the evil-doers
will not cease doing evil without physical punishment.

Editor :   The poet Tulsidas has said : " Of religion,
pity, or love, is the root, as egotism of the body. Therefore, we should not abandon pity so long as we are alive."
This appears to me to be a scientific truth. I believe in it
as much as I believe in two and two being four. The force
of love is the same as the force of the soul or truth. We
have evidence of its working at every step. The universe
would disappear without the existence of that force. But
you ask for historical evidence. It is, therefore, necessary
to know what history means. The Gujarati equivalent
means : " It so happened ". If that is the meaning of
history, it is possible to give copious evidence. But, if it
means the doings of kings and emperors, there can be no
evidence of soul-force or passive resistance in such history.
You cannot expect silver ore in a tin mine. History, as
we know it, is a record of the wars of the world, and so

there is a proverb among Englishmen that a nation which has no history, that is, no wars, is a happy nation. How kings played, how they became enemies of one another, how they murdered one another, is found accurately recorded in history, and if this were all that had happened in the world, it would have been ended long ago. If the story of the universe had commenced with wars, not a man would have been found alive today. Those people who have been warred against have disappeared as, for instance, the natives of Australia of whom hardly a man was left alive by the intruders. Mark, please, that these natives did not use soul-force in self-defence, and it does not require much foresight to know that the Australians will share the same fate as their victims. " Those that take the sword shall perish by the Sword." With us the proverb is that professional swimmers will find a watery grave.

The fact that there are so many men still alive in the world shows that it is based not on the force of arms but on the force of truth or love. Therefore, the greatest and most unimpeachable evidence of the success of this force is to be found in the fact that, in spite of the wars of the world, it still lives on.

Thousands, indeed tens of thousands, depend for their existence on a very active working of this force. Little quarrels of millions of families in their daily lives disappear before the exercise of this force. Hundreds of nations live in peace. History does not and cannot take note of this fact. History is really a record of every interruption of the even working of the force of love or of the soul. Two brothers quarrel ; one of them repents and re-awakens the love that was lying dormant in him ; the two again begin to live in peace ; nobody takes note of this. But if the two brothers, through the intervention of solicitors or some other reason, take up arms or go to law — which is another form of the exhibition of brute force — their doing would be immediately noticed in the press, they would be the talk of their neighbours and would probably go down to history. And what is true of families and communities is true of nations. There is no reason to believe that there is one law for families and another for nations. History, then, is a record of an interruption of the course of nature. Soul-force, being natural, is not noted in history.

Reader : According to what you say, it is plain that instances of this kind of passive resistance are not to be found in history. It is necessary to understand this passive resistance more fully. It will be better, therefore, if you enlarge upon it.

Editor : Passive resistance is a method of securing rights by personal suffering ; it is the reverse of resistance by arms. When I refuse to do a thing that is repugnant to my conscience, I use soul-force. For instance, the Government of the day has passed a law which is applicable to me. I do not like it. If by using violence I force the Government to repeal the law, I am employing what may be termed body-force. If I do not obey the law and accept the penalty for its breach, I use soul-force. It involves sacrifice of self.

Everybody admits that sacrifice of self is infinitely superior to sacrifice of others. Moreover, if this kind of force is used in a cause that is unjust, only the person using it suffers. He does not make others suffer for his mistakes. Men have before now done many things which were subsequently found to have been wrong. No man can claim that he is absolutely in the right or that a particular thing is wrong because he thinks so, but it is wrong for him so long as that is his deliberate judgment. It is therefore meet that he should not do that which he knows to be wrong, and suffer the consequence whatever it may be. This is the key to the use of soul-force.

Reader : You would then disregard laws — this is rank disloyalty. We have always been considered a law-abiding nation. You seem to be going even beyond the extremists. They say that we must obey the laws that have been passed, but that if the laws be bad, we must drive out the law-givers even by force.

Editor : Whether I go beyond them or whether I do not is a matter of no consequence to either of us. We simply want to find out what is right and to act accordingly. The real meaning of the statement that we are a law-abiding nation is that we are passive resisters. When we do not like certain laws, we do not break the heads of law-givers but we suffer and do not submit to the laws. That we should obey laws whether good or bad is a new-fangled notion. There was no such thing in former days. The people disregarded those laws they did not like and suffered the penalties for their breach. It is contrary to our manhood if we obey laws repugnant to our conscience. Such teaching is opposed to religion and means slavery. If the Government were to ask us to go about without any clothing, should we do so ? If I were a passive resister, I would say to them that I would have nothing to do with their law. But we have so forgotten ourselves and become so compliant that we do not mind any degrading law.

A man who has realized his manhood, who fears only God, will fear no one else. Man-made laws are not necessarily binding on him. Even the Government does not expect any such thing from us. They do not say : " You must do such and such a thing," but they say : " If you do not do it, we will punish you." We are sunk so low that we fancy that it is our duty and our religion to do what the law lays down. If man will only realize that it is unmanly to obey laws that are unjust, no man's tyranny will enslave him. This is the key to self-rule or home-rule.

It is a superstition and ungodly thing to believe that an act of a majority binds a minority. Many examples can be given in which acts of majorities will be found to have been wrong and those of minorities to have been right. All reforms owe their origin to the initiation of minorities in opposition to majorities. If among a band of robbers a knowledge of robbing is obligatory, is a pious man to accept the obligation ? So long as the superstition that men should obey unjust laws exists, so long will their slavery exist. And a passive resister alone can remove such a superstition.

To use brute-force, to use gunpowder, is contrary to passive resistance, for it means that we want our opponent to do by force that which we desire but he does not. And, if such a use of force is justifiable, surely he is entitled to do likewise by us. And so we should never come to an agreement. We may simply fancy, like the blind horse moving in a circle round a mill, that we are making progress. Those who believe that they are not bound to obey laws which are repugnant to their conscience have only the remedy of passive resistance open to them. Any other must lead to disaster.

Hind Swaraj or Indian Home Rule, chap. XVII

6

EVIDENCE BEFORE THE HUNTER COMMITTEE

(Extracts)

1. Examination by Lord Hunter

Q. I take it, Mr Gandhi, that you are the author of the Satyagraha movement.

A. Yes, Sir.

Q. Will you explain it briefly ?

A. It is a movement intended to replace methods of violence and a movement based entirely upon truth. It is, as I have conceived it, an extension of the domestic law on the political field, and my experience has led me to the conclusion that that movement, and that alone, can rid India of the possibility of violence spreading throughout the length and breadth of the land, for the redress of grievances.

Q. It was adopted by you in connection with the opposition to the Rowlatt Act. And in that connection you asked the people to sign the Satyagraha pledge.

A. Yes, Sir.

Q. Was it your intention to enlist as many men as possible in the movement ?

A. Yes, consistently with the principle of truth and non-violence. If I got a million men ready to act according to those principles, I would not mind enlisting them all.

Q. Is it not a movement essentially antagonistic to Government because you substitute the determination of the Satyagraha Committee for the will of the Government ?

A. That is not the spirit in which the movement has been understood by the people.

Q. I ask you to look at it from the point of view of the Government. If you were a Governor yourself, what would you say to a movement that was started with the object of breaking those laws which your Committee determined ?

A. That would not be stating the whole case of the Satyagraha doctrine. If I were in charge of the Government and brought face to face with a body who, entirely in search of truth, were determined to seek redress from unjust laws without inflicting violence, I would welcome it and would consider that they were the best constitution-alists, and, as a Governor I would take them by my side as advisers who would keep me on the right path.

Q. People differ as to the justice or injustice of parti-cular laws ?

A. That is the main reason why violence is elimina-ted and a Satyagrahi gives his opponent the same right of independence and feelings of liberty that he reserves to himself, and he will fight by inflicting injuries on his own person.

Lord Hunter : I was looking at it from the point of view of the continuance of Government. Would it be possible to continue the Government if you had set up against the Government a body of men who would not accept the Government view but the view of an inde-pendent Committee ?

A. I have found from my experience that it was possible to do so during the eight years of continuous struggle in South Africa. I found General Smuts, who went through the whole of that campaign, at the end of it saying that if all conducted themselves as the Satyagrahis had done, they should have nothing to fear.

Q. But there was no such pledge in that campaign as is prescribed here ?

A. Certainly there was. Every Satyagrahi was bound to resist all those laws which he considered to be unjust and which were not of a criminal character, in order to bend the Government to the will of the people.

Q. I understand your vow contemplates breaking of laws which a Committee may decide.

A. Yes, my Lord. I want to make it clear to the Committee that that part of the vow was meant to be a restraint on individual liberty. As I intended to make it a mass movement, I thought the constitution of some such Committee as we had appointed was necessary, so that no man should become a law unto himself, and, therefore, we conceived the plan that the Committee would be able to show what laws might be broken.

Q. We hear that doctors differ, and, even Satyagrahis might differ ?

A. Yes, I found it so to my cost.

Q. Supposing a Satyagrahi was satisfied that a particular law was a just law and that the Committee did not obey this law, what is a Satyagrahi to do ?

A. He is not bound to disobey that law. We had such Satyagrahis in abundance.

Q. Is it not rather a dangerous campaign ?

A. If you will conceive the campaign as designed in order to rid the country of violence, then you will share with me the same concern for it ; I think that at any cost a movement of this character should live in the country in a purified state.

Q. By your pledge are you not binding a man's conscience ?

A. Not according to my interpretation of it. If my interpretation of the pledge is found to be incorrect, I shall mend my error if I have to start the movement again. (*Lord Hunter* — No, no, Mr Gandhi, I do not pretend to advise you.)

I wish I could disabuse the Committee of the idea that it is a dangerous doctrine. It is conceived entirely with the object of ridding the country of the idea of violence.

Lord Hunter here briefly detailed the circumstances preceding the passage of the Rowlatt Act, the widespread general Indian opposition to the Act etc., and asked Mr Gandhi to describe the essence of his objection to the legislation.

A. I have read the Rowlatt Committee's report to the end and the legislation foreshadowed in it, and I came to the conclusion that the legislation was not warranted by the facts produced by the Committee. I thought it was very restrictive of human liberty and that no self-respecting person or nation could allow such legislation. When I saw the debates in the Legislative Council, I felt that the opposition to it was universal. When I found the agitation against it, I felt that for me as a self-respecting individual and a member of a vast Empire, there was no course left open, but to resist that law to the utmost.

Q. So far as the objects of that legislation are concerned, have you any doubt that they are to put down revolutionary and anarchical crimes ?

A. They are quite laudable objects.

Q. Your complaint, then, must be as regards the methods adopted ?

A. Entirely.

Q. The method is, I understand, that greater power has been given to the executive than they enjoyed before.

A. That is so.

Q. But is it not the same power that the executive enjoyed under the Defence of India Act ?

A. That is true, but that was essentially an emergency measure designed to secure the co-operation of everybody in order to put down any violence that may be offered by any section of the community in connection with the successful carrying on of the war. It was assented to with the greatest reluctance. The Rowlatt legislation is of a different character altogether, and now the

experience of the working of the former Act has strengthened my objections to the Rowlatt Act.

Q. Mr Gandhi, the Rowlatt legislation is only to
operate if the local Government is satisfied that there is
anarchy.

A. I would not, as a legislator, leave that power in
the hands of an executive whom I have known to run mad
in India at times.

Q. Then really, your objection comes to this, that
the Government of India, in the prosecution of a laudable
object, adopted a wrong method. Therefore, is not the
proper method of dealing with that, from a constitutional
point of view, to endeavour to get the legislation remedied
by satisfying Government of the inexpediency of it ?

A. I approached on bended knees Lord Chelmsford.
and pleaded with him and with every English officer I
had the pleasure of meeting, and placed my views before
them, but they said they were helpless, and that the
Rowlatt Committee's recommendations had to be given
effect to. We had exhausted all the methods open to us.

Q. If an opponent differs from you, you cannot
satisfy him all of a sudden. You must do it by degrees.
Is it not rather a drastic way of attempting it by refusing
to obey the law ?

A. I respectfully beg to differ from Your Lordship.
If I find that even my father has imposed upon me a law
which is repugnant to my conscience, I think it is the
least drastic course that I could adopt, to respectfully tell
him that I cannot obey it. By that course I do nothing
but justice to my father, and, if I may say so without any
disrespect to the Committee, I have myself followed that
course with the greatest advantage and I have preached
that ever since. If it is not disrespectful to say so to my
father, it is not so to a friend and for that matter to my
Government.

Lord Hunter : In the prosecution of your Satyagraha
movement against the Rowlatt legislation you resolved
upon a general *hartal* throughout India. That *hartal* was
to be a day when no business was to be done and people

were generally to indicate by their attitude that they disapproved of the Government's action. A *hartal* means a general cessation throughout the whole country. Would it not create a very difficult situation ?

A. Cessation for a great length of time would create a difficult situation.

Mr Gandhi here explained how the observance of the *hartal* in some part of the country on the 30th March, and all over the country on the 6th April came about not on account of any miscalculation, but on account of the people in one part coming to know of the Viceregal assent to the Act earlier than the people in other parts.

Q. You agree that the abstention from work should be entirely voluntary ?

A. Yes, entirely voluntary, in the sense that persuasion on the day of the *hartal* would not be allowed, whereas persuasion by means of leaflets and other propaganda work on the other days would be perfectly legitimate, so long as no physical force was employed.

Q. You disapprove of people interfering with *tongas* on the day of the *hartal* ?

A. Certainly.

Q. You would not object to the police interfering in the case of such a disapprovable interference on the people's part ?

A. I would not if they acted with proper restraint and forbearance.

Q. But you agree that on the day of the *hartal* it was highly improper to jostle with other people and stop *tongas* ?

A. From a Satyagrahi standpoint I would hold it to be criminal.

Lord Hunter : Your leading lieutenant in Delhi, Swami Shraddhananda — *Mr Gandhi* interrupting : I would not call him my lieutenant, but an esteemed co-worker. — Did he write you a letter on the subject, and indicate to you that after what had occurred in Delhi and the Punjab, it was manifest that you could not prosecute a general *hartal* without violence inevitably ensuing ?

A. I cannot recall the contents of that letter. I think he went much further and said that it was not possible that the law-breaking campaign could be carried on with impunity among the masses. He did not refer to *hartal* proceeding. There was a difference of opinion between me and Swami Shraddhananda when I suspended civil disobedience. I found it necessary to suspend it because I had not obtained sufficient control, to my satisfaction, over the people. What Swami Shraddhananda said was that Satyagraha could not be taken as a mass movement. But I did not agree with his view and I do not know that he is not converted to my view today. The suspension of civil disobedience was as much necessary as prosecution for offences against law. I would like the Committee to draw a sharp distinction between *hartal* and civil disobedience. *Hartal* was designed to strike the imagination of the people and the Government. Civil disobedience was a discipline for those who were to offer disobedience. I had no means of understanding the mind of India except by some such striking movement. *Hartal* was a proper indication to me how far I would be able to carry civil disobedience.

Q. If there is a *hartal* side by side with the preaching of Satyagraha would it not be calculated to promote violence ?

A. My experience is entirely to the contrary. It was an amazing scene for me to see people collected in their thousands — men, women and even little children and babies marching peacefully in procession. The peaceful *hartals* would not have been at all possible if Satyagraha was not preached in the right way.

But as I have said a *hartal* is a different thing from civil disobedience in practice.

*   *   *

Lord Hunter : Now, the only matters that we have got to deal with here are as regards Ahmedabad itself. In Ahmedabad, as we have been told, you enjoy great popularity among the mill workers ?

Mr Gandhi : Yes.

Lord Hunter : And your arrest seems to have caused great resentment on their part and led to the very unfortunate actions of the mob on April 10, 11 and 12 in Ahmedabad and Viramgam ?

Mr Gandhi : Yes.

Lord Hunter : So far as those incidents are concerned you have no personal knowledge of them ?

Mr Gandhi : No.

Lord Hunter : I don't know whether there is anything that you can communicate to us in connection with those events to help us to form an opinion.

Mr Gandhi : I venture to present the opinion that I considered that the action of the mob, whether at Ahmedabad or at Viramgam, was totally unjustified, and I think that it was a sad thing that they lost self-control. But, at the same time, I would like to say that the people among whom, rightly or wrongly, I was popular, were put to a severe test by Government. They should have known better. I do not say that the Government committed an unpardonable error of judgment and the mob committed no error. On the contrary, I hold that it was more unpardonable on the part of the mob than on the part of Government.

Proceeding, Mr Gandhi narrated how he endeavoured to do what he could to repair the error. He placed himself entirely at the disposal of the authorities. He had a long interview with Mr Pratt and other officials. He was to have held a meeting of the people on the 13th but he was told that it would not be possible to hold it that day, not on account of Colonel Fraser's order, because he was promised every assistance in connection with the meeting, but that the notice of the meeting would not reach all the people that day. The meeting took place on the 14th. There he adumbrated what had happened. There he had to use the terms *organized* and *educated* both of which terms had been so much quoted against him and against the people. The speech was in Gujarati. Mr Gandhi explained and hoped Sir Chimanlal Setalwad would bear him out on a reference to the Gujarati speech that the word only means those who can read and write, and that he used the word and expressed the opinion as he sensed the thing at that time.

He emphasized it was not a previous organization that he meant ; he only meant to say, and there could be no mistaking the actual words in his speech, that the acts were done in an *organized manner*. He further emphasized that he was speaking of Ahmedabad only, that he had then no knowledge of what had happened even at Viramgam, and that he would not retract a single statement from that speech. In his opinion, said Mr Gandhi, violence was done in an organized manner. It cannot be interpreted to mean a deep-laid conspiracy. He laid special emphasis on the fact that while he used these expressions he was addressing the people, and not the police authorities.

If Mr Guider stated that a single name of the offenders was not forthcoming from him, he was entirely mistaken about his mission and had put an improper valuation upon the term *organization*. The crimes committed by the mob were the result of their being deluded by the wicked rumour of the arrest of Miss Anasuya. There was a class of half-educated people who possessed false ideas obtained from sources such as cinematographs and from silly novels and from political leaders. He knew that school. He had mixed with them and endeavoured to wean them. He had so far succeeded in his endeavours that there were today hundreds of people who had ceased to belong to the school of revolution.

Proceeding, Mr Gandhi said he had now given the whole meaning of what he had said. He had never meant that there were University men behind the disturbances. He did not say they were incapable of those acts, but he was not aware of any highly educated man directing the mob.

Lord Hunter : Do you imply that there was a common purpose on the part of the rioters ?

Mr Gandhi : I don't say that. It would be exaggerating to say that, but I think the common purpose was restricted to two or three men or parties who instigated the crimes.

Q. Did the agitation take an anti-European character?

A. It was certainly an anti-Government movement. I would fain believe it was not anti-European, but I have not yet made up my mind as to that.

Lord Hunter : I do not know whether you want to answer this or not. According to the Satyagraha doctrine, is it right that people who have committed crimes should be punished by the civil authorities?

Mr Gandhi : It is a difficult question to answer, because (through punishment) you anticipate pressure from outside. I am not prepared to say that it is wrong, but there is a better method. But I think, on the whole, it would be proper to say that a Satyagrahi cannot possibly quarrel with any punishment that might be meted out to an offender, and therefore he cannot be anti-Government in that sense.

Lord Hunter : But apparently it is against the doctrine of Satyagraha to give assistance to Government by way of placing the information that a Satyagrahi has that would lead to the conviction of offenders?

Mr Gandhi : According to the principle of Satyagraha it is inconsistent, for the simple reason that a Satyagrahi's business is not to assist the police in the method which is open to the police, but he helps the authorities and the police to make the people more law-abiding and more respectable to authority.

Lord Hunter : Supposing a Satyagrahi has seen one of the more serious crimes committed in these riots in his own presence. Would there be no obligation on him to inform the police?

Mr Gandhi : Of course I answered that question to Mr Guider before and I think I must answer it to Your Lordship. I don't want to misguide the youth of the country, but even then he cannot go against his own brother. When I say brother, I do not, of course, make any distinction of country or nationality. A Satyagrahi is wholly

independent of such a distinction. The Satyagrahi's position is somewhat similar to that of a counsel defending
an accused. I have known criminals of the deadliest type
and I may humbly claim to have been instrumental in
weaning them from crimes. I should be forfeiting their
confidence if I disclosed the name of a single man. But
supposing I found myself wanting in weaning them I
would surely not take the next step to go and inform the
police about them ; I do not hesitate to say that for a
Satyagrahi it is the straightest thing not to give evidence
of a crime done even under his nose. But there can be
only the rarest uses of this doctrine and even today I am
not able to say whether I would not give evidence against
a criminal whom I saw caught in the act.

Young India, 21-1-'20

2. Examination by Sir Chimanlal Setalwad

Sir Chimanlal : With regard to your Satyagraha
doctrine, so far as I understand it, it involves the pursuit
of truth and in that pursuit you invite suffering on yourself and do not cause violence to anybody else.

Mr Gandhi : Yes, Sir.

Q.   However honestly a man may strive in his search
for truth his notions of truth may be different from the
notions of others. Who then is to determine the truth ?

A.   The individual himself would determine that.

Q.   Different individuals would have different views
as to truth. Would that not lead to confusion ?

A.   I do not think so.

Q.   Honestly striving after truth is different in every
case.

A.   That is why the non-violence part was a necessary corollary. Without that there would be confusion
and worse.

Q.   Must not the person wanting to pursue truth be
of high moral and intellectual equipment ?

A.   No. It would be impossible to expect that from
every one. If A has evolved a truth by his own efforts

which B, C and others are to accept I should not require them to have the equipment of A.

Q. Then it comes to this that a man comes to a decision and others of lower intellectual and moral equipment would have to blindly follow him.

A. Not blindly. All I wish to urge is that each individual, unless he wants to carry on his pursuit of truth independently, needs to follow someone who has determined truth.

Q. Your scheme involves the determination of truth by people of high moral and intellectual equipment and a large number of people may follow them blindly being themselves unable to arrive at similar conclusions by reason of their lower intellectual equipment.

A. I would exact from them nothing more than I would expect from an ordinary being.

Q. I take it that the strength of the propaganda must depend on the number of its followers.

A. No. In Satyagraha success is possible even if there is only one Satyagrahi of the proper stamp.

Q. Mr Gandhi, you said you do not consider yourself a perfect Satyagrahi yet. The large mass of people are then even less so.

A. No. I do not consider myself an extraordinary man. There may be people more capable of determining truth than myself. Forty thousand Indians in South Africa, totally uncultured, came to the conclusion that they could be Satyagrahis and if I could take you through those thrilling scenes in the Transvaal you will be surprized to hear what restraint your countrymen in South Africa exhibited.

Q. But there you were all unanimous.

A. I have more solidity of opinion here than in South Africa.

Q. But there you had a clear-cut issue, not here.

A. Here too we have a clear-cut issue, viz. the Rowlatt Act.

Mr Gandhi then explained how he presented

Satyagraha as an instrument of infinitely greater power than violence.

Q. Does not suffering and going on suffering require extraordinary self-control ?

A. No ; no extraordinary self-control is required. Every mother suffers. Your countrymen, I submit, have got such control and they have exhibited that in a very large measure.

Q. Take Ahmedabad. Did they exhibit control here ?

A. All I say is, throughout India where you find these isolated instances of violence you will find a very large number of people who exercised self-restraint. Ahmedabad and other places show that we had not attained proper mastery over self. The Kaira people in the midst of grave provocation last year acted with the greatest self-restraint.

Q. Do you mean to say these acts of violence were mere accidents ?

A. Not accidents. But they were rare and would be rarer for a clear conception of Satyagraha. The country, I think, has sufficiently well realized the doctrine to warrant a second trial. I do feel sure that the country is all the purer and better for having gone through the fire of Satyagraha.

Q. Ordinarily your doctrine contemplates co-operation with the Government and elimination of race-hatred and inviting self-suffering. Does not suffering create ill-will ?

A. It is contrary to my thirty years' experience that people have by suffering been filled with any ill-will against the Government. In South Africa after a bitter struggle the Indians have lived on the best of terms with the Government, and Gen. Smuts was the recipient of an address which was voluntarily voted by the Indians.

Q. Is it possible to take part in the movement without taking the Satyagraha vow ?

A. I would ask them to take part in the non-civil-resistance part of the movement. The masses unless they took the pledge were not to do the civil-disobedience part

of the pledge. For those who were not civil resisters, therefore, another vow was devised asking people to follow
truth at all costs and to refrain from violence. I had suspended civil resistance then, and as it is open to a leader
to emphasize one part of the vow, I eliminated the civil-
resistance part which was not for that season suited to the
people, and placed the truth part before them.

*   *   *

Q. Is not the underlying idea embarrassment of
Government ?

A. Certainly not. A Satyagrahi relies not upon
embarrassment but upon self-suffering for securing
relief.

Q. Would not ordered Government be impossible ?

A. Ordered Government cannot be impossible if
totally inoffensive people break the laws. But I would
certainly make Government impossible if I found it had
taken leave of its senses.

Q. In your message you ask people to refrain from
violence and still violence occurred. Does it not show that
the ordinary mind finds it very difficult to practise the
theory of non-violence ?

A. After having used methods of violence for years
it is difficult for them to practise abstention.

Young India, 21-1-'20

3. Examination by Pandit Jagatnarain

Q. It is alleged that the Satyagraha movement would
embarrass the Government. Are you not afraid of any
such result of your movement ?

A. The Satyagraha movement is not started with
the intention of embarrassing the Government while
ordinary political agitation is often started with that
object. If a Satyagrahi finds his activities resulting in
embarrassing the Government, he will not hesitate to
face it.

Q. But you will agree with me that every political
agitation depends for its success on the number of
followers ?

A. I do not regard the force of numbers as necessary in a just cause, and in such a cause every man, be he high or low, can have his remedy.

Q. But you would certainly try to have as many men in your movement as possible ?

A. Not exactly so. A Satyagrahi depends only on truth and his capacity to suffer for truth.

Q. But in politics, Mahatmaji, how can a single man's voice be heard ?

A. That is exactly what I have been attempting to disprove.

Q. Do you believe that an English officer will take any notice of isolated attempts ?

A. Why, that is my experience. Lord Bentinck became an ordinary Mr at the instance of Keshavachandra Sen.

Q. Oh, you cite an example of an extraordinary man.

A. Men of ordinary abilities also can develop morality. No doubt I regard illiteracy among my people as deplorable and I consider it necessary to educate them, but it is not at all impossible for an absolutely illiterate man to imbibe the Satyagraha principle. This is my long-standing experience.

Here Mr Gandhi briefly cleared the distinction between *hartal* and Satyagraha. *Hartal* was no integral part of Satyagraha. It should be resorted to only when necessary. He tried and tried it successfully in connection with the deportation of Mr Horniman and the Khilafat movement.

Q. You can resort to no other remedy to oppose the irresponsible, foreign officials and that is why you have started this movement. Is it not ?

A. I cannot say that with certainty. I can conceive the necessity of Satyagraha in opposition to the would-be full responsible self-government. Our ministers can never claim to defend themselves on the score of their ignorance, whereas such a defence is available today for the English officers.

Q. But with all the rights of self-government we shall be able to dismiss the ministers.

A. I cannot feel on that point so assured for ever. In England it often happens that ministers can continue in the executive even though they lose all the confidence of the public. The same thing may happen here too and therefore I can imagine a state of things in this country which would need Satyagraha even under Home Rule.

Q. Would you think that there should be no unrest coming after the Satyagraha movement ?

A. Not only I do not think so, I would be disappointed if there were no unrest in case Anasuyabehn and I were arrested. But that unrest will not take the shape of violence. It pains a Satyagrahi to see others suffering ; Satyagrahis will follow each other to jail. I do wish for such unrest.

Young India, 4-2-'20

7

THE THEORY AND PRACTICE OF SATYAGRAHA

[The following is taken from an article by Gandhiji contributed to the Golden Number of *Indian Opinion* which was issued in 1914 as a souvenir of the eight years' Satyagraha in South Africa :]

Carried out to its utmost limit, Satyagraha is independent of pecuniary or other material assistance ; certainly, even in its elementary form, of physical force or violence. Indeed, violence is the negation of this great spiritual force, which can only be cultivated or wielded by those who will entirely eschew violence. It is a force that may be used by individuals as well as by communities. It may be used as well in political as in domestic affairs. Its universal applicability is a demonstration of its permanence and invincibility. It can be used alike by men, women and children. It is totally untrue to say that it is a force to be used only by the weak so long as they are not capable of meeting violence by violence. This superstition arises from the incompleteness of the English expression, *passive resistance*. It is impossible for those who consider themselves to be weak to apply this force. Only those who realize that there is something in man which is superior to the brute nature in him and that the latter always yields to it, can effectively be Satyagrahis. This force is to violence, and, therefore, to all tyranny, all injustice, what light is to darkness. In politics, its use is based upon the immutable maxim, that government of the people is possible only so long as they consent either consciously or unconsciously to be governed. We did not want to be governed by the Asiatic Act of 1907 of the Transvaal, and it had to go before this mighty force. Two courses were open to us : to use violence when we were called upon to submit to the Act, or to suffer the penalties prescribed under the Act, and thus to draw out and exhibit the force of the soul within us for a period long enough to appeal to the sympathetic chord in the governors or the law-makers. We have taken long to achieve what we set about striving for. That was because our Satyagraha was not of the most complete type. All Satyagrahis do not understand the full value of the force, nor have we men who always from conviction refrain from violence. The use of this force requires the adoption of poverty, in the sense that we must be indifferent whether we have the wherewithal to feed or clothe ourselves. During the past struggle, all Satyagrahis, if any at all, were not prepared to go that length. Some again were only Satyagrahis so called. They came without any conviction, often with mixed motives, less often with impure motives. Some even, whilst engaged in the struggle, would gladly have resorted to violence but for most vigilant supervision. Thus it was that the struggle became prolonged ; for the exercise of the purest soul-force, in its perfect form, brings about instantaneous relief. For this exercise, prolonged training of the individual soul is an absolute necessity, so that a perfect Satyagrahi has to be almost, if not entirely, a perfect man. We cannot all suddenly become such men, but if my proposition is correct — as I know it to be correct — the greater the spirit of Satyagraha in us, the better men will we become. Its use, therefore, is, I think, indisputable, and it is a force, which, if it became universal, would revolutionize social ideals and do away with despotisms and the ever-growing militarism under which the nations of the West are groaning and are being almost crushed to death, and which fairly promises to overwhelm even the nations of the East. If the past struggle has produced even a few Indians who would dedicate themselves to the task of becoming Satyagrahis as nearly perfect as possible, they would not only have served themselves in the truest sense of the term, they would also have served humanity at large. Thus viewed, Satyagraha is the noblest and best education. It should come, not after the ordinary education in letters, of children, but it should precede it. It will not be denied, that a child, before it begins to write its alphabet and to gain worldly knowledge, should know what the soul is, what truth is, what love is, what powers are latent in the soul. It should be an essential of real education that a child should learn, that in the struggle of life, it can easily conquer hate by love, untruth by truth, violence by self-suffering.

Young India, 3-11-'27

SECTION SECOND : DISCIPLINE FOR SATYAGRAHA

8

SATYAGRAHA ASHRAM VOWS

[The vows were the principles which Gandhiji believed every Satyagrahi should follow in his daily life. The following were sent as a series of weekly discourses on the vows during 1930 from the Yeravda Jail to members of his Ashram at Sabarmati. We include discourses on only four of the vows here, viz. those of Truth, Non-violence, Chastity and Non-possession. The remaining seven are : Fearlessness, Control of the Palate, Non-stealing, Bread-Labour, Equality of Religions, Anti-untouchability and Swadeshi. The interested reader is referred for Gandhiji's discourses on them to his booklet *From Yeravda Mandir* (published by the Navajivan Publishing House, Ahmedabad). — Ed.]

Importance of Vows

Taking vows is not a sign of weakness, but of strength. To do at any cost something that one ought to do constitutes a vow. It becomes a bulwark of strength. A man who says that he will do something ' as far as possible ', betrays either his pride or his weakness. I have noticed in my own case, as well as in the case of others, that the limitation ' as far as possible ' provides a fatal loophole. To do something ' as far as possible ' is to succumb to the very first temptation. There is no sense in saying that one would observe truth ' as far as possible '. Even as no businessman will look at a note in which a man promises to pay a certain amount on a certain date ' as far as possible ', so will God refuse to accept a promissory note drawn by a man, who will observe truth as far as possible.

God is the very image of the vow. God would cease to be God if He swerved from His own laws even by a

37

hair's breadth. The sun is a greater keeper of observances ;
hence the possibility of measuring time and publishing
almanacs. All business depends upon men fulfilling their
promises. Are such promises less necessary in character
building or self-realization ? We should therefore never
doubt the necessity of vows for the purpose of self-purification and self-realization.

I

Truth

I deal with Truth first of all, as the Satyagraha Ashram
owes its very existence to the pursuit and the attempted
practice of Truth.

The word *Satya* (Truth) is derived from *Sat*, which
means ' being '. Nothing is or exists in reality except
Truth. That is why *Sat* or Truth is perhaps the most
important name of God. In fact it is more correct to say
that Truth is God, than to say that God is Truth. But as we
cannot do without a ruler or a general, names of God such
as ' King of Kings ' or ' the Almighty ' are and will remain
generally current. On deeper thinking, however, it will be
realized, that *Sat* or *Satya* is the only correct and fully
significant name for God.

And where there is Truth, there also is knowledge
which is true. Where there is no Truth, there can be no
true knowledge. That is why the word *Chit* or knowledge
is associated with the name of God. And where there is
true knowledge, there is always bliss (*Ananda*). Sorrow
has no place there. And even as Truth is eternal, so is
the bliss derived from it. Hence we know God as *Sat-chit-
ananda*, One who combines in Himself Truth, Knowledge
and Bliss.

Devotion to this Truth is the sole justification for
our existence. All our activities should be centred in
Truth. Truth should be the very breath of our life. When
once this stage in the pilgrim's progress is reached, all
other rules of correct living will come without effort, and
obedience to them will be instinctive. But without Truth

it would be impossible to observe any principles or rules in life.

Generally speaking, observation of the law of Truth is understood merely to mean that we must speak the truth. But we in the Ashram should understand the word *Satya* or Truth in a much wider sense. There should be Truth in thought, Truth in speech, and Truth in action. To the man who has realized this Truth in its fulness, nothing else remains to be known, because all knowledge is necessarily included in it. What is not included in it is not Truth, and so not true knowledge ; and there can be no inward peace without true knowledge. If we once learn how to apply this never-failing test of Truth, we will at once be able to find out what is worth doing, what is worth seeing, what is worth reading.

But how is one to realize this Truth, which may be likened to the philosopher's stone or the cow of plenty ? By single-minded devotion (*abhyasa*) and indifference to all other interests in life (*vairagya*) — replies the *Bhagavadgita*. In spite, however, of such devotion, what may appear as truth to one person will often appear as untruth to another person. But that need not worry the seeker. Where there is honest effort, it will be realized that what appear to be different truths are like the countless and apparently different leaves of the same tree. Does not God Himself appear to different individuals in different aspects ? Yet we know that He is one. But Truth is the right designation of God. Hence there is nothing wrong in every man following Truth according to his lights. Indeed it is his duty to do so. Then if there is a mistake on the part of any one so following Truth, it will be automatically set right. For the quest of Truth involves *tapas* — self-suffering, sometimes even unto death. There can be no place in it for even a trace of self-interest. In such selfless search for Truth nobody can lose his bearings for long. Directly he takes to the wrong path he stumbles, and is thus redirected to the right path. Therefore the pursuit of Truth is true *bhakti* (devotion). It is the path that leads to God. There is no place in it for cowardice, no

place for defeat. It is the talisman by which death itself
becomes the portal to life eternal.

In this connection it would be well to ponder over
the lives and examples of Harishchandra, Prahlad, Rama-
chandra, Imam Hasan and Imam Husain, the Christian
saints, etc. How beautiful it would be, if all of us, young
and old, men and women, devoted ourselves wholly to
Truth in all that we might do in our waking hours, whether
working, eating, drinking or playing, till dissolution of the
body makes us one with Truth ? God as Truth has been for
me a treasure beyond price ; may He be so to every one
of us.

II

Ahimsa or Love

We saw last week how the path of Truth is as narrow
as it is straight. Even so is that of *ahimsa*. It is like
balancing oneself on the edge of a sword. By concentration an acrobat can walk on a rope. But the concentration
required to tread the path of Truth and *ahimsa* is far
greater. The slightest inattention brings one tumbling to
the ground. One can realize Truth and *ahimsa* only by
ceaseless striving.

But it is impossible for us to realize perfect Truth
so long as we are imprisoned in this mortal frame. We can
only visualize it in our imagination. We cannot, through
the instrumentality of this ephemeral body, see face to
face Truth which is eternal. That is why in the last resort
one must depend on faith.

It appears that the impossibility of full realization of
Truth in this mortal body led some ancient seeker after
Truth to the appreciation of *ahimsa*. The question which
confronted him was : " Shall I bear with those who
create difficulties for me, or shall I destroy them ? " The
seeker realized that he who went on destroying others did
not make headway but simply stayed where he was, while
the man who suffered those who created difficulties marched ahead, and at times even took the others with him.

The first act of destruction taught him that the Truth which was the object of his quest was not outside himself but within. Hence the more he took to violence, the more he receded from Truth. For in fighting the imagined enemy without, he neglected the enemy within.

We punish thieves, because we think they harass us. They may leave us alone ; but they will only transfer their attentions to another victim. This other victim however is also a human being, ourselves in a different form, and so we are caught in a vicious circle. The trouble from thieves continues to increase, as they think it is their business to steal. In the end we see that it is better to endure the thieves than to punish them. The forbearance may even bring them to their senses. By enduring them we realize that thieves are not different from ourselves, they are our brethren, our friends, and may not be punished. But whilst we may bear with the thieves, we may not endure the infliction. That would only induce cowardice. So we realize a further duty. Since we regard the thieves as our kith and kin, they must be made to realize the kinship. And so we must take pains to devise ways and means of winning them over. This is the path of *ahimsa*. It may entail continuous suffering and the cultivating of endless patience. Given these two conditions, the thief is bound in the end to turn away from his evil ways. Thus step by step we learn how to make friends with all the world ; we realize the greatness of God — of Truth. Our peace of mind increases in spite of suffering ; we become braver and more enterprising ; we understand more clearly the difference between what is everlasting and what is not ; we learn how to distinguish between what is our duty and what is not. Our pride melts away, and we become humble. Our worldly attachments diminish, and the evil within us diminishes from day to day.

Ahimsa is not the crude thing it has been made to appear. Not to hurt any living thing is no doubt a part of *ahimsa*. But it is its least expression. The principle of *ahimsa* is hurt by every evil thought, by undue haste, by lying, by hatred, by wishing ill to anybody. It is also violated by our holding on to what the world needs. But the world needs even what we eat day by day. In the place where we stand there are millions of micro-organisms to whom the place belongs, and who are hurt by our presence there. What should we do then ? Should we commit suicide ? Even that is no solution, if we believe, as we do, that so long as the spirit is attached to the flesh, on every destruction of the body it weaves for itself another. The body will cease to be only when we give up all attachment to it. This freedom from all attachment is the realization of God as Truth. Such realization cannot be attained in a hurry. The body does not belong to us. While it lasts, we must use it as a trust handed over to our charge. Treating in this way, the things of the flesh, we may one day expect to become free from the burden of the body. Realizing the limitations of the flesh, we must strive day by day towards the ideal with what strength we have in us.

It is perhaps clear from the foregoing, that without *ahimsa* it is not possible to seek and find Truth. *Ahimsa* and Truth are so intertwined that it is practically impossible to disentangle and separate them. They are like the two sides of a coin, or rather of a smooth unstamped metallic disc. Who can say, which is the obverse, and which is the reverse ? Nevertheless *ahimsa* is the means ; Truth is the end. Means to be means must always be within our reach, and so *ahimsa* is our supreme duty. If we take care of the means, we are bound to reach the end sooner or later. When once we have grasped this point, final victory is beyond question. Whatever difficulties we encounter, whatever apparent reverses we sustain, we may not give up the quest for Truth which alone is, being God Himself.

III

Brahmacharya or Chastity

The third among our observances is *brahmacharya*. As a matter of fact all observances are deducible from

Truth, and are meant to subserve it. The man, who is wedded to Truth and worships Truth alone, proves unfaithful to her, if he applies his talents to anything else. How then can he minister to the senses ? A man, whose activities are wholly consecrated to the realization of Truth, which requires utter selflessness, can have no time for the selfish purpose of begetting children and running a household. Realization of Truth through self-gratification should, after what has been said before, appear a contradiction in terms.

If we look at it from the standpoint of *ahimsa* (non-violence), we find that the fulfilment of *ahimsa* is impossible without utter selflessness. *Ahimsa* means Universal Love. If a man gives his love to one woman, or a woman to one man, what is there left for all the world besides ? It simply means, " We two first, and the devil take all the rest of them." As a faithful wife must be prepared to sacrifice her all for the sake of her husband, and a faithful husband for the sake of his wife, it is clear that such persons cannot rise to the height of Universal Love, or look upon all mankind as kith and kin. For they have created a boundary wall round their love. The larger their family, the farther are they from Universal Love. Hence one who would obey the law of *ahimsa* cannot marry, not to speak of gratification outside the marital bond.

Then what about people who are already married ? Will they never be able to realize Truth ? Can they never offer up their all at the altar of humanity ? There is a way out for them. They can behave as if they were not married. Those who have enjoyed this happy condition will be able to bear me out. Many have to my knowledge successfully tried the experiment. If the married couple can think of each other as brother and sister, they are freed for universal service. The very thought that all the women in the world are his sisters, mothers or daughters will at once ennoble a man and snap his chains. The husband and wife do not lose any thing here, but only add to their resources and even to their family. Their love becomes free from the impurity of lust and so grows stronger. With the disappearance of this impurity, they can serve each other better, and the occasions for quarrelling become fewer. There are more occasions for quarrelling where the love is selfish and bounded.

If the foregoing argument is appreciated, a consideration of the physical benefits of chastity becomes a matter of secondary importance. How foolish it is intentionally to dissipate vital energy in sensual enjoyment! It is a grave misuse to fritter away for physical gratification that which is given to man and woman for the full development of their bodily and mental powers. Such misuse is the root cause of many a disease.

Brahmacharya, like all other observances, must be observed in thought, word and deed. We are told in the *Gita,* and experience will corroborate the statement, that the foolish man, who appears to control his body, but is nursing evil thoughts in his mind, makes a vain effort. It may be harmful to suppress the body, if the mind is at the same time allowed to go astray. Where the mind wanders, the body must follow sooner or later.

It is necessary here to appreciate a distinction. It is one thing to allow the mind to harbour impure thoughts; it is a different thing altogether if it strays among them in spite of ourselves. Victory will be ours in the end, if we non-co-operate with the mind in its evil wanderings.

We experience every moment of our lives, that often while the body is subject to our control, the mind is not. This physical control should never be relaxed, and in addition we must put forth a constant endeavour to bring the mind under control. We can do nothing more, nothing less. If we give way to the mind, the body and the mind will pull different ways, and we shall be false to ourselves. Body and mind may be said to go together, so long as we continue to resist the approach of every evil thought.

The observance of *brahmacharya* has been believed to be very difficult, almost impossible. In trying to find a reason for this belief, we see that the term *brahmacharya* has been taken in a narrow sense. Mere control of animal passion has been thought to be tantamount to observing *brahmacharya.* I feel, that this conception is incomplete and wrong. *Brahmacharya* means control of all the organs of sense. He, who attempts to control only one organ, and allows all the others free play, is bound to find his effort futile. To hear suggestive stories with the ears, to see suggestive sights with the eyes, to taste stimulating food with the tongue, to touch exciting things with the hands, and then at the same time expect to control the only remaining organ is like putting one's hands in the fire, and expecting to escape being burnt. He therefore who is resolved to control the one must be likewise determined to control the rest. I have always felt, that much harm has been done by the narrow definition of *brahmacharya.* If we practise simultaneous self-control in all directions, the attempt will be scientific and possible of success. Perhaps the palate is the chief sinner. That is why in the Ashram we have assigned to control of the palate a separate place among our observances.

Let us remember the root meaning of *brahmacharya.* *Charya* means course of conduct ; *brahma-charya* conduct adapted to the search of *Brahma,* i.e., Truth. From this etymological meaning arises the special meaning, viz., control of all the senses. We must entirely forget the incomplete definition which restricts itself to the sexual aspect only.

IV

Non-possession

Possession implies provision for the future. A seeker after Truth, a follower of the law of Love cannot hold anything against tomorrow. God never stores for the morrow ; He never creates more than what is strictly needed for the moment. If therefore we repose faith in His providence, we should rest assured that He will give us every day our daily bread, meaning everything that we require. Saints and devotees, who have lived in such faith, have always derived a justification for it from their experience. Our ignorance or negligence of the Divine Law, which gives to man from day to day his daily bread and no more, has given rise to inequalities with all the miseries attendant upon them. The rich have a superfluous store of things which they do not need, and which are therefore neglected and wasted ; while millions are starved to death for want of sustenance. If each retained possession only of what he needed, no one would be in want, and all would live in contentment. As it is, the rich are discontented no less than the poor. The poor man would fain become a millionaire, and the millionaire a multi-millionaire. The rich should take the initiative in dispossession with a view to a universal diffusion of the spirit of contentment. If only they keep their own property within moderate limits, the starving will be easily fed, and will learn the lesson of contentment along with the rich.

Perfect fulfilment of the ideal of Non-possession requires, that man should, like the birds, have no roof over his head, no clothing and no stock of food for the morrow. He will indeed need his daily bread, but it will be God's business, and not his, to provide it. Only the fewest possible, if any at all, can reach this ideal. We ordinary seekers may not be repelled by the seeming impossibility. But we must keep the ideal constantly in view, and in the light thereof, critically examine our possessions, and try to reduce them. Civilization, in the real sense of the term, consists not in the multiplication, but in the deliberate and voluntary reduction of wants. This alone promotes real happiness and contentment, and increases the capacity for service. Judging by this criterion, we find that in the Ashram we possess many things, the necessity for which cannot be proved, and we thus tempt our neighbours to thieve.

From the standpoint of pure Truth, the body too is a possession. It has been truly said that desire for enjoyment creates bodies for the soul. When this desire vanishes, there remains no further need for the body, and man is free from the vicious cycle of births and deaths. The soul is omnipresent ; why should she care to be confined within the cagelike body, or do evil and even kill for the sake of that cage ? We thus arrive at the ideal of total renunciation, and learn to use the body for the purposes of service so long as it exists, so much so that service, and not bread, becomes with us the staff of life. We eat and drink, sleep and wake, for service alone. Such an attitude of mind brings us real happiness, and the beatific vision in the fulness of time. Let us all examine ourselves from this standpoint.

We should remember, that Non-possession is a principle applicable to thoughts, as well as to things. A man who fills his brain with useless knowledge violates that inestimable principle. Thoughts, which turn us away from God, or do not turn us towards Him, constitute impediments in our way.

From Yeravda Mandir, chapters I to III & VI

9

YAJNA OR SACRIFICE

Yajna means an act directed to the welfare of others, done without desiring any return for it, whether of a temporal or spiritual nature. ' Act ' here must be taken in its widest sense, and includes thought and word, as well as deed. ' Others ' embraces not only humanity, but all life. Therefore, and also from the standpoint of *ahimsa,* it is not a *yajna* to sacrifice lower animals even with a view to the service of humanity. It does not matter that animal sacrifice is alleged to find a place in the *Vedas.* It is enough for us, that such sacrifice cannot stand the fundamental tests of Truth and Non-violence. I readily admit my incompetence in *Vedic* scholarship. But the incompetence, so far as this subject is concerned, does not worry me, because even if the practice of animal sacrifice be proved to have been a feature of *Vedic* society, it can form no precedent for a votary of *ahimsa.*

Again a primary sacrifice must be an act, which conduces the most to the welfare of the greatest number in the widest area, and which can be performed by the largest number of men and women with the least trouble.

It will not therefore be a *yajna,* much less a *mahayajna,* to wish or to do ill to any one else, even in order to serve a so-called higher interest. And the *Gita* teaches, and experience testifies, that all action that cannot come under the category of *yajna* promotes bondage.

The world cannot subsist for a single moment without *yajna* in this sense, and therefore the *Gita,* after having dealt with true wisdom in the second chapter, takes up in the third the means of attaining it, and declares in so many words, that *yajna* came with the Creation itself. This body therefore has been given us, only in order that we may serve all Creation with it. And therefore, says the *Gita,* he who eats without offering *yajna* eats stolen food. Every single act of one who would lead a life of purity should be in the nature of *yajna.* *Yajna* having come to us with our birth, we are debtors all our lives, and thus for ever bound to serve the universe. And even as a bondslave receives food, clothing and so on from the master whom he serves, so should we gratefully accept such gifts as may be assigned to us by the Lord of the universe. What we receive must be called a gift; for as debtors we are entitled to no consideration for the discharge of our obligations. Therefore we may not blame the Master, if we fail to get it. Our body is His to be cherished or cast away according to His will. This is not a matter for complaint or even pity; on the contrary, it is a natural and even a pleasant and desirable state, if only we realize our proper place in God's scheme. We do indeed need strong faith, if we would experience this supreme bliss. " Do not worry in the least about yourself, leave all worry to God," — this appears to be the commandment in all religions.

This need not frighten any one. He who devotes himself to service with a clear conscience will day by day grasp the necessity for it in greater measure, and will continually grow richer in faith. The path of service can hardly be trodden by one, who is not prepared to renounce self-interest, and to recognize the conditions of his birth. Consciously or unconsciously every one of us does render some service or other. If we cultivate the habit of doing this service deliberately, our desire for service will steadily grow stronger, and will make not only for our own happiness, but that of the world at large.

Again, not only the good, but all of us are bound to place our resources at the disposal of humanity. And if such is the law, as evidently it is, indulgence ceases to hold a place in life and gives way to renunciation. The duty of renunciation differentiates mankind from the beast.

Some object, that life thus understood becomes dull and devoid of art, and leaves no room for the householder. But renunciation here does not mean abandoning the world and retiring into the forest. The spirit of renunciation should rule all the activities of life. A householder does not cease to be one, if he regards life as a duty rather than as an indulgence. A merchant, who operates in the sacrificial spirit, will have crores passing through his hands, but he will, if he follows the law, use his abilities for service. He will therefore not cheat or speculate, will lead a simple life, will not injure a living soul and will lose millions rather than harm anybody. Let no one run away with the idea that this type of merchant exists only in my imagination. Fortunately for the world, it does exist in the West as well as in the East. It is true, such merchants may be counted on one's fingers' ends, but the type ceases to be imaginary, as soon as even one living specimen can be found to answer to it. No doubt such sacrificers obtain their livelihood by their work. But livelihood is not their objective, but only a by-product of their vocation. A life of sacrifice is the pinnacle of art, and is full of true joy. *Yajna* is not *yajna* if one feels it to be burdensome or annoying. Self-indulgence leads to destruction, and renunciation to immortality. Joy has no independent existence. It depends upon our attitude to life. One man will enjoy theatrical scenery, another the ever new scenes which unfold themselves in the sky. Joy, therefore, is a matter of individual and national education. We shall delight in things which we have been taught to delight in as children. And illustrations can be easily cited of different national tastes.

Again, many sacrificers imagine that they are free to receive from the people everything they need, and many things they do not need, because they are rendering disinterested service. Directly this idea sways a man, he ceases to be a servant, and becomes a tyrant over the people.

One who would serve will not waste a thought upon his own comforts, which he leaves to be attended to or neglected by his Master on high. He will not therefore encumber himself with everything that comes his way ; he will take only what he strictly needs and leave the rest. He will be calm, free from anger and unruffled in mind even if he finds himself inconvenienced. His service, like virtue, is its own reward, and he will rest content with it.

Again, one dare not be negligent in service, or be behindhand with it. He, who thinks that he must be diligent only in his personal business, and unpaid public business may be done in any way and at any time he chooses, has still to learn the very rudiments of the science of sacrifice. Voluntary service of others demands the best of which one is capable, and must take precedence over service of self. In fact, the pure devotee consecrates himself to the service of humanity without any reservation whatever.

From Yeravda Mandir, chapters XIV-XV

10

PROTECTING HINDUISM

For self-defence, I would restore the spiritual culture. The best and most lasting self-defence is self-purification. I refuse to be lifted off my feet because of the scares that haunt us today. If Hindus would but believe in themselves and work in accordance with their traditions, they will have no reason to fear bullying. The moment they recommence the real spiritual training the Mussalman will respond. He cannot help it. If I can get together a band of young Hindus with faith in themselves and, therefore, faith in the Mussalmans, the band will become a shield for the weaker ones. They (the young Hindus) will teach how to die without killing. I know no other way. When our ancestors saw affliction surrounding them, they went in for *tapasya* — purification. They realized the helplessness of the flesh and in their helplessness they prayed till they compelled the Maker to obey their call. ' Oh yes,' says my Hindu friend, ' but then God sent some one to wield arms.' I am not concerned with denying the truth of the retort. All I say to the friend is that as a Hindu he may not ignore the cause and secure the result. It will be time to fight, when we have done enough *tapasya*. Are we purified enough I ask ? Have we even done willing penance for the sin of untouchability, let alone the personal purity of individuals ? Are our religious preceptors all that they should be ? We are beating the air whilst we simply concentrate our attention upon picking holes in the Mussalman conduct.

Young India, 19-6-'24

11

MORAL REQUIREMENTS FOR SATYAGRAHA

Reader : I deduce that passive resistance * is a splendid weapon of the weak, but that when they are strong they may take up arms.

Editor : This is gross ignorance. Passive resistance, that is, soul-force, is matchless. It is superior to the force of arms. How, then, can it be considered only a weapon of the weak ? Physical-force men are strangers to the courage that is requisite in a passive resister. Do you believe that a coward can ever disobey a law that he dislikes ? Extremists are considered to be advocates of brute force. Why do they, then, talk about obeying laws ? I do not blame them. They can say nothing else.

---

* Throughout this chapter the words *passive resistance* are generally used for Satyagraha.

When they succeed in driving out the English and they themselves become governors, they will want you and me to obey their laws. And that is a fitting thing for their constitution. But a passive resister will say he will not obey a law that is against his conscience, even though he may be blown to pieces at the mouth of a cannon.

What do you think ? Wherein is courage required — in blowing others to pieces from behind a cannon, or with a smiling face to approach a cannon and be blown to pieces ? Who is the true warrior — he who keeps death always as a bosom-friend, or he who controls the death of others ? Believe me that a man devoid of courage and manhood can never be a passive resister.

This, however, I will admit : that even a man weak in body is capable of offering this resistance. One man can offer it just as well as millions. Both men and women can indulge in it. It does not require the training of an army ; it needs no jiu-jitsu. Control over the mind is alone necessary, and when that is attained, man is free like the king of the forest and his very glance withers the enemy.

Passive resistance is an all-sided sword, it can be used anyhow ; it blesses him who uses it and him against whom it is used. Without drawing a drop of blood it produces far-reaching results. It never rusts and cannot be stolen. Competition between passive resisters does not exhaust. The sword of passive resistance does not require a scabbard. It is strange indeed that you should consider such a weapon to be a weapon merely of the weak.

Reader : You have said that passive resistance is a speciality of India. Have cannons never been used in India ?

Editor : Evidently, in your opinion, India means its few princes. To me it means its teeming millions on whom depends the existence of its princes and our own.

Kings will always use their kingly weapons. To use force is bred in them. They want to command, but those who have to obey commands do not want guns : and these are in a majority throughout the world. They have to learn either body-force or soul-force. Where they learn the former, both the rulers and the ruled become like so many mad men ; but where they learn soul-force, the commands of the rulers do not go beyond the point of their swords, for true men disregard unjust commands. Peasants have never been subdued by the sword, and never will be. They do not know the use of the sword, and they are not frightened by the use of it by others. That nation is great which rests its head upon death as its pillow. Those who defy death are free from all fear. For those who are labouring under the delusive charms of brute-force, this picture is not overdrawn. The fact is that, in India, the nation at large has generally used passive resistance in all departments of life. We cease to co-operate with our rulers when they displease us. This is passive resistance.

I remember an instance when, in a small principality, the villagers were offended by some command issued by the prince. The former immediately began vacating the village. The prince became nervous, apologized to his subjects and withdrew his command. Many such instances can be found in India. Real Home Rule is possible only where passive resistance is the guiding force of the people. Any other rule is foreign rule.

Reader : Then you will say that it is not at all necessary for us to train the body ?

Editor : I will certainly not say any such thing. It is difficult to become a passive resister unless the body is trained. As a rule, the mind, residing in a body that has become weakened by pampering, is also weak, and where there is no strength of mind there can be no strength of soul. We shall have to improve our physique by getting rid of infant marriages and luxurious living. If I were to ask a man with a shattered body to face a cannon's mouth I should make a laughing-stock of myself.

Reader : From what you say, then, it would appear that it is not a small thing to become a passive resister, and, if that is so, I should like you to explain how a man may become one.

Editor : To become a passive resister is easy enough but it is also equally difficult. I have known a lad of fourteen years become a passive resister ; I have known also sick people do likewise ; and I have also known physically strong and otherwise happy people unable to take up passive resistance. After a great deal of experience it seems to me that those who want to become passive resisters for the service of the country have to observe perfect chastity, adopt poverty, follow truth, and cultivate fearlessness.

Chastity is one of the greatest disciplines without which the mind cannot attain requisite firmness. A man who is unchaste loses stamina, becomes emasculated and cowardly. He whose mind is given over to animal passions is not capable of any great effort. This can be proved by innumerable instances. What, then, is a married person to do is the question that arises naturally ; and yet it need not. When a husband and wife gratify the passions, it is no less an animal indulgence on that account. Such an indulgence, except for perpetuating the race, is strictly prohibited. But a passive resister has to avoid even that very limited indulgence because he can have no desire for progeny. A married man, therefore, can observe perfect chastity. This subject is not capable of being treated at greater length. Several questions arise : How is one to carry one's wife with one, what are her rights, and other similar questions. Yet those who wish to take part in a great work are bound to solve these puzzles.

Just as there is necessity for chastity, so is there for poverty. Pecuniary ambition and passive resistance cannot well go together. Those who have money are not expected to throw it away, but they are expected to be indifferent about it. They must be prepared to lose every penny rather than give up passive resistance.

Passive resistance has been described in the course of our discussion as truth-force. Truth, therefore, has necessarily to be followed and that at any cost. In this connection, academic questions such as whether a man may not lie in order to save a life, etc., arise, but these questions occur only to those who wish to justify lying. Those who want to follow truth every time are not placed in such a quandary ; and if they are, they are still saved from a false position.

Passive resistance cannot proceed a step without fearlessness. Those alone can follow the path of passive resistance who are free from fear, whether as to their possessions, false honour, their relatives, the government, bodily injuries or death.

These observances are not to be abandoned in the belief that they are difficult. Nature has implanted in the human breast ability to cope with any difficulty or suffering that may come to man unprovoked. These qualities are worth having, even for those who do not wish to serve the country. Let there be no mistake, as those who want to train themselves in the use of arms are also obliged to have these qualities more or less. Everybody does not become a warrior for the wish. A would-be warrior will have to observe chastity and to be satisfied with poverty as his lot. A warrior without fearlessness cannot be conceived of. It may be thought that he would not need to be exactly truthful, but that quality follows real fearlessness. When a man abandons truth, he does so owing to fear in some shape or form. The above four attributes, then, need not frighten any one. It may be as well here to note that a physical-force man has to have many other useless qualities which a passive resister never needs. And you will find that whatever extra effort a swordsman needs is due to lack of fearlessness. If he is an embodiment of the latter, the sword will drop from his hand that very moment. He does not need its support. One who is free from hatred requires no sword. A man with a stick suddenly came face to face with a lion and instinctively raised his weapon in self-defence. The man saw that he had only prated about fearlessness when there was none in him. That moment he dropped the stick and found himself free from all fear.

Hind Swaraj or Indian Home Rule, chap. XVII

12

CONDITIONS FOR SUCCESSFUL SATYAGRAHA

There can be no Satyagraha in an unjust cause. Satyagraha in a just cause is vain, if the men espousing it are not determined and capable of fighting and suffering to the end ; and the slightest use of violence often defeats a just cause. Satyagraha excludes the use of violence in any shape or form, whether in thought, speech, or deed. Given a just cause, capacity for endless suffering and avoidance of violence, victory is a certainty.

Young India, 27-4-'21

13

NON-RETALIATION

Victory is impossible until we are able to keep our temper under the gravest provocation. Calmness under fire is a soldier's indispensable quality. A non-co-operator is nothing if he cannot remain calm and unperturbed under a fierce fire of provocation.

There should be no mistake. There is no civil disobedience possible, until the crowds behave like disciplined soldiers. And we cannot resort to civil disobedience, unless we can assure every Englishman that he is as safe in India as he is in his own home. It is not enough that we give the assurance. Every Englishman and Englishwoman must feel safe, not by reason of the bayonet at their disposal but by reason of our living creed of non-violence. That is the condition not only of success but our own ability to carry on the movement in its present form. There is no other way of conducting the campaign of non-co-operation.

Young India, 25-8-'21

14

COURAGE AND DISCIPLINE NECESSARY

The pledge of non-violence does not require us to co-operate in our humiliation. It, therefore, does not require us to crawl on our bellies or to draw lines with our noses or to walk to salute the Union Jack or to do anything degrading at the dictation of officials. On the contrary our creed requires us to refuse to do any of these things even though we should be shot. It was, therefore, for instance, no part of the duty of the Jalianwala Bagh people to run away or even to turn their backs when they were fired upon. If the message of non-violence had reached them, they would have been expected when fire was opened on them to march towards it with bare breasts and die rejoicing in the belief that it meant the freedom of their country. Non-violence laughs at the might of the tyrant and stultifies him by non-retaliation and non-retiral. We played into General Dyer's hands because we acted as he had expected. He wanted us to run away from his fire, he wanted us to crawl on our bellies and to draw lines with our noses. That was a part of the game of 'frightfulness'. When we face it with eyes front, it vanishes like an apparition. We may not all evolve that type of courage. But I am certain that Swaraj is unattainable this year if some of us have not the courage which enables us to stand firm like a rock without retaliating. The might of the tyrant recoils upon himself when it meets with no response, even as an arm violently waved in the air suffers dislocation.

And just as we need the cool courage described above, we need perfect discipline and training in voluntary obedience to be able to offer civil disobedience. Civil disobedience is the active expression of non-violence. Civil disobedience distinguishes the non-violence of the strong from the passive, i.e. negative non-violence of the weak. And as weakness cannot lead to Swaraj, negative non-violence must fail to achieve our purpose.

Have we then the requisite discipline? Have we, a friend asked me, evolved the spirit of obedience to our own rules and resolutions? Whilst we have made tremendous headway during the past twelve months, we have certainly not made enough to warrant us in embarking upon civil disobedience with easy confidence. Rules voluntarily passed by us and rules which carry no sanction save the disapproval of our own conscience must be like debts of honour held far more binding than rules superimposed upon us or rules whose breach we can purge by paying the penalty thereof. It follows that if we have not learnt the discipline of obeying our own rules, in other words carrying out our own promises, we are ill adapted for disobedience that can be at all described as civil. I do, therefore, suggest to every Congressman, every non-co-operator, and above all to every member of the All India Congress Committee to set himself or herself right with the Congress and his or her creed by carrying on the strictest self-examination and by correcting himself or herself wherever he or she might have failed.

Young India, 20-10-'21

15

THE NEED FOR HUMILITY

The spirit of non-violence necessarily leads to humility. Non-violence means reliance on God, the Rock of Ages. If we would seek His aid, we must approach Him with a humble and a contrite heart. Non-co-operationists may not trade upon their amazing success at the Congress. We must act, even as the mango tree which droops as it bears fruit. Its grandeur lies in its majestic lowliness. But one hears of non-co-operationists being insolent and intolerant in their behaviour towards those who differ from them. I know that they will lose all their majesty and glory, if they betray any inflation. Whilst we may not be dissatisfied with the progress made so far, we have little to our credit to make us feel proud. We have to sacrifice much more than we have done to justify pride, much less elation. Thousands, who flocked to the Congress *pandal*, have undoubtedly given their intellectual assent to the doctrine but few have followed it out in practice. Leaving aside the pleaders, how many parents have withdrawn their children from schools ? How many of those who registered their vote in favour of non-co-operation have taken to hand-spinning or discarded the use of all foreign cloth ?

Non-co-operation is not a movement of brag, bluster or bluff. It is a test of our sincerity. It requires solid and silent self-sacrifice. It challenges our honesty and our capacity for national work. It is a movement that aims at translating ideas into action. And the more we do, the more we find that much more must be done than we had expected. And this thought of our imperfection must make us humble.

A non-co-operationist strives to compel attention and to set an example not by his violence but by his unobtrusive humility. He allows his solid action to speak for his creed. His strength lies in his reliance upon the correctness of his position. And the conviction of it grows most in his opponent when he least interposes his speech between his action and his opponent. Speech, especially when it is haughty, betrays want of confidence and it makes one's opponent sceptical about the reality of the act itself. Humility therefore is the key to quick success. I hope that every non-co-operationist will recognize the necessity of being humble and self-restrained. It is because so little is really required to be done and because all of that little depends entirely upon ourselves that I have ventured the belief that Swaraj is attainable in less than one year.

Young India, 12-1-'21

16

WORK IN JAILS

An esteemed friend asks me whether now that the Government have provided an opportunity for hundreds to find themselves imprisoned and as thousands are responding, will it not be better for the prisoners to refuse to do any work in the gaols at all? I am afraid that the suggestion comes from a misapprehension of the moral position. We are not out to abolish gaols as an institution. Even under Swaraj we would have our gaols. Our civil disobedience, therefore, must not be carried beyond the point of breaking the unmoral laws of the country. Breach of the laws to be civil assumes the strictest and willing obedience to gaol discipline because disobedience of a particular rule assumes a willing acceptance of the sanction provided for its breach. And immediately a person quarrels both with the rule and the sanction for its breach, he ceases to be civil and lends himself to the precipitation of chaos and anarchy. A civil resister is, if one may be permitted such a claim for him, a philanthropist and a friend of the State. An anarchist is an enemy of the State and is, therefore, a misanthrope. I have permitted myself to use the language of war because the so-called constitutional method has become so utterly ineffective. But I hold the opinion firmly that civil disobedience is the purest type of constitutional agitation. Of course it becomes degrading and despicable if its civil, i.e., non-violent character is a mere camouflage. If the honesty of non-violence be admitted, there is no warrant for condemnation even of the fiercest disobedience because of the likelihood of its leading to violence. No big or swift movement can be carried on without bold risks and life will not be worth living if it is not attended with large risks. Does not the history of the world show that there would have been no romance in life if there had been no risks? It is the clearest proof of a degenerate atmosphere that one finds respectable people, leaders of society, raising their hands in horror and indignation at the slightest approach of danger or upon an outbreak of any violent commotion. We do want to drive out the beast in man, but we do not want on that account to emasculate him. And in the process of finding his own status, the beast in him is bound now and again to put up his ugly appearance. As I have often stated in these pages what strikes me down is not the sight of blood under every conceivable circumstance. It is blood spilt by the non-co-operator or his supporters in breach of his declared pledge, which paralyses me as I know it ought to paralyse every honest non-co-operator.

Therefore, to revert to the original argument, as civil resisters we are bound to guard against universal indiscipline. Gaol discipline must be submitted to until gaol government itself becomes or is felt to be corrupt and immoral. But deprivation of comfort, imposition of restrictions and such other inconveniences do not make gaol government corrupt. It becomes that when prisoners are humiliated or treated with inhumanity as when they are kept in filthy dens or are given food unfit for human consumption. Indeed, I hope that the conduct of non-co-operators in the gaol will be strictly correct, dignified and yet submissive. We must not regard gaolers and warders as our enemies but as fellow human beings not utterly devoid of the human touch. Our gentlemanly behaviour is bound to disarm all suspicion or bitterness. I know that this path of discipline on the one hand and fierce defiance on the other is a very difficult path, but there is no royal road to Swaraj. The country has deliberately chosen the narrow and the straight path. Like a straight line it is the shortest distance. But even as you require a steady and experienced hand to draw a straight line, so are steadiness of discipline and firmness of purpose absolutely necessary if we are to walk along the chosen path with an unerring step.

Young India, 15-12-'21

17

A MODEL PRISONER

"Should non-co-operators shout *Bande Mataram* inside jails against jail discipline which may excite ordinary prisoners to violence, should non-co-operators go on hunger strike for the improvement of food or other conveniences, should they strike work inside jails on *hartal* days and other days? Are non-co-operators entitled to break rules of jail discipline unless they affect their conscience?" Such is the text of a telegram I received from a non-co-operator friend in Calcutta. From another part of India when a friend, again a non-co-operator, heard of the indiscipline of non-co-operator prisoners, he asked me to write on the necessity of observing jail discipline. As against this I know prisoners who are scrupulously observing in a becoming spirit all the discipline imposed upon them.

It is necessary, when thousands are going to jail to understand exactly the position a non-co-operator prisoner can take up consistently with his pledge of non-violence. Non-co-operation, when its limitations are not recognized, becomes a licence instead of being a duty and therefore becomes a crime. The dividing line between right and wrong is often so thin as to become indistinguishable. But it is a line that is breakable and unmistakable.

What is then the difference between those who find themselves in jails for being in the right and those who are there for being in the wrong? Both wear often the same dress, eat the same food and are subject outwardly to the same discipline. But while the latter submit to discipline most unwillingly and would commit a breach of it secretly, and even openly if they could, the former will willingly and to the best of their ability conform to jail discipline and prove worthier and more serviceable to their cause than when they are outside. We have observed that the most distinguished among the prisoners are of greater service inside jails than outside. The coefficient of service is raised to the extent of the strictness with which jail discipline is observed.

Let it be remembered that we are not seeking to destroy jails as such. I fear that we shall have to maintain jails even under Swaraj. It will go hard with us, if we let the real criminals understand that they will be set free or be very much better treated when Swaraj is established. Even in reformatories by which I would like to replace every jail under Swaraj, discipline will be exacted. Therefore, we really retard the advent of Swaraj if we encourage indiscipline. Indeed the swift programme of Swaraj has been conceived on the supposition that we being a cultured people are capable of evolving high discipline within a short time.

Indeed whilst on the one hand civil disobedience authorizes disobedience of unjust laws or unmoral laws of a State which one seeks to overthrow, it requires meek and willing submission to the penalty of disobedience and, therefore, cheerful acceptance of jail discipline and its attendant hardships.

It is now, therefore, clear that a civil resister's resistance ceases and his obedience is resumed as soon as he is under confinement. In confinement he claims no privileges because of the civility of his disobedience. Inside the jail by his exemplary conduct he reforms even the criminals surrounding him, he softens the hearts of jailors and others in authority. Such meek behaviour springing from strength and knowledge ultimately dissolves the tyranny of the tyrant. It is for this reason that I claim that voluntary suffering is the quickest and the best remedy for the removal of abuses and injustices.

It is now manifest that shouts of *Bande Mataram* or any other in breach of jail discipline are unlawful for a non-co-operator to indulge in. It is equally unlawful for him to commit a stealthy breach of jail regulations. A non-co-operator will do nothing to demoralize his fellow prisoners. The only occasion when he can openly disobey jail regulations or hunger-strike is when an attempt is made to humiliate him or when the warders themselves break, as they often do, the rules for the comfort of prisoners or when food that is unfit for human consumption is issued as it often is. A case for civil disobedience also arises when there is interference with any obligatory religious practice.

Young India, 29-12-'21

18

SATYAGRAHI PRISONER'S CONDUCT

Whether all of us realize or not the method of non-co-operation is a process of touching the heart and appealing to reason, not one of frightening by rowdyism. Rowdyism has no place in a non-violent movement.

I have often likened Satyagrahi prisoners to prisoners of war. Once caught by the enemy, prisoners of war act towards the enemy as friends. It will be considered dishonourable on the part of a soldier as a prisoner of war to deceive the enemy. It does not affect my argument that the Government does not regard Satyagrahi prisoners as prisoners of war. If we act as such, we shall soon command respect. We must make the prison a neutral institution in which we may, nay, must co-operate to a certain extent.

We would be highly inconsistent and hardly self-respecting if on the one hand we deliberately break prison rules and in the same breath complain of punishment and strictness. We may not, for instance, resist and complain of search and at the same time conceal prohibited things in our blankets or our clothes. There is nothing in Satyagraha that I know whereby we may under certain circumstances tell untruths or practise other deception.

When we say that if we make the lives of prison officials uncomfortable, the Government will be obliged to sue for peace, we either pay them a subtle compliment or regard them as simpletons. We pay a subtle compliment when we consider that even though we may make prison officials' lives uncomfortable, the Government will look on in silence and hesitate to award us condign punishment so as utterly to break our spirit. That is to say we regard the administrators to be so considerate and humane that they will not severely punish us even though we give them sufficient cause. As a matter of fact, they will not and do not hesitate to throw over-board all idea of decency and award not only authorized but even unauthorized punishments on given occasions.

But it is my deliberate conviction that had we but acted with uniform honesty and dignity, behoving Satyagrahis, we would have disarmed all opposition on the part of the Government and such strictly honourable behaviour on the part of so many prisoners would have at least shamed the Government into confessing their error in imprisoning so many honourable and innocent men. For is it not their case that our non-violence is but a cloak for our violence ? Do we not therefore play into their hands every time we are rowdy ?

In my opinion therefore as Satyagrahis we are bound, when we become prisoners,

1. to act with the most scrupulous honesty ;

2. to co-operate with the prison officials in their administration ;

3. to set by our obedience to all reasonable discipline an example to co-prisoners ;

4. to ask for no favours and claim no privileges which the meanest of prisoners do not get and which we do not need strictly for reasons of health ;

5. not to fail to ask what we do so need and not to get irritated if we do not obtain it ;

6. to do all the tasks allotted, to the utmost of our ability.

It is such conduct which will make the Government position uncomfortable and untenable. It is difficult for them to meet honesty with honesty for their want of faith and unpreparedness for such a rare eventuality. Rowdyism they expect and meet with a double dose of it. They were able to deal with anarchical crime but they

have not yet found out any way of dealing with non-violence save by yielding to it.

The idea behind the imprisonment of Satyagrahis is
that he expects relief through humble submission to suffering. He believes that meek suffering for a just cause
has a virtue all its own and infinitely greater than the virtue
of the sword. This does not mean that we may not resist
when the treatment touches our self-respect. Thus for
instance we must resist to the point of death the use of
abusive language by officials or if they were to throw our
food at us which is often done. Insult and abuse are
no part of an official's duty. Therefore we must resist
them. But we may not resist search because it is part of
prison regulations.

Nor are my remarks about mute suffering to be con-
strued to mean that there should be no agitation against
putting innocent prisoners like Satyagrahis in the same
class as confirmed criminals. Only as prisoners we may
not ask for favours. We must be content to live with the
confirmed criminals and even welcome the opportunity of
working moral reform in them. It is however expected of
a government that calls itself civilized to recognize the
most natural divisions.

Young India, 5-6-'24

19

PRE-REQUISITES FOR SATYAGRAHA *

Public opposition is effective only where there is
strength behind it. What does a son do when he objects
to some action of his father? He requests the father to
desist from the objectionable course, i.e. presents respectful petitions. If the father does not agree in spite of
repeated prayers, he non-co-operates with him to the
extent even of leaving the paternal roof. This is pure

* From Gandhiji's Presidential Speech at the 3rd Kathiawad
Political Conference, Bhavnagar.

justice. Where father and son are uncivilized, they quarrel, abuse each other and often even come to blows. An obedient son is ever modest, ever peaceful and ever loving. It is only his love which on due occasion compels him to non-co-operate. The father himself understands this loving non-co-operation. He cannot endure abandonment by or separation from the son, is distressed at heart and repents. Not that it always happens thus. But the son's duty of non-co-operation is clear.

Such non-co-operation is possible between a prince and his people. In particular circumstances it may be the people's duty. Such circumstances can exist only where the latter are by nature fearless and are lovers of liberty. They generally appreciate the laws of the State and obey them voluntarily without the fear of punishment. Reasoned and willing obedience to the laws of the State is the first lesson in non-co-operation.

The second is that of tolerance. We must tolerate many laws of the State, even when they are inconvenient. A son may not approve of some orders of the father and yet he obeys them. It is only when they are unworthy of tolerance and immoral that he disobeys them. The father will at once understand such respectful disobedience. In the same way it is only when a people have proved their active loyalty by obeying the many laws of the State that they acquire the right of Civil Disobedience.

The third lesson is that of suffering. He who has not the capacity of suffering cannot non-co-operate. He who has not learnt to sacrifice his property and even his family when necessary can never non-co-operate. It is possible that a prince enraged by non-co-operation will inflict all manner of punishments. There lies the test of love, patience, and strength. He who is not ready to undergo the fiery ordeal cannot non-co-operate. A whole people cannot be considered fit or ready for non-co-operation when only an individual or two have mastered these three lessons. A large number of the people must be thus prepared before they can non-co-operate. The result of hasty non-co-operation can only lead to harm. Some patriotic young men who do not understand the limitations noted by me grow impatient. Previous preparation is needed for non-co-operation as it is for all important things. A man cannot become a non-co-operator by merely wishing to be one. Discipline is obligatory. I do not know that many have undergone the needful discipline in any part of Kathiawad. And when the requisite discipline has been gone through probably non-co-operation will be found to be unnecessary.

As it is, I observe the necessity for individuals to prepare themselves in Kathiawad as well as in other parts of India. Individuals must cultivate the spirit of service, renunciation, truth, non-violence, self-restraint, patience, etc. They must engage in constructive work in order to develop these qualities. Many reforms would be effected automatically if we put in a good deal of silent work among the people.

Young India, 8-1-'25

20

MY POLITICAL PROGRAMME

[Some American friends sent Gandhiji a gift of 145 dollars to be spent on that part of his work which appealed to them most, viz. anti-untouchability and Hindu-Muslim unity, and said that they knew too little about his political programme to wish to help in that part of his work also. In reply, Gandhiji wrote as follows: — Ed.]

My political programme is extremely simple. If the donors had added the spinning wheel to untouchability and unity, they would have practically completed it. My opinion is becoming daily more and more confirmed that we shall achieve our real freedom only by effort from within, i.e., by self-purification and self-help, and therefore, by the strictest adherence to truth and non-violence. Civil Disobedience is no doubt there in the background. But Civil Disobedience asks for and needs not a single farthing for its support. It needs and asks for stout hearts with a faith that will not flinch from any danger and will

shine the brightest in the face of severest trial. Civil
Disobedience is a terrifying synonym for suffering. But
it is better often to understand the terrible nature of a
thing if people will truly appreciate its benignant counter-
part. Disobedience is a right that belongs to every human
being and it becomes a sacred duty when it springs from
civility, or, which is the same thing, love. The anti-
untouchability reformers are offering Civil Disobedience
against entrenched orthodoxy. Protagonists of Hindu-
Muslim unity are resisting with their whole soul those
who will divide classes and sects. Just as there may be
this resistance against those who will hinder the removal
of untouchability or promotion of unity, so must there be
resistance against a rule that is stunting India's manhood.
It is daily grinding down the starving millions of this
vast country. Heedless of future consequences the rulers
are pursuing a course of conduct regarding intoxicating
drinks and drugs that must, if it remains unchecked, corrupt the toilers of the land and make posterity ashamed
of us who are making use of this immoral source of revenue
for educating our children. But· the condition of this
terrible resistance — resistance against orthodoxy, resistance against enemies of unity, and resistance against
Government — is possible of fulfilment only by a strong,
and if need be, a long course of self-purification and
suffering.

Young India, 1-4-'26

21

LIMITATIONS OF SATYAGRAHA

All Civil Disobedience is a part or branch of Satyagraha, but all Satyagraha is not Civil Disobedience. And
seeing that the Nagpur friends have suspended what they
were pleased to call Satyagraha or Civil Disobedience, let
me suggest for their information and that of others how
Satyagraha can be legitimately offered with reference to
the Bengal detenus. If they will not be angry with me

or laugh at me, let me commence by saying that they can offer Satyagraha by developing the power of the people through *khadi*, and through *khadi* achieving boycott of foreign cloth. They can offer Satyagraha by becoming precursors of Hindu-Muslim unity, by allowing their heads to be broken whenever there is a quarrel between the two, and whilst there is no active quarrel in their parts by performing silent acts of service to those of the opposite faith to theirs. If such constructive methods are too flat for them, and if they will be satisfied by nothing less than Civil Disobedience in spite of the violence of thought, word and deed raging round us, I suggest the following prescription of individual Civil Disobedience, which even one man can offer, not indeed in the hope of securing immediate release of detenus, but certainly in the hope of the individual sacrifice ultimately eventuating in such release. Let a batch, or only one person, say from Nagpur, march on foot to the Government House in Calcutta, and if a march is irksome or impossible then let him, her, or them beg enough money for trainfare from friends, and having reached Calcutta let only one Satyagrahi march to the Government House and walk on to the point where he or she is stopped. There let him or her stop and demand the release of detenus or his or her own arrest. To preserve intact the civil nature of this disobedience the Satyagrahi must be wholly unarmed, and in spite of insults, kicks or worse must meekly stand the ground, and be arrested without the slightest opposition. He may carry his own food in his pocket, a bottleful of water, take his *Gita*, the Koran, the Bible, the Zend Avesta or the Granth Sahib, as the case may be, and his *takli*. If there are many such real Satyagrahis, they will certainly transform the atmosphere in an immensely short time, even as one gentle shower transforms the plains of India into a beautiful green carpet in one single day.

The question will legitimately be asked, ' If you really mean what you say, why don't you take the lead, never mind whether any one follows you or not ? ' My answer is : I do not regard myself as pure enough to undertake such a heroic mission. I am trying every moment of my life to attain the requisite purity of thought, word and deed. As it is, I confess that I am swayed by many passions. Anger wells up in my breast when I see or hear about what I consider to be misdeeds. All I can humbly claim for myself is that I can keep these passions and moods under fair subjection, and prevent them from gaining mastery over me. But the standard of purity that I want, for any such heroic measure is not to have such passions at all and yet to hate the wrong. When I feel that I have become incapable even of thinking evil, and I hold it to be possible for every God-fearing man to attain that state, I shall wait for no man's advice, and even at the risk of being called the maddest of men, I shall not hesitate to knock at the Viceregal gate or go wherever God leads me, and demand what is due to this country which is being ground to dust today.

Meanwhile let no man mock at Satyagraha. Let no man parody it. If it is at all possible, leave Satyagraha alone, and the whole field is open for unchecked action. On a chartless sea in which there is no light-house a captain dares whither he wills. But a captain who knowing the existence of a light-house and its position, sails anyhow, or takes no precaution for knowing the light-house from deceiving stars, will be considered unfit for his post. If the reader can bear with me, let him understand that I claim to be the keeper of the light-house called Satyagraha in the otherwise chartless sea of Indian politics. And, therefore, it is that I have suggested, that those who make for Satyagraha will do well to go to its keeper. But I know that I have no patent rights in Satyagraha. I can, therefore, merely rely upon the indulgence of fellow-workers for recognition of my office.

Young India, 14-7-'27

A GREAT SATYAGRAHI

[In his speech at Chidambaram, Gandhiji paid this tribute to the great ' untouchable ' saint Nandanar :]

I know that Chidambaram must be a place of pilgrimage for me. I have never claimed to be the one original Satyagrahi. What I have claimed is to have made the application of that doctrine on an almost universal scale, and it yet remains to be seen and demonstrated that it is a doctrine which is capable of assimilation by thousands upon thousands of peoples in all ages and climes. I know, therefore, that mine is an experiment still in the making and it, therefore, always keeps me humble and rooted to the soil, and in that state of humility I always cling to every true example of Satyagraha that comes under my notice as a child clings to its mother's breast, and so when I heard and read the story of Nandanar and his lofty Satyagraha, and his great success, my head bowed before his spirit, and all day long I have felt elevated to be able to be in a place hallowed by the holy feet of Nanda, and it will not be without a wrench that I shall be leaving this place in a few minutes' time.

Nanda broke down every barrier and won his way to freedom not by brag, not by bluster, but by the purest form of self-suffering. He did not swear against his persecutors, he would not even condescend to ask his persecutors for what was his due. But he shamed them into doing justice by his lofty prayer, by the purity of his character, and if one may put it in human language he compelled God Himself to descend and made Him open the eyes of his persecutors. And what Nanda did in his time and in his own person, it is open to every one of us to do today in our own person.

Young India, 22-9-'27

NEILL STATUE SATYAGRAHA

In accordance with the promise made by the volunteers connected with this movement, they have sent me papers giving the particulars I had asked for. From them it appears that during the six weeks that the struggle had been on when the papers were sent to me thirty volunteers had courted imprisonment. Of these 29 are Hindus and one Mussalman, one lady aged 35 and one girl aged 9, her daughter. Of these thirty, two apologized, and got themselves released. The apology of a few, if it does not become infectious, does not matter. 'Blacklegs' will be found in every struggle. The men who have gone to gaol are not noted men. This is no loss, rather it is a gain in a Satyagraha struggle which requires no prestige save that of truth, and no strength save that of self-suffering which comes only from an immovable faith in one's* cause and from a completely non-violent spirit.

The volunteers must not be impatient. Impatience is a phase of violence. A Satyagrahi has nothing to do with victory. He is sure of it, but he has also to know that it comes from God. His is but to suffer.

The papers give me an account of income and expenditure. Let the Satyagrahis understand that they have to use every pice they get as a miser uses his hoards. I suggest their getting a local man of note to take charge of their moneys and a philanthropic auditor to audit their accounts free of charge. Strictest honesty and care are necessary in the handling of public funds. This is an indispensable condition of growth of a healthy public life.

The third paper I have before me is their appeal to the public. A Satyagrahi's appeal must contain moderate language. The appeal before me though unexceptionable admits of improvement. 'Not only Neill but all of his nefarious breed must go,' is a sentence that mars the

appeal. General Neill is no more. What we have to deal
with is the statue and not even the statue as such. We
seek to destroy the principle for which the statue stands.
We wish to injure no man. And we wish to gain our object
by enlisting public opinion not excluding English opinion
in our favour by self-suffering. Here there is no room for
the language of anger and hate.

So much for the volunteers.

The public owe a duty to them. They may not go to
gaol but they can supervise, control and guide and help
the movement in many ways. Agitation for the removal
of the statue is agitation for the removal of but a symptom
of a grave disease. And while the removal of the statue
will not cure the disease it will alleviate the agony and
point the way to reaching the disease itself. It is also often
possible to reach a deep-seated disease by dealing with
some of its symptoms. So long therefore as the Satyagrahi volunteers fight the battle in a clean manner and
strictly in accordance with the conditions applicable to
Satyagraha they deserve public support and sympathy.

Young India, 13-10-'27

24

A HIMALAYAN MISCALCULATION

Almost immediately after the Ahmedabad meeting I
went to Nadiad. It was here that I first used the expression
Himalayan miscalculation which obtained such a wide
currency afterwards. Even at Ahmedabad I had begun to
have a dim perception of my mistake. But when I reached
Nadiad and saw the actual state of things there and
heard reports about a large number of people from Kheda
district having been arrested, it suddenly dawned upon me
that I had committed a grave error in calling upon the
people in the Kheda district and elsewhere to launch upon
civil disobedience prematurely, as it now seemed to me.
I was addressing a public meeting. My confession
brought down upon me no small amount of ridicule. But

I have never regretted having made that confession. For I have always held that it is only when one sees one's own mistakes with a convex lens, and does just the reverse in the case of others, that one is able to arrive at a just relative estimate of the two. I further believe that a scrupulous and conscientious observance of this rule is necessary for one who wants to be a Satyagrahi.

Let us now see what that Himalayan miscalculation was. Before one can be fit for the practice of civil disobedience one must have rendered a willing and respectful obedience to the State laws. For the most part we obey such laws for fear of the penalty for their breach, and this holds good particularly in respect of such laws as do not involve a moral principle. For instance, an honest, respectable man will not suddenly take to stealing whether there is a law against stealing or not, but this very man will not feel any remorse for failure to observe the rule about carrying headlights on bicycles after dark. Indeed, it is doubtful whether he would even accept advice kindly about being more careful in this respect. But he would observe any obligatory rule of this kind, if only to escape the inconvenience of facing a prosecution for a breach of the rule. Such compliance is not, however, the willing and spontaneous obedience that is required of a Satyagrahi. A Satyagrahi obeys the laws of society intelligently and of his own free will, because he considers it to be his sacred duty to do so. It is only when a person has thus obeyed the laws of society scrupulously that he is in a position to judge as to which particular rules are good and just and which unjust and iniquitous. Only then does the right accrue to him of the civil disobedience of certain laws in well-defined circumstances. My error lay in my failure to observe this necessary limitation. I had called upon the people to launch upon civil disobedience before they had thus qualified themselves for it, and this mistake seemed to me of Himalayan magnitude. As soon as I entered the Kheda district, all the old recollections of the Kheda Satyagraha struggle came back to me, and I wondered how I

could have failed to perceive what was so obvious. I realized
that before a people could be fit for offering civil disobedience, they should thoroughly understand its deeper implications. That being so, before re-starting civil disobedience
on a mass scale, it would be necessary to create a band of
well-tried, pure-hearted volunteers who thoroughly understood the strict conditions of Satyagraha. They could
explain these to the people, and by sleepless vigilance keep
them on the right path.

With these thoughts filling my mind I reached Bombay, raised a corps of Satyagrahi volunteers through the
Satyagraha Sabha there, and with their help commenced
the work of educating the people with regard to the
meaning and inner significance of Satyagraha. This was
principally done by issuing leaflets of an educative character bearing on the subject.

But whilst this work was going on, I could see that
it was a difficult task to interest the people in the peaceful
side of Satyagraha. The volunteers too failed to enlist
themselves in large numbers. Nor did all those who
actually enlisted take anything like a regular systematic
training, and as the days passed by, the number of fresh
recruits began gradually to dwindle instead of to grow.
I realized that the progress of the training in civil disobedience was not going to be as rapid as I had at first
expected.

The Story of My Experiments with Truth, pt. V, chap. XXXIII

25

QUALIFICATIONS FOR SATYAGRAHA

Satyagraha presupposes self-discipline, self-control, self-purification, and a recognized social status in the person offering it. A Satyagrahi must never forget the distinction between evil and the evil-doer. He must not harbour ill-will or bitterness against the latter. He may not even employ needlessly offensive language against the evil person, however unrelieved his evil might be. For it should be an article of faith with every Satyagrahi that there is none so fallen in this world but can be converted by love. A Satyagrahi will always try to overcome evil by good, anger by love, untruth by truth, *himsa* by *ahimsa*. There is no other way of purging the world of evil. Therefore a person who claims to be a Satyagrahi always tries by close and prayerful self-introspection and self-analysis to find out whether he is himself completely free from the taint of anger, ill-will and such other human infirmities, whether he is not himself capable of those very evils against which he is out to lead a crusade. In self-purification and penance lies half the victory of a Satyagrahi. A Satyagrahi has faith that the silent and undemonstrative action of truth and love produces far more permanent and abiding results than speeches or such other showy performances.

But although Satyagraha can operate silently, it requires a certain amount of action on the part of a Satyagrahi. A Satyagrahi, for instance, must first mobilize public opinion against the evil which he is out to eradicate, by means of a wide and intensive agitation. When public opinion is sufficiently roused against a social abuse even the tallest will not dare to practise or openly to lend support to it. An awakened and intelligent public opinion is the most potent weapon of a Satyagrahi. When a person supports a social evil in total disregard of un-animous public opinion, it indicates a clear justification for his social ostracism. But the object of social ostracism should never be to do injury to the person against whom it is directed. Social ostracism means complete non-co-operation on the part of society with the offending individual; nothing more, nothing less, the idea being that a person who deliberately sets himself to flout society has no right to be served by society. For all practical purposes this should be enough. Of course, special action may be indicated in special cases and the practice may have to be varied to suit the peculiar features of each individual case.

Young India, 8-8-'29

26

SOME RULES OF SATYAGRAHA

Satyagraha literally means insistence on truth. This insistence arms the votary with matchless power. This power or force is connoted by the word *Satyagraha*. Satyagraha, to be genuine, may be offered against one's wife or one's children, against rulers, against fellow citizens, even against the whole world.

Such a universal force necessarily makes no distinction between kinsmen and strangers, young and old, man and woman, friend and foe. The force to be so applied can never be physical. There is in it no room for violence. The only force of universal application can, therefore, be that of *ahimsa* or love. In other words it is soul-force.

Love does not burn others, it burns itself. Therefore, a Satyagrahi, i.e. a civil resister, will joyfully suffer even unto death.

It follows, therefore, that a civil resister, whilst he will strain every nerve to compass the end of the existing rule, will do no intentional injury in thought, word or deed to the person of a single Englishman. This necessarily brief explanation of Satyagraha will perhaps enable the

reader to understand and appreciate the following rules :
As an Individual
1. A Satyagrahi, i.e., a civil resister will harbour no anger.

2. He will suffer the anger of the opponent.

3. In so doing he will put up with assaults from the opponent, never retaliate ; but he will not submit, out of fear of punishment or the like, to any order given in anger.

4. When any person in authority seeks to arrest a civil resister, he will voluntarily submit to the arrest, and he will not resist the attachment or removal of his own property, if any, when it is sought to be confiscated by the authorities.

5. If a civil resister has any property in his possession as a trustee, he will refuse to surrender it, even though in defending it he might lose his life. He will however, never retaliate.

6. Non-retaliation excludes swearing and cursing.

7. Therefore a civil resister will never insult his opponent, and therefore also not take part in many of the newly coined cries which are contrary to the spirit of *ahimsa*.

8. A civil resister will not salute the Union Jack, nor will he insult it or officials, English or Indian.

9. In the course of the struggle if any one insults an official or commits an assault upon him, a civil resister will protect such official or officials from the insult or attack even at the risk of his life.

As a Prisoner
10. As a prisoner, a civil resister, will behave courteously towards prison officials, and will observe all such discipline of the prison as is not contrary to self-respect ; as for instance, whilst he will *salaam* officials in the usual manner, he will not perform any humiliating gyrations and refuse to shout 'Victory to *Sarkar*' or the like. He will take cleanly cooked and cleanly served food, which is not contrary to his religion, and will refuse to take food insultingly served or served in unclean vessels.

11.   A civil resister will make no distinction between an ordinary prisoner and himself, will in no way regard himself as superior to the rest, nor will he ask for any conveniences that may not be necessary for keeping his body in good health and condition. He is entitled to ask for such conveniences as may be required for his physical or spiritual well-being.

12.   A civil resister may not fast for want of conveniences whose deprivation does not involve any injury to one's self-respect.

As a Unit

13.   A civil resister will joyfully obey all the orders issued by the leader of the corps, whether they please him or not.

14.   He will carry out orders in the first instance even though they appear to him insulting, inimical or foolish, and then appeal to higher authority. He is free before joining to determine the fitness of the corps to satisfy him, but after he has joined it, it becomes a duty to submit to its discipline irksome or otherwise. If the sum total of the energy of the corps appears to a member to be improper or immoral, he has a right to sever his connection, but being within it, he has no right to commit a breach of its discipline.

15.   No civil resister is to expect maintenance for his dependents. It would be an accident if any such provision is made. A civil resister entrusts his dependents to the care of God. Even in ordinary warfare wherein hundreds of thousands give themselves up to it, they are able to make no previous provision. How much more, then, should such be the case in Satyagraha ? It is the universal experience that in such times hardly anybody is left to starve.

In Communal Fights

16.   No civil resister will intentionally become a cause of communal quarrels.

17.   In the event of any such outbreak, he will not take sides, but he will assist only that party which is demonstrably in the right. Being a Hindu he will be

generous towards Mussalmans and others, and will sacrifice himself in the attempt to save non-Hindus from a Hindu attack. And if the attack is from the other side, he will not participate in any retaliation but will give his life in protecting Hindus.

18. He will, to the best of his ability, avoid every occasion that may give rise to communal quarrels.

19. If there is a procession of Satyagrahis they will do nothing that would wound the religious susceptibilities of any community, and they will not take part in any other processions that are likely to wound such susceptibilities.

Young India, 27-2-'30

27

FULL SURRENDER

As a Satyagrahi I believe in the absolute efficacy of full surrender. Numerically Hindus happen to be the major community. Therefore, they may give to the minorities what they may want. But even if the Hindus were in a minority, as a Satyagrahi and Hindu I should say that the Hindus would lose nothing in the long run by full surrender.

To this argument a retort has thoughtlessly been made, "Why then do you not advise India to surrender to the English? Give them the domination they want and be happy." The hasty retort ignores the vital fact that I have not advised surrender to the bayonet. In the code of the Satyagrahi there is no such thing as surrender to brute force. Or the surrender then is the surrender of suffering and not to the will of the wielder of the bayonet. A Satyagrahi's surrender has to come out of his strength, not out of weakness. The surrender advised by me is not of honour but of earthly goods. There is no loss of honour in surrendering seats and positions of emoluments. There is loss of honour in haggling about them. Let the Englishmen give up the bayonet and live in our midst as simple

friends and I should plead for them. The law of surrender
and suffering is a universal law admitting of no exceptions.
    Young India, 30-4-'31

28

TO WEAKEN COMMUNALISM

My implicit faith in non-violence does mean yielding
to minorities when they are really weak. The best way
to weaken communalists is to yield to them. Resistance
will only rouse their suspicion and strengthen their opposition. A Satyagrahi resists when there is threat of force
behind obstruction. I know that I do not carry the Congressmen in general with me in this what to me appears
as very sensible and practical point of view. But if we
are to come to Swaraj through non-violent means, I know
that this point of view will be accepted.
    Young India, 2-7-'31

29

POLITICAL POWER *v.* SATYAGRAHA

If I want political power it is for the sake of the
reforms for which the Congress stands. Therefore when
the energy to be spent in gaining that power means so
much loss of energy required for the reforms, as threatens
to be the case if the country is to engage in a duel with
the Mussalmans or Sikhs, I would most decidedly advise
the country to let the Mussalmans and Sikhs take all the
power and I would go on with developing the reforms.

If we were to analyse the activities of the Congress
during the past twelve years, we would discover that the
capacity of the Congress to take political power has increased in exact proportion to its ability to achieve success
in the constructive effort. That is to me the substance of
political power. Actual taking over of the Government

machinery is but a shadow, an emblem. And it could easily be a burden if it came as a gift from without, the people having made no effort to deserve it.

It is now perhaps easy to realize the truth of my statement that the needful can be 'gained more quickly and more certainly by Satyagraha than by political power '. Legislation in advance of public opinion has often been demonstrated to be futile. Legal prohibition of theft in a country in which the vast majority are thieves would be futile. Picketing and the other popular activities are therefore the real thing. If political power was a thing apart from these reforms, we would have to suspend the latter and concentrate on the former. But we have follow- ed the contrary course. We have everywhere emphasized the necessity of carrying on the constructive activities as being the means of attaining Swaraj. I am convinced that whenever legal prohibition of drinks, drugs and foreign cloth comes, it will come because public opinion had de- manded it. It may be said that public opinion demands it today but the foreign Government does not respond. This is only partly right. Public opinion in this country is only now becoming a vital force and developing the real sanction which is Satyagraha.

Young India, 2-7-'31

30

FOR ' FOLLOWERS '

A friend sends me the following :

" It will be very helpful if you will kindly guide your follow- ers about their conduct when they have to engage in a political controversy. Your guidance on the following points is parti- cularly needed :

(a) Vilification so as to lower the opponent in public estima- tion ;

(b) Kind of criticism of the opponent permissible ;

(c) Limit to which hostility should be carried ;

(d) Whether effort should be made to gain office and power."

I have said before in these pages that I claim no followers. It is enough for me to be my own follower. It is
by itself a sufficiently taxing performance. But I know
that many claim to be my followers. I must therefore
answer the questions for their sakes. If they will follow
what I endeavour to stand for rather than me they will
see that the following answers are derived from truth and
ahimsa.

(a)   Vilification of an opponent there can never be.
But this does not exclude a truthful characterization of
his acts. An opponent is not always a bad man because
he opposes. He may be as honourable as we may claim to
be and yet there may be vital differences between him
and us.

(b)   Our criticism will therefore be if we *believe* him
to be guilty of untruth to meet it with truth, of discourtesy
with courtesy, of bullying with calm courage, of violence
with suffering, of arrogance with humility, of evil with
good. " My follower " would seek not to condemn but to
convert.

(c)   There is no question of any limit to which hostility may be carried. For there should be no hostility to
persons. Hostility there must be to acts when they are
subversive of morals or the good of society.

(d)   Office and power must be avoided. Either may
be accepted when it is clearly for greater service.

Young India, 7-5-'31

31

MAINTENANCE ALLOWANCE

[In the course of his speech at the Deshaseva Mandal, Sind, on
the occasion of its second anniversary Gandhiji said :]

The question has been asked me whether the
workers who join such institutions should receive some
allowance for their livelihood or not. There are some
who think it a humiliation to receive any allowance and
would prefer to work without any. They do not seem to

realize that if we act on that principle we shall have to search for millionaire workers. Millionaires are few and far between and it is very rarely that we get volunteer workers from that class. I must say that there is a subtle self-conceit in the insistence that we should work without drawing any allowance. There is not only no humiliation in receiving an allowance for one's livelihood but a clear duty. Gokhale began his life of service with an allowance of Rs 40 a month and never in his life drew more than Rs 75 monthly. He contented himself with that much all his life. He did not feel it below his dignity to draw an humble allowance for his livelihood, but considered it an act of duty and of merit. Why then should we pretend to have a higher sense of self-respect than he ? Even a millionaire's son, if he becomes a member should, instead of depending on his millions, make a gift of his millions to such a society and draw his monthly allowance as other members may be doing.

There is one thing more which I should like to bring home to you. Bodies like these ought to be governed by strict rules and regulations. A man without a pledge or a code of conduct is like a ship without a rudder.

I am told that a worker in Sind finds it difficult to live without less than a hundred rupees a month. I find it difficult to swallow this. It may be so in Sind because we have artificially increased our wants. But my experience tells me that it is possible to do with very much less. Lalaji's Servants of the People Society and Gokhale's Servants of India Society we know because of the great names of their founders, but there are many other societies of volunteer workers where the individual allowance is not more than Rs 25 to Rs 30. In Utkal Rs 25 to Rs 30 is an exception and Rs 15 is the rule. We have, therefore, to cut our coat according to our cloth, and limit our needs in accordance with the conditions of our people.

Young India, 30-4-'31

A NON-VIOLENT ARMY

The Congress should be able to put forth a non-violent army of volunteers numbering not a few thousands but lakhs who would be equal to every occasion where the police and the military are required. Thus, instead of one brave Pashupatinath Gupta who died in the attempt to secure peace, we should be able to produce hundreds. And a non-violent army acts unlike armed men, as well in times of peace as of disturbances. They would be constantly engaged in constructive activities that make riots impossible. Theirs will be the duty of seeking occasions for bringing warring communities together, carrying on peace propaganda, engaging in activities that would bring and keep them in touch with every single person, male and female, adult and child, in their parish or division. Such an army should be ready to cope with any emergency, and in order to still the frenzy of mobs should risk their lives in numbers sufficient for the purpose. A few hundred, maybe a few thousand, such spotless deaths will once for all put an end to the riots. Surely a few hundred young men and women giving themselves deliberately to mob fury will be any day a cheap and braver method of dealing with such madness than the display and use of the police and the military.

Harijan, 26-3-'38

TO VOLUNTEERS

I have received several letters offering the writers' names for enrolment as volunteers ready to immolate themselves at times of rioting and the like. To these writers I would suggest that they enlist co-workers themselves, form local corps, and begin training in accordance with the suggestion I have made. Let them not confine themselves merely to preparedness for emergencies, but for the daily walk of life in all its departments, personal, domestic, social, economic, political, religious. Only thus will they find themselves more than ready for dealing with emergencies in their own localities or beats. They may not aim, except indirectly, at influencing events happening hundreds of miles away from their scene of activity. That ability will come, if the right beginning is made in the first instance.

Harijan, 23-4-'38

34

REQUISITE QUALIFICATIONS

The four days' fast set me thinking of the qualifications required in a Satyagrahi. Though they were carefully considered and reduced to writing in 1921 they seem to have been forgotten.

In Satyagraha, it is never the numbers that count ; it is always the quality, more so when the forces of violence are uppermost.

Then it is often forgotten that it is never the intention of a Satyagrahi to embarrass the wrong-doer. The appeal is never to his fear ; it is, must be, always to his heart. The Satyagrahi's object is to convert, not to coerce, the wrong-doer. He should avoid artificiality in all his doings. He acts naturally and from inward conviction.

Keeping these observations before his mind's eye, the reader will perhaps appreciate the following qualifications which, I hold, are essential for every Satyagrahi in India :

1. He must have a living faith in God, for He is his only Rock.

2. He must believe in truth and non-violence as his creed and therefore have faith in the inherent goodness of human nature which he expects to evoke by his truth and love expressed through his suffering.

3. He must be leading a chaste life and be ready and willing for the sake of his cause to give up his life and his possessions.

4. He must be a habitual *khadi*-wearer and spinner. This is essential for India.

5. He must be a teetotaller and be free from the use of other intoxicants in order that his reason may be always unclouded and his mind constant.

6. He must carry out with a willing heart all the rules of discipline as may be laid down from time to time.

7. He should carry out the jail rules unless they are specially devised to hurt his self-respect.

The qualifications are not to be regarded as exhaustive. They are illustrative only.

Harijan, 25-3-'39

35

QUALIFICATIONS OF A PEACE BRIGADE

Some time ago I suggested the formation of a Peace Brigade whose members would risk their lives in dealing with riots, especially communal. The idea was that this Brigade should substitute the police and even the military. This reads ambitious. The achievement may prove impossible. Yet, if the Congress is to succeed in its non-violent struggle, it must develop the power to deal peacefully with such situations.

Let us therefore see what qualifications a member of the contemplated Peace Brigade should possess.

(1)   He or she must have a living faith in non-violence. This is impossible without a living faith in God. A non-violent man can do nothing save by the power and grace of God. Without it he won't have the courage to die without anger, without fear and without retaliation. Such courage comes from the belief that God sits in the hearts of all and that there should be no fear in the presence of God. The knowledge of the omnipresence of God also means respect for the lives of even those who may be called opponents or *goondas*. This contemplated intervention is a process of stilling the fury of man when the brute in him gets mastery over him.

(2)   This messenger of peace must have equal regard for all the principal religions of the earth. Thus, if he is a Hindu, he will respect the other faiths current in India. He must therefore possess a knowledge of the general principles of the different faiths professed in the country.

(3)   Generally speaking this work of peace can only be done by local men in their own localities.

(4)   The work can be done singly or in groups. Therefore no one need wait for companions. Nevertheless one would naturally seek companions in one's own locality and form a local brigade.

(5)   This messenger of peace will cultivate through personal service contacts with the people in his locality or chosen circle, so that when he appears to deal with ugly situations, he does not descend upon the members of a riotous assembly as an utter stranger liable to be looked upon as a suspect or an unwelcome visitor.

(6)   Needless to say, a peace-bringer must have a character beyond reproach and must be known for his strict impartiality.

(7)   Generally, there are previous warnings of coming storms. If these are known, the peace brigade will not wait till the conflagration breaks out but will try to handle the situation in anticipation.

(8)   Whilst, if the movement spreads, it might be well if there are some whole-time workers, it is not absolutely necessary that there should be. The idea is to have as many good and true men and women as possible. These can be had only if volunteers are drawn from those who are engaged in various walks of life but have leisure enough to cultivate friendly relations with the people living in their circle and otherwise possess the qualifications required of a member of the Peace Brigade.

(9)   There should be a distinctive dress worn by the members of the contemplated brigade so that in course of time they will be recognized without the slightest difficulty.

These are but general suggestions. Each centre can work out its own constitution on the basis here suggested.

Lest false hopes may be raised, I must warn workers against entertaining the hope that I can play any active part in the formation of Peace Brigades. I have not the health, energy or time for it. I find it hard enough to cope with the tasks I dare not shirk. I can only guide and make suggestions through correspondence or these columns. Therefore let those who appreciate the idea and feel they have the ability, take the initiative themselves. I know that the proposed Brigade has great possibilities and that the idea behind it is quite capable of being worked out in practice.

Harijan, 18-6-'38

THE NECESSITY OF TRAINING

I am not likely, lightly and in the near future, to advise mass Satyagraha anywhere. There is neither adequate training nor discipline among the people. I have not the shadow of a doubt that the people at large should pass one or more positive tests. Mere abstention from physical violence will not answer our purpose. In the centre of this programme of positive tests I unhesitatingly put the spinning wheel and all it means. If there is quick response, this can be a short course. But it may well be a long course if the people do not make an enthusiastic response. I know no other programme than the fourfold constructive programme of 1920. If the people do not take it up whole-heartedly, it is proof enough for me that they have no *ahimsa* in them, or not the *ahimsa* of my conception, or say they have no confidence in the present leadership. For me there is no other test but what I have ever put before the nation since 1920. The new light tells me that I must not weaken as I have done before in exacting the discipline I have mentioned. I can quite clearly see my way to advise civil disobedience wherever the conditions mentioned are amply fulfilled. That civil disobedience will be individual, but in terms of *ahimsa* far more effective than any mass civil disobedience of the past. I must own that the past movements have been more or less tainted. I have no regret for them. For I knew no better then. I had the sense and humility to retrace my steps whenever I discovered blunders. Hence the nation has gone forward from step to step. But the time has come for a radical change in the direction indicated.

Harijan, 10-6-'39

PHYSICAL TRAINING FOR THE SATYAGRAHI

Ahimsa requires certain duties which can be done only by those with a trained physique. It is, therefore, most necessary to consider what kind of physical training a non-violent person should receive.

Very few of the rules applying to a violent army will apply to a non-violent body. A violent army will not have its arms for show but for definitely destructive purposes. A non-violent body will have no use for such weapons and will, therefore, beat its swords into plough-shares and spears into pruning hooks, and will shrink from the thought of using them as lethal weapons. The violent soldier will be trained in the use of violence by being taught to shoot. The non-violent soldier will have no time for this pastime. He will get all his training through nursing the sick, saving those in danger at the risk of his own life, patrolling places which may be in fear of thieves and dacoits, and in laying down his life, if necessary, in dissuading them from their purpose. Even the uniforms of the two will differ. The violent man will wear a coat of mail for his protection, and his uniform will be such as can dazzle people. The uniform of the non-violent man will be simple, in conformity with the dress of the poor, and betokening humility. Its purpose will be just to keep him from heat and cold and rain. A violent soldier's protection will be his arms, no matter how much he takes God's name. He will not shrink from spending millions on armaments. The first and last shield and buckler of the non-violent person will be his unwavering faith in God. And the minds of the two will be as poles asunder. The violent man will always be casting about for plans to work the destruction of his enemy and will pray to God to fulfil his purpose. The national anthem of the British people is worth considering in this connection. It prays to God to save the King, to frustrate the enemy's knavish tricks, and to destroy him. Millions of Englishmen sing this anthem aloud with one voice standing respectfully. If God is the Incarnation of Mercy, He is not likely to listen to such prayer, but it cannot but affect the minds of those who sing it, and in times of war it simply kindles their hatred and anger to white heat. The one condition of winning a violent war is to keep the indignation against the enemy burning fiercely.

In the dictionary of the non-violent there is no such word as an external enemy. But even for the supposed enemy he will have nothing but compassion in his heart. He will believe that no man is intentionally wicked, that there is no man but is gifted with the faculty to discriminate between right and wrong, and that if that faculty were to be fully developed, it would surely mature into non-violence. He will therefore pray to God that He may give the supposed enemy a sense of right and bless him. His prayer for himself will always be that the spring of compassion in him may ever be flowing, and that he may ever grow in moral strength so that he may face death fearlessly.

Thus since the minds of both will differ as the poles, their physical training will also differ in the same degree.

We all know more or less what military training is like. But we have hardly ever thought that non-violent training must be of a different kind. Nor have we ever cared to discover whether in the past such training was given anywhere in the world. I am of opinion that it used to be given in the past and is even now being given in a haphazard way. The various exercises of *Hatha Yoga* are in this direction. The physical training given by means of these imparts among other things physical health, strength, agility, and the capacity to bear heat and cold. Shri Kuvalayanandji is making scientific researches in the technique and benefits of these exercises. I have no knowledge of the progress he has made, nor do I know whether he is making his experiments with *ahimsa* as his goal. My reference to *Hatha Yoga* is meant only with a view to showing that this ancient type of non-violent training still exists, though I know that there is room in it for improvement. I do not know either that the author of this science had any idea of mass non-violence. The exercises had at their back the desire for individual salvation. The object of the various exercises was to strengthen and purify the body in order to secure control of the mind. The mass non-violence we are now thinking of applies to people of all religions and therefore the rules .that may be framed must be such as can be accepted by all believers in *ahimsa*. And then as we are thinking of a non-violent army, that is to say, of bringing into being a Satyagraha *sangha*, we can but build anew accepting the old as our foundation. Let us then think of the physical training required by a Satyagrahi. If the Satyagrahi is not healthy in mind and body, he may perhaps fail in mustering complete fearlessness. He should have the capacity to stand guard at a single spot day and night ; he must not fall ill ˙even if he has to bear cold and heat and rain ; he must have the strength to go to places of peril, to rush to scenes of fire, and the courage to wander about alone in desolate jungles and haunts of death ; he will bear, without a grumble, severe beatings, starvation and worse, and will keep to his post of duty without flinching ; he will have the resourcefulness and capacity to plunge into a seemingly impenetrable scene of rioting ; he will have the longing and capacity to run with the name of God on his lips to the rescue of men living on the top storeys of buildings enveloped in flames ; he will have the fearlessness to plunge into a flood in order to rescue people being carried off by it or to jump down a well to save a drowning person.

This list can be extended *ad libitum*. The substance of it all is that we should cultivate the capacity to run to the rescue of people in danger and distress and to suffer cheerfully any amount of hardship that may be inflicted upon us. He who accepts this fundamental principle will easily be able to frame rules of physical training for Satya-grahis. I have a firm conviction that the very foundation of this training is faith in God. If that is absent, all the training one may have received is likely to fail at the critical moment.

Let no one poohpooh my statement by saying that the Congress has many people who are ashamed to take the name of God. I am simply trying to state the view in terms of the science of Satyagraha as I have known and developed it. The only weapon of the Satyagrahi is God, by whatsoever name one knows Him. Without Him the Satyagrahi is devoid of strength before an opponent armed with monstrous weapons. Most people lie prostrate before physical might. But he who accepts God as his only Protector will remain unbent before the mightiest earthly power.

As faith in God is essential in a Satyagrahi, even so is *brahmacharya*. Without *brahmacharya* the Satyagrahi will have no lustre, no inner strength to stand unarmed against the whole world. *Brahmacharya* may have here the restricted meaning of conservation of the vital energy brought about by sexual restraint, and not the comprehensive definition I have given of it. He who intends to live on spare diet and without any external remedies, and still wants to have physical strength, has need to conserve his vital energy. It is the richest capital man can ever possess. He who can preserve it ever gains renewed strength out of it. He who uses it up, consciously or unconsciously, will ultimately be impotent. His strength will fail him at the right moment. I have often written about the ways and means of conserving this energy. Let the reader turn to my writings and carry out the instructions. He who lusts with the eye or the touch can never conserve his vital energy, nor the man who lusts after flesh-pots. Those who hope to conserve this energy without strict observance of the rules will no more succeed than those who hope to swim against the current without being exhausted. He who restrains himself physically and sins with his thoughts will fare worse than he who, without professing to observe *brahmacharya*, lives the life of a restrained householder. For he who lusts with the thought will ever remain unsated and will end his life a moral wreck and burden on the earth. Such a one can never be a full Satyagrahi. Nor can one who hankers after wealth and fame.

This is the foundation of the physical training for a Satyagrahi. The detailed structure of the course can easily be built in consonance with this foundation.

It should now be clear that in the physical training of a Satyagrahi there is no room for lethal weapons like the sword or the spear. For far more terrible weapons than we have seen are in existence today, and newer ones are being invented every day. Of what fear will a sword rid him who has to cultivate the capacity to overcome all fear — real or imaginary ? I have not yet heard of a man having shed all fear by learning sword-play. Mahavir and others who imbibed *ahimsa* did not do so because they knew the use of weapons, but because, in spite of the knowledge of their use, they shed all fear.

A slight introspection will ,show that he who has always depended on the sword will find it difficult to throw it away. But having deliberately discarded it he is likely to find his *ahimsa* more lasting than that of him who, not knowing its use, fancies he will not fear it. But that does not mean that in order to be truly non-violent one must beforehand possess and know the use of arms. By parity of reasoning, one might say that only a thief can be honest, only a diseased person can be healthy, and only a dissolute person can be a *brahmachari*. The fact is that we have formed the habit of thinking along traditional grooves and will not get out of them. And as we cannot take a detached view, we cannot draw the right conclusions and get caught in delusive snares.

If I have the time, I hope to present the reader with a model course of training.

Harijan, 13-10-'40

BRAHMACHARYA FOR SATYAGRAHA

There must be power in the word of a Satyagraha general — not the power that the possession of limitless arms gives, but the power that purity of life, strict vigilance, and ceaseless application produce. This is impossible without the observance of *brahmacharya*. It must be as full as it is humanly possible. *Brahmacharya* here does not mean mere physical self-control. It means much more. It means complete control over all the senses. Thus an impure thought is a breach of *brahmacharya* ; so is anger. All power comes from the preservation and sublimation of the vitality that is responsible for creation of life. If the vitality is husbanded instead of being dissipated, it is transmuted into creative energy of the highest order. This vitality is continuously and even unconsciously dissipated by evil, or even rambling, disorderly, unwanted, thoughts. And since thought is the root of all speech and action, the quality of the latter corresponds to that of the former. Hence perfectly controlled thought is itself power of the highest potency and can become self-acting. That seems to me to be the meaning of the silent prayer of the heart. If man is after the image of God, he has but to will a thing in the limited sphere allotted to him and it becomes. Such power is impossible in one who dissipates his energy in any way whatsoever, even as steam kept in a leaky pipe yields no power. The sexual act divorced from the deliberate purpose of generation is a typical and gross form of dissipation and has therefore been specially and rightly chosen for condemnation. But in one who has to organize vast masses of mankind for non-violent action the full control described by me has to be attempted and virtually achieved.

This control is unattainable save by the grace of God. There is a verse in the second chapter of the *Gita* which freely rendered means : " Sense-effects remain in abeyance whilst one is fasting or whilst the particular sense is starved, but the hankering does not cease except when one sees God face to face." This control is not mechanical or temporary. Once attained it is never lost.

Harijan, 23-7-'38

39

DISCIPLINE — SATYAGRAHI AND MILITARY

I have not yet known a general who has not altered time and again the plans of his campaign and made eleventh-hour alterations in his orders. The ordinary fighting soldier knows nothing of these plans. In fact they are a closely guarded secret unknown to all but the general himself. That is why Tennyson wrote those immortal lines — " Theirs not to reason why, theirs not to make reply, theirs but to do and die." But these words apply, if you please, to a Satyagrahi army more appropriately than to the ordinary army. For a military general may change his plans in view of the changing situations every day. Military strategy depends on the changing tactics of the enemy. The Satyagrahi general has to obey his inner voice, for over and above the situation outside, he examines himself constantly and listens to the dictates of the Inner Self. But both in Satyagraha and military warfare the position of the soldier is very nearly the same. He knows no rest, no certainty of movements, the only certainty for him is to face heavy odds and even death. His promise to be under discipline and to obey the general's command applies even during the period of suspension of hostilities. But I have not asked for this kind of discipline. I have always tried to carry conviction to my co-workers, to carry their hearts and their reason with me. I shall go on doing so always, but where you cannot follow you will have to have faith. In ordinary warfare a soldier cannot reason why. In our warfare there is enough scope for reasoning, but there is a limit to it. You will go on arguing until you are convinced, but when no conviction comes, you must fall back on faith.

Harijan, 10-6-'39

40

SCORCHED EARTH

There is no bravery in my poisoning my well or filling it in so that my brother who is at war with me may not use the water. Let us assume that I am fighting him in the orthodox manner. Nor is there sacrifice in it, for it does not purify me, and sacrifice, as its root meaning implies, presupposes purity. Such destruction may be likened to cutting one's nose to spite one's face. Warriors of old had wholesome laws of war. Among the excluded things were poisoning wells and destroying food crops. But I do claim that there are bravery and sacrifice in my leaving my wells, crops and homestead intact, bravery in that I deliberately run the risk of the enemy feeding himself at my expense and pursuing me, and sacrifice in that the sentiment of leaving something for the enemy purifies and ennobles me.

Harijan, 12-4-'42

TRAINING FOR A NON-VIOLENT ARMY

Q. What should be the training and discipline for a non-violent army ? Should not certain aspects of conventional military training form a part of the syllabus ?

A. A very small part of the preliminary training received by the military is common to the non-violent army. These are discipline, drill, singing in chorus, flag hoisting, signalling and the like. Even this is not absolutely necessary and the basis is different. The positively necessary training for a non-violent army is an immovable faith in God, willing and perfect obedience to the chief of the non-violent army and perfect inward and outward co-operation between the units of the army.

Harijan, 12-5-'46

42

CONSTRUCTIVE PREPARATION

Advising Rajkot workers on how to produce an atmosphere of non-violence of the brave, Gandhiji said :

" This depends on individual workers cultivating non-violence in thought, word and deed, by means of a concentrated effort in the fulfilment of the fourfold constructive programme. Maximum of work and minimum of speech must be your motto. In the centre of the programme is the spinning wheel — no haphazard programme of spinning, but scientific understanding of every detail, including the mechanics and the mathematics of it, study of cotton and its varieties, and so on. There is the programme of literacy. You must concentrate exclusively on it, and not talk of any other thing. The work should be systematic and according to time-table. Don't talk of politics — not even of non-violence — but talk to them of the advantages of literacy. There is prohibition of drink and intoxicating drugs and of gambling. There is medical relief by means of the propagation of simple rules of hygiene and sanitation and elementary preventive measures, and of cheap home remedies and training intelligent village folk in these.

" There should not be one house in Rajkot with which you have not established contact from the point of view of pure service. You have to cultivate the Mussalmans, serve them unselfishly. There are the Harijans. Establish living contact with them.

" All this constructive work should be for its own sake. And yet be sure that it will develop the quality required for non-violent responsible government. That is how I began my work in South Africa. I began with serving them. I did not know that I was training them for civil disobedience. I did not know myself that I was so training myself. But you all know what happened in the end.

" This constructive programme may go on endlessly. Why should you be tired of it? Do you know the Hundred Years' War in England? If they fought for a hundred years, we should be prepared to fight for a thousand years, inasmuch as we are a continent. That we will have given our contribution to the fight for freedom, will be our reward.

" That is the mass constructive programme I want you to do, and that is the basis of the training for the non-violence of the brave. It is whole and indivisible, and those who do not believe in it whole-heartedly must leave me and work according to their own lights."

Harijan, 10-6-'39

SECTION THIRD: NON-CO-OPERATION AND CIVIL DISOBEDIENCE

43

THE NATIONAL WEEK

[The Rowlatt Act was passed in the third week of March 1919. It was meant to deal with the situation arising from the expiry of the Defence of India Act soon after World War I. It gave arbitrary powers to the authorities to arrest, confine, imprison or otherwise punish persons who were suspected to be concerned in movements prejudicial to the security of the State. Gandhiji regarded the Act as subversive of the elementary principles of justice and destructive of civil liberties, and therefore by no means to be tolerated.

During World War I, Lloyd George, the then Premier of England made solemn promises to Indian Muslims that the suzerainty of their religious head, the Khalif, who was also the Sultan of Turkey, will be respected. Indian Muslims were thus induced to fight against their co-religionists of Turkey. But after the war, these pledges were broken and Turkey was deprived of her territories which were then distributed between England and France under the guise of mandates. This enraged not only the Muslims but also the other communities in India, who naturally looked upon this act as downright betrayal by Britain of her plighted word. This was the origin of the Khilafat movement, in which Hindus joined with the Muslims against the British.

These two issues led to intense agitation culminating on the 13th April, 1919, in the Jalianwala massacre, where peaceful people who had assembled in a political meeting in a small park were mercilessly killed by gun-fire ordered by a British commanding officer. Thereupon political passions rose to white heat, and Gandhiji organized his non-co-operation movement against the British Govt. in India. He also instituted the week, April 6th to 13th, of terrible happenings in 1919, as a National Week of prayer and fasting celebrated ever since, even to this day. — Ed.]

The sixth of April again saw the inauguration of a definite plan of Hindu-Muslim unity and Swadeshi.

It was the 6th of April which broke the spirit underlying the Rowlatt Act and made it a dead letter. The 13th of April saw not merely the terrific tragedy but in that tragedy Hindu-Muslim blood flowed freely in a mingled stream and sealed the compact.

How to commemorate or celebrate these two great national events? I venture to suggest that those who will, should devote the 6th of April next to fast (twenty-four hours' abstention from food) and prayer.

The whole of the week beginning from the 6th should be devoted to some work connected with the tragedy of the 13th.

Then the 13th. That day of days should be devoted to fasting and prayer. It should be free from ill-will or anger. We want to cherish the memory of the innocent dead. We do not want to remember the wickedness of the deed. The nation will rise by readiness to sacrifice, not by preparing to revenge. On that day I would also have the nation to remember the mass excesses and feel penitent for them.

I would further urge that during the week each one does his or her best in his or her own person to realize more fully than ever the principles of Satyagraha, Hindu-Muslim unity and Swaraj. In order to emphasize Hindu-Muslim unity, I would advise joint meetings of Hindus and Mussalmans on Friday the 12th April at 7 p.m., urging that the Khilafat question be decided in accordance with the just Muslim sentiments.

Thus this national week should be a week of purification, self-examination, sacrifice, exact discipline and expression of cherished national sentiments. There should be no trace of bitterness, no violence of language, but absolute fearlessness and firmness.

I respectfully trust that all parties and all classes will see their way to take their full share in the observances of the National Week and make it an event for the true and definite progress in national awakening.

Young India, 10-3-'20 (reprinted in the issue of 30-3-'22)

44

THE SATYAGRAHA WEEK

First and foremost in the programme for the holy National Week I put fasting and prayer. I have said enough to emphasize the necessity of both these for the unfoldment of our national life. I speak of these from personal experience. But writing to a friend on this very matter of prayer, I came across a beautiful thing from Tennyson, which I present to the readers of *Young India*, if per chance I might convert them to a definite belief in the efficacy of prayer.

Here is the gem :

" .... More things are wrought by prayer
" Than this world dreams of. Wherefore, let thy voice
" Rise like a fountain for me night and day.
" For what are men better than sheep or goats
" That nourish a blind life within the brain,
" If, knowing God, they lift not hands of prayer
" Both for themselves and those who call them friend ?
" For so the whole round earth is every way
" Bound by gold chains about the feet of God."

Throughout my wanderings in India, I have had the privilege of mixing with men of all creeds, of mixing with thousands of women, hundreds upon hundreds of students. I have discussed with them national problems with a passion which I am unable to describe. I have found that we have not yet reached a conscious recognition of our national state. We have not had the discipline necessary for a realization of that state and I venture to say that there is nothing so powerful as fasting and prayer that would give us the requisite discipline, spirit of self-sacrifice, humility and resoluteness of will without which there can be no real progress. I hope, therefore, that millions throughout India will open the Satyagraha Week with sincere fasting and prayer.

I do not wish, during this week, to emphasize the civil-resistance part of Satyagraha. I would like us to contemplate Truth and Non-violence, and to appreciate their

invincibility. Indeed, if all of us regulated our lives by
this eternal law of *Satya* and *Ahimsa*, there will be no
occasion for civil or other resistance. Civil resistance comes
into play when only a small body of men endeavour to
follow truth in the face of opposition. It is difficult to know
what is truth, when to defend it to the point of civil
resistance, and how to avoid error in the shape of violence
in one's pursuit after truth. There may well be differences
of opinion as to the advisability of preaching civil resistance as a creed during a week devoted to national uplift,
in which one seeks the co-operation of all without distinction of party, class or creed.

Young India, 30-3-'22

45

JALIANWALA BAGH

There was an unfortunate hitch about the purchase
of this Bagh for the nation. Thanks to the efforts of the
Hon'ble Pandit Madan Mohan Malaviya, Sannyasi Swami
Shri Shraddhananda and the local leaders, it has now
become the property of the nation subject to full payment
of the purchase price within three months from the 6th
instant. The purchase price is Rs 5,36,000. And the amount
must be raised within the prescribed period.

It is, therefore, necessary to examine the propriety
of making this purchase on behalf of the nation, especially
as it has been questioned even in enlightened quarters.
With the Cawnpore Memorial before us the attitude is not
to be wondered at. But with all respect to objectors, I
cannot help saying that if the Bagh had not been acquired,
it would have been a national disgrace. Can we afford
to forget those five hundred or more men who were killed
although they had done nothing wrong either morally or
legally ? If they had died knowingly and willingly, if
realizing their innocence they had stood their ground and
faced the shots from the fifty rifles, they would have gone

down to history as saints, heroes and patriots. But even as it was, the tragedy became one of first class national importance. Nations are born out of travail and suffering. We should forfeit all title to be considered a nation, if we failed to treasure the memory of those, who in our battle for political freedom might, innocently or for the crimes of others, lose their lives or otherwise suffer. We were unable to protect our helpless countrymen when they were ruthlessly massacred. We may decline, if we will, to avenge the wrong. The nation will not lose if we did. But shall we — can we afford to — decline to perpetuate the memory and to show to the surviving members of the families of the dead that we are sharers in their sufferings, by erecting a national tombstone and by telling the world thereby that in the death of these men each one of us has lost dear relations ? If national instinct does not mean at least this much kinship, it has no meaning for me. I hold it to be our duty to tell the present generation and generations yet unborn that in our march towards true freedom, we must be prepared for repetitions of the wrongs such as the Jalianwala Bagh massacre. We must provide against them, we must not seek them, but we must be ready to face them if they came again. I would not have us flinch from the battle of national life. The supreme lesson of the Amritsar Congress was that the sufferings of the Punjab did not dishearten the nation but that the nation treated them as a matter of course. Some of us made stupid mistakes and the innocent suffered for them. We must in future try to avoid the mistakes but in spite of our best effort, we may fail to convert every one to sanity. We must, therefore, be ready for the repetition of the sufferings of the guiltless by telling the country now that they and theirs shall not be forgotten, but that the memory of the innocent dead shall be regarded as a sacred trust, and that the surviving relations shall have the right to look to the nation for maintenance in case of need. This is the primary meaning of the memorial. And has not the blood of the Mohammedan mixed with that of the

Hindu ? Has not the blood of the Sikh mixed with that of the Sanatanist and the Samajist ? The memorial should be a national emblem of an honest and sustained effort to achieve Hindu-Muslim unity.

But the objector's objection still remains unanswered. Will not the memorial also perpetuate bitterness and ill-will ? It will depend upon the trustees. And if I know them, I know that that is not their intention at all. I know that such was not the intention of the vast assembly. I do not wish to convey that bitterness was not there. It was there, and not in any way suppressed. But the idea of the memorial had nothing of bitterness in it. The people want to, they must be encouraged to, forget the doer and his madness. What General Dyer did we may all do if we had his irresponsibility and opportunity. To err is human, and it must be held to be equally human to forgive if we, though being fallible, would like rather to be forgiven than punished and reminded of our misdeeds. Nor does this mean that we may not ask for General Dyer's dismissal. A lunatic cannot be kept in a position from which he can do harm to his neighbours. But just as we do not bear ill-will towards a lunatic, so too may we not bear ill-will even towards General Dyer. I would therefore eschew from the memorial all idea of bitterness and ill-will, but treat it as a sacred memory and regard the Bagh as a place of pilgrimage to be visited by all irrespective of class, creed or colour. I would invite Englishmen to appreciate our feeling in the matter, ask them by subscribing to the memorial in the spirit of the Royal Proclamation to make common cause with us in our endeavour to regain consciousness, to realize the same freedom that they enjoy under the same constitution and to realize Hindu-Muslim unity without which there can be no true progress for India.

Young India, 18-2-'20

46

NEITHER A SAINT NOR A POLITICIAN

A kind friend has sent me the following cutting from the April number of the *East and West* :

"Mr Gandhi has the reputation of a saint but it seems that the politician in him often dominates his decisions. He has been making great use of *hartals* and there can be no gainsaying that under his direction *hartal* is becoming a powerful political weapon for uniting the educated and the uneducated on a single question of the day. The *hartal* is not without its disadvantages. It is teaching direct action, and direct action however potent does not work for unity. Is Mr Gandhi quite sure that he is serving the highest behests of *ahimsa*, harmlessness ? His proposal to commemorate the shooting at Jalianwala Bagh is not likely to promote concord. It is a tragic incident into which our Government was betrayed, but is the memory of its bitterness worth retaining ? Can we not commemorate the event by raising a temple of peace, to help the widows and orphans, to bless the souls of those who died without knowing why ? The world is full of politicians and petti-foggers who, in the name of patriotism, poison the inner sweetness of man and, as a result, we have wars and feuds and such shameless slaughter as turned Jalianwala Bagh into a shambles. Shall we not now try for a larger symbiosis such as Buddha and Christ preached, and bring the world to breathe and prosper together ? Mr Gandhi seemed destined to be the apostle of such a movement, but circumstances are forcing him to seek the way of raising resistances and group unities. He may yet take up the larger mission of uniting the world."

I have given the whole of the quotation. As a rule I do not notice criticism of me or my methods except when thereby I acknowledge a mistake or enforce still further the principles criticized. I have a double reason for noticing the extract. For, not only do I hope further to elucidate the principles I hold dear, but I want to show my regard for the author of the criticism whom I know and whom I have admired for many years for the singular beauty of his character. The critic regrets to see in me a politician whereas he expected me to be a saint. Now I think that the word *saint* should be ruled out of present life. It is too sacred a word to be lightly applied to anybody, much less to one like myself who claims only to be a humble searcher after truth, knows his limitations, makes mistakes, never hesitates to admit them when he makes them, and frankly confesses that he, like a scientist, is making experiments about some 'of the eternal verities' of life, but cannot even claim to be a scientist because he can show no tangible proof of scientific accuracy in his methods or such tangible results of his experiments as modern science demands. But though by disclaiming sainthood I disappoint the critic's expectations, I would have him to give up his regrets by answering him that the politician in me has never dominated a single decision of mine, and if I seem to take part in politics, it is only because politics encircle us today like the coil of a snake from which one cannot get out, no matter how much one tries. I wish therefore to wrestle with the snake, as I have been doing with more or less success consciously since 1894, unconsciously, as I have now discovered, ever since reaching years of discretion. Quite selfishly, as I wish to live in peace in the midst of a bellowing storm howling round me, I have been experimenting with myself and my friends by introducing religion into politics. Let me explain what I mean by religion. It is not the Hindu religion, which I certainly prize above all other religions, but the religion which transcends Hinduism, which changes one's very nature, which binds one indissolubly to the truth within and which ever purifies. It is the permanent element in human nature which counts no cost too great in order to find full expression and which leaves the soul utterly restless until it has found itself, known its Maker and appreciated the true correspondence between the Maker and itself.

It was in that religious spirit that I came upon *hartal*. I wanted to show that it is not a knowledge of letters that would give India consciousness of herself, or that would bind the educated together. The *hartal* illuminated the whole of India as if by magic on the 6th of April, 1919. And had it not been for the interruption of the 10th of April, brought about by Satan whispering fear into the ears of a Government conscious of its own wrong and inciting to anger a people that were prepared for it by utter distrust of the Government, India would have risen to an unimaginable height. The *hartal* had not only been taken up by the great masses of people in a truly religious spirit but it was intended to be a prelude to a series of direct actions.

But my critic deplores direct action. For, he says, " it does not work for unity." I join issue with him. Never has anything been done on this earth without direct action. I rejected the word *passive resistance* because of its insufficiency and its being interpreted as a weapon of the weak. It was direct action in South Africa which told and told so effectively that it converted General Smuts to sanity. He was in 1906 the most relentless opponent of Indian aspirations. In 1914, he took pride in doing tardy justice by removing from the Statute Book of the Union a disgraceful measure which, in 1909 he had told Lord Morley, would be never removed, for he then said South Africa would never tolerate repeal of a measure which was twice passed by the Transvaal Legislature. But what is more, direct action sustained for eight years left behind it not only no bitterness but the very Indians who put up such a stubborn fight against General Smuts ranged themselves round his banner in 1915 and fought under him in East Africa. It was direct action in Champaran which removed an agelong grievance. A meek submission when one is chafing under a disability or a grievance which one would gladly see removed, not only does not make for unity, but makes the weak party acid, angry and prepares him for an opportunity to explode. By allying myself with the weak party, by teaching him direct, firm, but harmless action, I make him feel strong and capable of defying the physical might. He feels braced for the struggle, regains confidence in himself and knowing that the remedy lies with himself, ceases to harbour the spirit of revenge and learns to be satisfied with a redress of the wrong he is seeking to remedy.

It is working along the same line that I have ventured to suggest a memorial about Jalianwala Bagh. The

writer in *East and West* has ascribed to me a proposal
which has never once crossed my mind. He thinks that
I want "to commemorate the shooting at Jalianwala
Bagh ". Nothing can be further from my thought than
to perpetuate the memory of a black deed. I dare say
that before we have come to our own we shall have a
repetition of the tragedy and I will prepare the nation
for it by treasuring the memory of the innocent dead. The
widows and the orphans have been and are being helped,
but we cannot " bless the souls of those who died without
knowing why," if we will not acquire the ground which
has been hallowed by innocent blood and there erect a
suitable memorial for them. It is not to serve, if I can
help it, as a reminder of a foul deed, but it shall serve as an
encouragement to the nation that it is better to die helpless and unarmed and as victims rather than as tyrants.
I would have the future generations remember that we
who witnessed the innocent dying did not ungratefully
refuse to cherish their memory. As Mrs Jinnah truly
remarked when she gave her mite to the fund, the memorial would at least give us an excuse for living. After all
it will be the spirit in which the memorial is erected that
will decide its character.

What was the larger ' symbiosis ' that Buddha and
Christ preached ? Buddha fearlessly carried the war into
the enemy's camp and brought down on its knees an arro-
gant priesthood. Christ drove out the money-changers
from the temple of Jerusalem and drew down curses from
Heaven upon the hypocrites and the pharisees. Both were
for intensely direct action. But even as Buddha and
Christ chastized they showed unmistakable gentleness and
love behind every act of theirs. They would not raise a
finger against their enemies, but would gladly surrender
themselves rather than the truth for which they lived.
Buddha would have died resisting the priesthood, if the
majesty of his love had not proved to be equal to the
task of bending the priesthood. Christ died on the cross
with a crown of thorns on his head defying the might of
a whole empire. And if I raise resistances of a non-violent

character I simply and humbly follow in the footsteps of the great teachers named by my critic.

Lastly, the writer of the paragraph quarrels with my 'grouping unities' and would have me to take up 'the larger mission of uniting the world'. I once told him under a common roof that I was probably more cosmopolitan than he. I abide by that expression. Unless I group unities I shall never be able to unite the whole world. Tolstoy once said that if we would but get off the backs of our neighbours the world would be quite all right without any further help from us. And if we can only serve our immediate neighbours by ceasing to prey upon them, the circle of unities thus grouped in the right fashion will ever grow in circumference till at last it is conterminous with that of the whole world. More than that it is not given to any man to try or achieve. यथा पिंडे तथा ब्रह्मांडे* is as true today as ages ago when it was first uttered by an unknown *rishi*.

Young India, 12-5-'20

47

THE LAW OF SUFFERING

No country has ever risen without being purified through the fire of suffering. Mother suffers so that her child may live. The condition of wheat growing is that the seed grain should perish. Life comes out of Death. Will India rise out of her slavery without fulfilling this eternal law of purification through suffering?

If my advisers are right, evidently India will realize her destiny without travail. For their chief concern is that the events of April, 1919, should not be repeated. They fear non-co-operation because it would involve the sufferings of many. If Hampdon had argued thus he would not have withheld payment of ship-money, nor would Wat Tayler have raised the standard of revolt.

* As the atom, so the universe.

English and French histories are replete with instances of men continuing their pursuit of the right irrespective of the amount of suffering involved. The actors did not stop to think whether ignorant people would not have involuntarily to suffer. Why should we expect to write our history differently? It is possible for us, if we would, to learn from the mistakes of our predecessors to do better, but it is impossible to do away with the law of suffering which is the one indispensable condition of our being. The way to do better is to avoid, if we can, violence from our side and thus quicken the rate of progress and to introduce greater purity in the methods of suffering. We can, if we will, refrain, in our impatience, from bending the wrong-doer to our will by physical force as Sinn Feiners are doing today, or from coercing our neighbours to follow our methods as was done last year by some of us in bringing about *hartal*. Progress is to be measured by the amount of suffering undergone by the sufferer. The purer the suffering, the greater is the progress. Hence did the sacrifice of Jesus suffice to free a sorrowing world. In his onward march he did not count the cost of suffering entailed upon his neighbours whether it was undergone by them voluntarily or otherwise. Thus did the sufferings of a Harishchandra suffice to re-establish the kingdom of truth. He must have known that his subjects would suffer involuntarily by his abdication. He did not mind because he could not do otherwise than follow truth.

I have already stated that I do not deplore the massacre of Jalianwala Bagh so much as I deplore the murders of Englishmen and destruction of property by ourselves. The frightfulness at Amritsar drew away public attention from the greater though slower frightfulness at Lahore where attempt was made to emasculate the inhabitants by slow processes. But before we rise higher we shall have to undergo such processes many more times till they teach us to take up suffering voluntarily and to find joy in it. I am convinced that the Lahorians never deserved the cruel insults that they were subjected to;

they never hurt a single Englishman ; they never destroyed any property. But a wilful ruler was determined to
crush the spirit of a people just trying to throw off his
chafing yoke. And if I am told that all this was due to
my preaching Satyagraha, my answer is that I would
preach Satyagraha all the more forcibly for that so long
as I have breath left in me, and tell the people that next
time they would answer O'Dwyer's insolence not by
opening shops by reason of threats of forcible sales but
by allowing the tyrant to do his worst and let him sell
their all but their unconquerable souls. Sages of old
mortified the flesh so that the spirit within might be set
free, so that their trained bodies might be proof against
any injury that might be inflicted on them by tyrants
seeking to impose their will on them. And if India wishes
to revive her ancient wisdom and to avoid the errors of
Europe, if India wishes to see the Kingdom of God established on earth instead of that of Satan which has
enveloped Europe, then I would urge her sons and
daughters not to be deceived by fine phrases, the terrible
subtleties that hedge us in, the fears of suffering that
India may have to undergo, but to see what is happening
today in Europe and from it understand that we must
go through suffering even as Europe has gone through,
but not the process of making others suffer. Germany
wanted to dominate Europe and the Allies wanted to do
likewise by crushing Germany. Europe is no better for
Germany's fall. The Allies have proved themselves to be
just as deceitful, cruel, greedy and selfish as Germany was
or would have been. Germany would have avoided the
sanctimonious humbug that one sees associated with the
many dealings of the Allies.

The miscalculation that I deplored last year was not
in connection with the sufferings imposed upon the people,
but about the mistakes made by them and violence done
by them owing to their not having sufficiently understood
the message of Satyagraha. What then is the meaning of
non-co-operation in terms of the law of suffering ? We
must voluntarily put up with the losses and inconveniences

that arise from having to withdraw our support from a Government that is ruling against our will. Possession of power and riches is a crime under an unjust Government, poverty in that case is a virtue, says Thoreau. It may be that in the transition state we may make mistakes ; there may be avoidable suffering. These things are preferable to national emasculation.

We must refuse to wait for the wrong to be righted till the wrong-doer has been roused to a sense of his iniquity. We must not, for fear of ourselves or others having to suffer, remain participators in it. But we must combat the wrong by ceasing to assist the wrong-doer directly or indirectly.

If a father does an injustice it is the duty of his children to leave the parental roof. If the headmaster of a school conducts his institution on an immoral basis, the pupils must leave the school. If the chairman of a corporation is corrupt the members thereof must wash their hands clean of his corruption by withdrawing from it ; even so if a Government does a grave injustice the subjects must withdraw co-operation wholly or partially, sufficiently to wean the ruler from his wickedness. In each case conceived by me there is an element of suffering whether mental or physical. Without such suffering it is not possible to attain freedom.

Young India, 16-6-'20

48

HOW TO WORK NON-CO-OPERATION

Perhaps the best way of answering the fears and criticism as to non-co-operation is to elaborate more fully the scheme of non-co-operation. The critics seem to imagine that the organizers propose to give effect to the whole scheme at once. The fact however is that the organizers have fixed definite, progressive four stages. The first is the giving up of titles and resignation of honorary posts. If there is no response or if the response received is not effective, recourse will be had to the second stage. The second stage involves much previous arrangement. Certainly not a single servant will be called out unless he is either capable of supporting himself and his dependents or the Khilafat Committee is able to bear the burden. All the classes of servants will not be called out at once and never will any pressure be put upon a single servant to withdraw himself from Government service. Nor will a single private employee be touched, for the simple reason that the movement is not anti-English. It is not even anti-Government. Co-operation is to be withdrawn because the people must not be party to a wrong — a broken pledge — a violation of deep religious sentiment. Naturally, the movement will receive a check, if there is any undue influence brought to bear upon any Government servant, or if any violence is used or countenanced by any member of the Khilafat Committee. The second stage must be entirely successful, if the response is at all on an adequate scale. For no Government — much less the Indian Government — can subsist if the people cease to serve it. The withdrawal therefore of the police and the military — the third stage — is a distant goal. The organizers however wanted to be fair, open and above suspicion. They did not want to keep back from Government or the public a single step they had in contemplation even as a remote contingency. The fourth, i.e. suspension of taxes, is still more remote. The organizers recognize that suspension of general taxation is fraught with the greatest danger. It is likely to bring a sensitive class in conflict with the police. They are therefore not likely to embark upon it, unless they can do so with the assurance that there will be no violence offered by the people.

I admit, as I have already done, that non-co-operation is not unattended with risk, but the risk of supineness in the face of a grave issue is infinitely greater than the danger of violence ensuing from organizing non-co-operation. To do nothing is to invite violence for a certainty.

It is easy enough to pass resolutions or write articles

condemning non-co-operation. But it is no easy task to restrain the fury of a people incensed by a deep sense of wrong. I urge those who talk or work against non-co-operation to descend from their chairs and go down to the people, learn their feelings and write, if they have the heart, against non-co-operation. They will find, as I have found, that the only way to avoid violence is to enable them to give such expression to their feelings as to compel redress. I have found nothing save non-co-operation. It is logical and harmless. It is the inherent right of a subject to refuse to assist a government that will not listen to him.

Non-co-operation as a voluntary movement can only succeed, if the feeling is genuine and strong enough to make people suffer to the utmost. If the religious sentiment of the Mohammedans is deeply hurt and if the Hindus entertain neighbourly regard towards their Muslim brethren, they both will count no cost too great for achieving the end. Non-co-operation will not only be an effective remedy but will also be an effective test of the sincerity of the Muslim claim and the Hindu profession of friendship.

Young India, 5-5-'20

49

HOW AND WHEN TO ACT

The following is a statement issued by the Non-co-operation Committee for public information and guidance :

Many questions have been asked of the Non-co-operation Committee as to its expectation and the methods to be adopted for beginning non-co-operation.

The Committee wish it to be understood that whilst they expect every one to respond to their recommendation to the full, they are desirous of carrying the weakest members also with them. The Committee want to enlist the passive sympathy, if not the active co-operation, of the whole of the country in the method of non-co-operation.

Those, therefore, who cannot undergo physical

sacrifice will help by contributing funds or labour to the movement.

Should non-co-operation become necessary, the Committee has decided upon the following as part of the first stage :

(1)   Surrender of all titles of honour and honorary offices.

(2)   Non-participation in Government loans.

(3)   Suspension by lawyers of practice and settlement of civil disputes by private arbitration.

(4)   Boycott of Government schools by parents.

(5)   Boycott of the Reformed Councils.

(6)   Non-participation in Government parties, and such other functions.

(7)   Refusal to accept any civil or military post, in Mesopotamia, or to offer as Units for the army especially for service in the Turkish territories now being administered in violation of pledges.

(8)   Vigorous prosecution of Swadeshi, inducing the people, at the time of this national and religious awakening, to appreciate their primary duty to their country by being satisfied with its own productions and manufactures.

Swadeshi must be pushed forward without waiting for the 1st of August, for it is an eternal rule of conduct not to be interrupted even when the settlement arrives.

In order not to commit themselves, people will refrain now from taking service either civil or military. They will also suspend taking Government loans, new or old.

For the rest, it should be remembered that non-co-operation does not commence before 1st August next.

Every effort is being, and will still be, made to avoid resort to such a serious breach with the Government by urging His Majesty's Ministers to secure the revision of a Treaty which has been so universally condemned.

Those who realize their responsibility and gravity of the cause will not act independently, but in concert with the Committee. Success depends entirely upon disciplined

and concerted non-co-operation and the later is dependent
upon strict obedience to instructions, calmness and absolute freedom from violence.

Young India, 7-7-'20

50

AT THE CALL OF THE COUNTRY

Dr Sapru delivered before the Khilafat Conference
at Allahabad an impassioned address sympathizing with
the Mussalmans in their trouble but dissuaded them from
embarking on non-co-operation. He was frankly unable
to suggest a substitute but was emphatically of opinion
that whether there was a substitute or not non-co-operation was a remedy worse than the disease. He said further that the Mussalmans will be taking upon their
shoulders a serious responsibility if, whilst they appealed
to the ignorant masses to join them, they could not appeal
to the Indian judges to resign, and if they did they would
not succeed.

I acknowledge the force of Dr Sapru's last argument.
At the back of Dr Sapru's mind is the fear that non-co-
operation by the ignorant people would lead to distress
and chaos and would do no good. In my opinion any
non-co-operation is bound to do some good. Even the
Viceregal door-keeper saying, " Please Sir, I can serve the
Government no longer because it has hurt my national
honour," and resigning is a step mightier and more
effective than the mightiest speech declaiming against the
Government for its injustice.

Nevertheless, it would be wrong to appeal to the door-
keeper until one has appealed to the highest in the land.
And as I propose, if the necessity arose, to ask the door-
keepers of the Government to dissociate themselves from
an unjust Government, I propose now to address an appeal
to the Judges and the Executive Councillors to join the
protest that is rising from all over India against the double
wrong done to India, on the Khilafat and the Punjab questions. In both national honour is involved.

I take it that these gentlemen have entered upon their high offices not for the sake of emolument, nor I hope for the sake of fame, but for the sake of serving their country. It was not for money, for, they were earning more than they do now. It must not be for fame, for, they cannot buy fame at the cost of national honour. The only consideration that can at the present moment keep them in office must be service of the country.

When the people have faith in the Government, when it represents the popular will, the judges and the executive officials possibly serve the country. But when that Government does not represent the will of the people, when it supports dishonesty and terrorism, the judges and the executive officials by retaining office become instruments of dishonesty and terrorism. And the least therefore that these holders of high offices can do is to cease to become agents of a dishonest and terrorizing Government.

For the judges the objection will be raised that they are above politics, and so they are and should be. But the doctrine is true only in so far as the Government is on the whole for the benefit of the people and at least represents the will of the majority. Not to take part in politics means not to take sides. But when a whole country has one mind, one will, when a whole country has been denied justice, it is no longer a question of party politics, it is a matter of life and death. It then becomes the duty of every citizen to refuse to serve a Government which misbehaves and flouts national wish. The judges are at that moment bound to follow the nation if they are ultimately its servants.

There remains another argument to be examined. It applies to both the judges and the members of the executive. It will be urged that my appeal could only be meant for the Indians and what good can it do by Indians renouncing offices which have been won for the nation by hard struggle. I wish that I could make an effective appeal to the English as well as the Indians. But I confess that I have written with the mental reservation that the appeal is addressed only to the Indians. I must therefore examine the argument just stated. Whilst it is true that these offices have been secured after a prolonged struggle, they are of use not because of the struggle but because they are intended to serve the nation. The moment they cease to possess that quality, they become useless and as in the present case harmful, no matter how hard-earned and therefore valuable they may have been at the outset.

I would submit too to our distinguished countrymen who occupy high offices that their giving up their offices will bring the struggle to a speedy end and would probably obviate the danger attendant upon the masses being called upon to signify their disapproval by withdrawing co-operation. If the title-holders gave up their titles, if the holders of honorary offices gave up their appointments and if the high officials gave up their posts, and the would-be councillors boycotted the councils, the Government would quickly come to its senses, and give effect to the people's will. For the alternative before the Government then would be nothing but despotic rule pure and simple. That would probably mean military dictatorship. The world's opinion has advanced so far that Britain dare not contemplate such dictatorship with equanimity. The taking of the steps suggested by me will constitute the peacefullest revolution the world has ever seen. Once the infallibility of non-co-operation is realized, there is an end to all bloodshed and violence in any shape or form.

Undoubtedly a cause must be grave to warrant the drastic method of national non-co-operation. I do say that the affront such as has been put upon Islam cannot be repeated for a century. Islam must rise now or 'be fallen' if not for ever, certainly for a century. And I cannot imagine a graver wrong than the massacre of Jalianwala and the barbarity that followed it, the white-wash by the Hunter Committee, the dispatch of the Government of India, Mr Montagu's letter upholding the Viceroy and the then Lieutenant-Governor of the Punjab, the refusal to remove officials who made of the lives of the Punjabis 'a hell' during the Martial Law period. These acts constitute a complete series of continuing wrongs against India which if India has any sense of honour, she must right at the sacrifice of all the material wealth she possesses. If she does not, she will have bartered her soul for a ' mess of pottage '.

Young India, 21-7-'20

51

THE FIRST OF AUGUST

It is hardly likely that before the 1st August there will be on the part of His Majesty's Ministers promise of a revision of the peace terms and the consequent suspension of the inauguration of non-co-operation. The first of August next will be as important an event in the history of India as was the 6th of April last year. The sixth of April marked the beginning of the end of the Rowlatt Act. No one can consider the Rowlatt Act can possibly live in the face of the agitation that has only been suspended — never given up. It must be clear to any one that the power that wrests justice from an unwilling Government in the matter of the Punjab and the Khilafat will be the power that will secure repeal of the Rowlatt Act. And that power is the power of Satyagraha whether it is known by the name of civil disobedience or non-co-operation.

Many people dread the advent of non-co-operation, because of the events of last year. They fear madness from the mob and consequent repetition of last year's reprisals almost unsurpassed in their ferocity in the history of modern times. Personally I do not mind Governmental fury as I mind mob fury. The latter is a sign of national distemper and therefore more difficult to deal with than the former which is confined to a small corporation. It is easier to oust a Government that has rendered itself unfit to govern than it is to cure unknown people in a mob of their madness. But great movements cannot be stopped altogether because a Government or a people or both go wrong. We learn and profit through our mistakes and failures. No general worth the name gives up a battle because he has suffered reverses, or which is the same thing, made mistakes. And so we must approach non-co-operation with confidence and hope. As in the past, the commencement is to be marked by fasting and prayer — a sign of the religious character of the demonstration. There should also be on that day suspension of business, and meetings to pass resolutions praying for revision of the peace terms and justice for the Punjab, and inculcating non-co-operation until justice has been done.

The giving up of titles and honorary posts should also commence from the first of August. Doubt has been expressed as to the sufficiency of notice regarding surrender of titles and honorary posts. It is however quickly dispelled by bearing in mind that the first of August marks the commencement of the surrender of titles. It is not the only day on which surrender has to take place. Indeed I do not expect a very large response on the first day. A vigorous propaganda will have to be carried on and the message delivered to every title- or post-holder and the argument presented to him proving the duty of such surrender.

But the greatest thing in this campaign of non-co-operation is to evolve order, discipline, co-operation among the people and co-ordination among the workers. Effective non-co-operation depends upon complete organization. Thousands of men who have filled meetings throughout the Punjab have convinced me that the people want to withdraw co-operation from the Government but they must know how. Most people do not understand the complicated machinery of the Government. They do not realize that every citizen silently but none-the-less certainly sustains the Government of the day in ways of which he has no knowledge. Every citizen therefore renders himself responsible for every act of his Government. And it is quite proper to support it so long as the actions of the Government are bearable. But when they hurt him and his nation, it becomes his duty to withdraw his support.

But as I have said, every citizen does not know how to do so in an orderly manner. Disorderliness comes from anger, orderliness out of intelligent resistance. The first condition therefore of real success is to ensure entire absence of violence. Violence done to persons representing the Government or to persons who don't join our ranks, i.e., the supporters of the Government, means in every case retrogression in our case, cessation of non-co-operation and useless waste of innocent lives. Those, therefore, who wish to make non-co-operation a success in the quickest possible time will consider it their first duty to see that in their neighbourhood complete order is kept.

Young India, 28-7-'20

52

WHO IS DISLOYAL ?

Mr Montagu has discovered a new definition of disloyalty. He considers my suggestion to boycott the visit of the Prince of Wales to be disloyal, and some newspapers taking the cue from him have called persons who have made the suggestion ' unmannerly '. They have even attributed to these ' unmannerly ' persons the suggestion of ' boycotting the Prince '. I draw a sharp and fundamental distinction between boycotting the Prince and boycotting any welcome arranged for him. Personally I would extend the heartiest welcome to His Royal Highness if he came or could come without official patronage and the protecting wings of the Government of the day. Being the heir to a constitutional monarch, the Prince's movements are regulated and dictated by the ministers, no matter how much the dictation may be concealed beneath diplomatically polite language. In suggesting the boycott therefore the promoters have suggested boycott of an insolent bureaucracy and dishonest ministers of His Majesty.

You cannot have it both ways. It is true that under a constitutional monarchy, the royalty is above politics. But you cannot send the Prince on a political visit for the purpose of making political capital out of him, and then complain that those, who will not play your game and, in order to checkmate you, proclaim a boycott of the Royal visit, do not know constitutional usage. For the Prince's visit is not for pleasure. His Royal Highness is to come, in Mr Lloyd George's words, as the 'ambassador of the British nation', in other words, his own ambassador in order to issue a certificate of merit to him and possibly to give the ministers a new lease of life. The wish is designed to consolidate and strengthen a power that spells mischief for India. Even as it is, Mr Montagu has foreseen that the welcome will probably be excelled by any hitherto extended to Royalty, meaning that the people are not really and deeply affected and stirred by the official atrocities in the Punjab and the manifestly dishonest breach of official declarations on the Khilafat. With the knowledge that India was bleeding at heart, the Government of India should have told His Majesty's ministers that the moment was inopportune for sending the Prince. I venture to submit that it is adding insult to injury to bring the Prince and through his visit to steal honours and further prestige for a Government that deserves to be dismissed with disgrace. I claim that I prove my loyalty by saying that India is in no mood, is too deeply in mourning to take part in any welcome to His Royal Highness, and that the ministers and the Indian Government show their disloyalty by making the Prince a cat's paw of their deep political game. If they persist, it is the clear duty of India to have nothing to do with the visit.

Young India, 4-8-'20

53

NON-VIOLENCE AND SWADESHI

Before a crowded meeting of Mussalmans in the Muzaffarabad at Bombay held on the 29th July, speaking on the impending non-co-operation which commenced on the 1st of August, Mr Gandhi said the time for speeches on non-co-operation was past and the time for practice had arrived. But two things were needful for complete success : an environment free from any violence on the part of the people and a spirit of self-sacrifice. Non-co-operation, as the speaker had conceived it, was an impossibility in an atmosphere surcharged with the spirit of violence. Violence was an exhibition of anger and any such exhibition was dissipation of valuable energy. Subduing of one's anger was a storing up of national energy, which, when set free in an ordered manner, would produce astounding results. His conception of non-co-operation did not involve rapine, plunder, incendiarism and all the concomitants of mass madness. His scheme presupposed ability on their part to control all the forces of evil. If, therefore, any disorderliness was found on the part of the people which they could not control, he for one would certainly help the Government to control them. In the presence of disorder it would be for him a choice of evil, and evil though he considered the present Government to be, he would not hesitate for the time being to help the Government to control disorder. But he had faith in the people. He believed that they knew that the cause could only be won by non-violent methods. To put it at the lowest, the people had not the power, even if they had the will, to resist with brute strength the unjust Governments of Europe who had, in the intoxication of their success, disregarding every canon of justice, dealt so cruelly by the only Islamic Power in Europe.

Matchless Weapon

In non-co-operation they had a matchless and powerful weapon. It was a sign of religious atrophy to sustain an unjust Government that supported an injustice by resorting to untruth and camouflage. So long therefore as the Government did not purge itself of the canker of injustice and untruth, it was their duty to withdraw all help from it, consistently with their ability to preserve order in the social structure. The first stage of non-co-operation was, therefore, so arranged as to involve minimum of danger to public peace and minimum of sacrifice on the part of those who participated in the movement. And if they might not help an evil Government nor receive any favours from it, it followed that they must give up all titles of honour which were no longer a proud possession. Lawyers, who were in reality honorary officers of the Court, should cease to support Courts that upheld the prestige of an unjust Government and the people must be able to settle their disputes and quarrels by private arbitration. Similarly, parents should withdraw their children from the public schools and they must evolve a system of national education or private education totally independent of the Government. An insolent Government, conscious of its brute strength, might laugh at such withdrawals by the people especially as the Law Courts and schools were supposed to help the people, but he had not a shadow of doubt that the moral effect of such a step could not possibly be lost even upon a Government whose conscience had become stifled by the intoxication of power.

Swadeshi

He had hesitation in accepting Swadeshi as a plank in non-co-operation. To him Swadeshi was as dear as life itself. But he had no desire to smuggle in Swadeshi through the Khilafat movement, if it could not legitimately help that movement. But conceived as non-co-operation was in a spirit of self-sacrifice, Swadeshi had a legitimate place in the movement. Pure Swadeshi meant sacrifice of their liking for fineries. He asked the nation to sacrifice its liking for the fineries of Europe and Japan and be satisfied with the coarse but beautiful fabrics woven on their handlooms out of yarns spun by millions of their sisters. If the nation had become really awakened to a sense of the danger to its religions and its self-respect, it could not but perceive the absolute and immediate necessity of the adoption of Swadeshi in its intense form, and if the people of India adopted Swadeshi with religious zeal he begged to assure them that its adoption would arm them with a new power and would produce an unmistakable impression throughout the whole world. He, therefore, expected the Mussalmans to give the lead by giving up all the fineries they were so fond of and adopt the simple cloth that could be produced by the manual labour of their sisters and brethren in their own cottages. And he hoped that the Hindus would follow suit. It was a sacrifice in which the whole nation, every man, woman and child, could take part.

Young India, 4-8-'20

54

PROGRAMME FOR SATYAGRAHA

[From a letter written by Gandhiji to Hakim Ajmal Khan from Sabarmati Jail, dated 12th March, 1922.]

A staunch Mussalman, you have shown in your own life what Hindu-Muslim unity means.

We all now realize, as we have never before realized, that without that unity we cannot attain our freedom, and I make bold to say that without that unity the Mussalmans of India cannot render the Khilafat all the aid they wish. Divided, we must ever remain slaves. This unity, therefore, cannot be a mere policy to be discarded when it does not suit us. We can discard it only when we are tired of Swaraj. Hindu-Muslim unity must be our creed to last for all time and under all circumstances.

Nor must that unity be a menace to the minorities — the Parsees, the Christians, the Jews or the powerful Sikhs. If we seek to crush any of them, we shall some day want to fight each other.

I have been drawn so close to you chiefly because I know that you believe in Hindu-Muslim unity in the full sense of the term.

This unity, in my opinion, is unattainanble without our adopting non-violence as a firm policy. I call it a policy because it is limited to the preservation of that unity. But it follows that thirty crores of Hindus and Mussalmans, united not for a time but for all time, can defy all the powers of the world and should consider it a cowardly act to resort to violence in their dealings with the English administrators. We have hitherto feared them and their guns in our simplicity. The moment we realize our combined strength, we shall consider it unmanly to fear them and, therefore, ever to think of striking them. Hence am I anxious and impatient to persuade my countrymen to feel non-violent, not out of our weakness but out of our strength. But you and I know that we have not yet evolved the non-violence of the strong. And we have not done so, because the Hindu-Muslim union has not gone much beyond the stage of policy. There is still too much mutual distrust and consequent fear. I am not disappointed. The progress we have made in that direction is indeed phenomenal. We seem to have covered in eighteen months' time the work of a generation. But infinitely more is necessary. Neither the classes nor the masses feel instinctively that our union is necessary as the breath of our nostrils.

For this consummation we must, it seems to me, rely more upon quality than quantity. Given a sufficient number of Hindus and Mussalmans with almost a fanatical faith in everlasting friendship between the Hindus and the Mussalmans of India, we shall not be long before the unity permeates the masses. A few of us must first clearly understand that we can make no headway without accepting non-violence in thought, word and deed for the full realization of our political ambition. I would, therefore, beseech you and the members of the Working Committee and the All-India Congress Committee to see that our ranks contain no workers who do not fully realize the essential truth I have endeavoured to place before you. A living faith cannot be manufactured by the rule of majority.

To me the visible symbol of all-India unity and, there-fore, of the acceptance of non-violence as an indispensable means for the realization of our political ambition is un-doubtedly the *charkha*, i.e. khaddar. Only those who believe in *cultivating* a non-violent spirit and eternal friendship between Hindus and Mussalmans will daily and religiously spin. Universal hand-spinning and the univer-sal manufacture and use of hand-spun and hand-woven khaddar will be a substantial, if not absolute, proof of real unity and non-violence. And it will be a recognition of a living kinship with the dumb masses. Nothing can possibly unify and revivify India as the acceptance by all India of the spinning wheel as a daily sacrament and khaddar wear as a privilege and a duty.

Whilst, therefore, I am anxious that more title-holders should give up their titles, lawyers law-courts, scholars Government schools or colleges, Councillors the Councils, and the soldiers and the civilians their posts, I would urge the nation to restrict its activity in this direction only to the consolidation of the results already achieved and to trust its strength to command further abstentions from association with a system we are seeking to mend or end.

Moreover, the workers are too few. I would not waste a single worker today on destructive work when we have such an enormous amount of constructive work. But perhaps the most conclusive argument against devoting further time to destructive propaganda is the fact that the spirit of intolerance which is a form of violence has never been so rampant as now. Co-operators are estranged from us ; they fear us. They say that we are establishing a worse bureaucracy than the existing one. We must remove every cause for such anxiety. We must go out of our way to win them to our side. We must make Englishmen safe from all harm from our side. I should not have to labour the point, if it was clear to every one as it is to you and to me that our pledge of non-violence implies utter humility and goodwill even towards our bitterest opponent. This neces-sary spirit will be automatically realized, if only India will devote her sole attention to the work of construction suggested by me.

I flatter myself with the belief that my imprisonment is quite enough for a long time to come. I believe in all humility that I have no ill-will against any one. Some of my friends would not have to be as non-violent as I am. But we contemplated the imprisonment of the most innocent. If I may be allowed that claim, it is clear that I should not be followed to prison by anybody at all. We do want to paralyze the Government considered as a system — not, however, by intimidation, but by the irresistible pressure of our innocence. In my opinion it would be intimidation to fill the jails anyhow. And why should more innocent men seek imprisonment till one considered to be the most innocent has been found inadequate for the purpose.

My caution against further courting of imprisonment does not mean that we are now to shirk imprisonment. If the Government will take away every *non-violent* non-co-operator, I should welcome it. Only it should not be because of our civil disobedience, defensive or aggressive. Nor, I hope, will the country fret over those who are in jail. It will do them and the country good to serve the full term of their imprisonment. They can be fitly discharged before their time only by an act of the Swaraj Parliament. And I entertain an absolute conviction that universal adoption of khaddar is Swaraj.

I have refrained from mentioning untouchability. I am sure every good Hindu believes that it has got to go. Its removal is as necessary as the realization of Hindu-Muslim unity.

I have placed before you a programme which is in my opinion the quickest and the best. No impatient Khilafatist can devise a better. May God give you health and wisdom to guide the country to her destined goal.

Young India, 16-3-'22

55

THE DOCTRINE OF THE SWORD

In this age of the rule of brute force, it is almost impossible for any one to believe that any one else could possibly reject the law of the final supremacy of brute force. And so I receive anonymous letters advising me that I must not interfere with the progress of non-co-operation even though popular violence may break out. Others come to me and, assuming that secretly I must be plotting violence, inquire when the happy moment for declaring open violence will arrive. They assure me that the English will never yield to anything but violence secret or open. Yet others, I am informed, believe that I am the most rascally person living in India because I never give out my real intention, and that they have not a shadow of doubt that I believe in violence just as much as most people do.

Such being the hold that the doctrine of the sword has on the majority of mankind, and as success of non-co-operation depends principally on absence of violence during its pendency, and as my views in this matter affect the conduct of a large number of people, I am anxious to state them as clearly as possible.

I do believe that where there is only a choice between cowardice and violence I would advise violence. Thus when my eldest son asked me what he should have done, had he been present when I was almost fatally assaulted in 1908, whether he should have run away and seen me killed or whether he should have used his physical force which he could and wanted to use, and defended me, I told him that it was his duty to defend me even by using violence. Hence it was that I took part in the Boer War, the so-called Zulu rebellion and the late War. Hence also do I advocate training in arms for those who believe in the method of violence. I would rather have India resort to arms in order to defend her honour than that she should in a cowardly manner become or remain a helpless witness to her own dishonour.

But I believe that non-violence is infinitely superior to violence, forgiveness is more manly than punishment. क्षमा वीरस्य भूषणम् । (Forgiveness adorns a soldier). But abstinence is forgiveness only when there is the power to punish ; it is meaningless when it pretends to proceed from a helpless creature. A mouse hardly forgives a cat when it allows itself to be torn to pieces by her. I therefore appreciate the sentiment of those who cry out for the condign punishment of General Dyer and his ilk. They would tear him to pieces if they could. But I do not believe India to be helpless. I do not believe myself to be a helpless creature. Only I want to use India's and my strength for a better purpose.

Let me not be misunderstood. Strength does not come from physical capacity. It comes from an indomitable will. An average Zulu is any way more than a match for an average Englishman in bodily capacity. But he flees from an English boy, because he fears the boy's revolver or those who will use it for him. He fears death and is nerveless in spite of his burly figure. We in India may in a moment realize that one hundred thousand Englishmen need not frighten three hundred million human beings. A definite forgiveness would therefore mean a definite recognition of our strength. With enlightened forgiveness must come a mighty wave of strength in us, which would make it impossible for a Dyer and a Frank Johnson to heap affront upon India's devoted head. It matters little to me that for the moment I do not drive my point home. We feel too downtrodden not to be angry and revengeful. But I must not refrain from saying that India can gain more by waiving the right of punishment. We have better work to do, a better mission to deliver to the world.

I am not a visionary. I claim to be a practical idealist. The religion of non-violence is not meant merely for *rishis* and saints. It is meant for the common people as well. Non-violence is the law of our species as violence is the law of the brute. The spirit lies dormant in the brute and he knows no law but that of physical might. The dignity of man requires obedience to a higher law — to the strength of the spirit.

I have therefore ventured to place before India the ancient law of self-sacrifice. For Satyagraha and its off-shoots, non-co-operation and civil resistance, are nothing but new names for the law of suffering. The *rishis*, who discovered the law of non-violence in the midst of violence, were greater geniuses than Newton. They were themselves greater warriors than Wellington. Having themselves known the use of arms, they realized their uselessness and taught a weary world that its salvation lay not through violence but through non-violence.

Non-violence in its dynamic condition means conscious suffering. It does not mean meek submission to the will of the evil-doer, but it means the pitting of one's whole soul against the will of the tyrant. Working under this law of our being, it is possible for a single individual to defy the whole might of an unjust empire, to save his honour, his religion, his soul and lay the foundation for that empire's fall or its regeneration.

And so I am not pleading for India to practise non-violence because she is weak. I want her to practise non-violence being conscious of her strength and power. No training in arms is required for realization of her strength. We seem to need it because we seem to think that we are but a lump of flesh. I want India to rcognize that she has a soul that cannot perish and that can rise triumphant above every physical weakness and defy the physical combination of a whole world. What is the meaning of Rama, a mere human being, with his host of monkeys, pitting himself against the insolent strength of ten-headed Ravana surrounded in supposed safety by the raging waters on all sides of Lanka ? Does it not mean the conquest of physical might by spiritual strength ? However, being a practical man, I do not wait till India recognizes the practicability of the spiritual life in the political world. India considers herself to be powerless and paralyzed before the machine-guns, the tanks and the aeroplanes of the English. And she takes up non-co-operation out of her weakness.

It must still serve the same purpose, namely, bring her delivery from the crushing weight of British injustice if a sufficient number of people practise it.

I isolate this non-co-operation from Sinn Feinism, for, it is so conceived as to be incapable of being offered side by side with violence. But I invite even the school of violence to give this peaceful non-co-operation a trial. It will not fail through its inherent weakness. It may fail because of poverty of response. Then will be the time for real danger. The high-souled men, who are unable to suffer national humiliation any longer, will want to vent their wrath. They will take to violence. So far as I know, they must perish without delivering themselves or their country from the wrong. If India takes up the doctrine of the sword, she may gain momentary victory. Then India will cease to be the pride of my heart. I am wedded to India because I owe my all to her. I believe absolutely that she has a mission for the world. She is not to copy Europe blindly. India's acceptance of the doctrine of the sword will be the hour of my trial. I hope I shall not be found wanting. My religion has no geographical limits. If I have a living faith in it, it will transcend my love for India herself. My life is dedicated to service of India through the religion of non-violence which I believe to be the root of Hinduism.

Meanwhile I urge those who distrust me not to disturb the even working of the struggle that has just commenced, by inciting to violence in the belief that I want violence. I detest secrecy as a sin. Let them give non-violent non-co-operation a trial and they will find that I had no mental reservation whatsoever.

Young India, 11-8-'20

56

RENUNCIATION OF MEDALS

[Mr Gandhi has addressed the following letter to the Viceroy :]

It is not without a pang that I return the Kaiser-i-Hind gold medal granted to me by your predecessor for my humanitarian work in South Africa, the Zulu War medal granted in South Africa for my services as officer in charge of the Indian volunteer ambulance corps in 1906 and the Boer War medal for my services as assistant superintendent of the Indian volunteer stretcher-bearer corps during the Boer War of 1899-1900. I venture to return these medals in pursuance of the scheme of non-co-operation inaugurated today in connection with the Khilafat movement. Valuable as these honours have been to me, I cannot wear them with an easy conscience so long as my Mussalman countrymen have to labour under a wrong done to their religious sentiment. Events that have happened during the past month have confirmed me in the opinion that the Imperial Government have acted in the Khilafat matter in an unscrupulous, immoral and unjust manner and have been moving from wrong to wrong in order to defend their immorality. I can retain neither respect nor affection for such a Government.

The attitude of the Imperial and Your Excellency's Governments on the Punjab question has given me additional cause for grave dissatisfaction. I had the honour, as Your Excellency is aware, as one of the Congress commissioners to investigate the causes of the disorders in the Punjab during the April of 1919. And it is my deliberate conviction that Sir Michael O'Dwyer was totally unfit to hold the office of Lieutenant Governor of the Punjab and that his policy was primarily responsible for infuriating the mob at Amritsar. No doubt the mob excesses were unpardonable ; incendiarism, murder of five innocent Englishmen and the cowardly assault on Miss Sherwood were most deplorable and uncalled for. But the punitive measures taken by General Dyer, Col. Frank

Johnson, Col. O'Brien, Mr Bosworth Smith, Rai Shriram Sud, Mr Malik Khan and other officers were out of all proportion to the crime of the people and amounted to wanton cruelty and inhumanity almost unparalleled in modern times. Your Excellency's light-hearted treatment of the official crime, your exoneration of Sir Michael O'Dwyer, Mr Montagu's dispatch and above all the shameful ignorance of the Punjab events and callous disregard of the feelings of Indians betrayed by the House of Lords, have filled me with the gravest misgivings regarding the future of the Empire, have estranged me completely from the present Government and have disabled me from tendering, as I have hitherto whole-heartedly tendered, my loyal co-operation.

In my humble opinion the ordinary method of agitating by way of petitions, deputations and the like is no remedy for moving to repentance a Government so hopelessly indifferent to the welfare of its charge as the Government of India has proved to be. In European countries, condonation of such grievous wrongs as the Khilafat and the Punjab would have resulted in a bloody revolution by the people. They would have resisted at all cost national emasculation such as the said wrongs imply. But half of India is too weak to offer violent resistance and the other half is unwilling to do so. I have therefore ventured to suggest the remedy of non-co-operation which enables those who wish, to dissociate themselves from the Government and which if it is unattended by violence and undertaken in an ordered manner, must compel it to retrace its steps and undo the wrongs committed. But whilst I shall pursue the policy of non-co-operation in so far as I can carry the people with me, I shall not lose hope that you will yet see your way to do justice. I, therefore, respectfully ask Your Excellency to summon a conference of the recognized leaders of the people and in consultation with them find a way that would placate the Mussalmans and do reparation to the unhappy Punjab.

Young India, 4-8-'20

57

NON-PAYMENT OF FINES

All the readers of *Young India* may not know that Ahmedabad came under a heavy fine for the misdeeds of the April of last year. The fine was collected from the residents of Ahmedabad but some were exempted at the discretion of the Collector. Among those who were called upon to pay fines were income-tax payers. They had to pay a third of the tax paid by them. Mr V. J. Patel, a noted barrister, and Dr Kanuga, a leading medical practitioner, were among those who were unable to pay. They had admittedly helped the authorities to quell the disturbance. No doubt they were Satyagrahis but they had endeavoured to still the mob fury even at some risk to their own persons. But the authorities would not exempt them. It was a difficult thing for them to use discretion in individual cases. It was equally difficult for these two gentlemen to pay any fine when they were not to blame at all. They did not wish to embarrass the authorities and yet they were anxious to preserve their self-respect. They carried on no agitation but simply notified their inability to pay the fines in the circumstances set forth above. Therefore, an attachment order was issued. Dr Kanuga is a very busy practitioner and his cash box is always full. The watchful attaching official attached his cash box and extracted enough money to discharge the writ of execution. A lawyer's business cannot be conducted on those lines. Mr Patel sported no cash box. A sofa of his sitting room was therefore attached and advertised for sale and duly sold. Both these Satyagrahis thus completely saved their consciences.

Wiseacres may laugh at the folly of allowing writs of attachment and paying for the collection of fines. Multiply such instances and imagine the consequence to the authorities of executing thousands of writs. Writs are possible when they are confined to a few recalcitrants.

They are troublesome when they have to be executed against many high-souled persons who have done no wrong and who refuse payment to vindicate a principle. They may not attract much notice when isolated individuals resort to this method of protest. But clean examples have a curious method of multiplying themselves. They bear publicity and the sufferers instead of incurring odium receive congratulations. Men like Thoreau brought about the abolition of slavery by their personal examples. Says Thoreau, " I know this well, that if one thousand, if one hundred, if ten men whom I could name, — if ten *honest* men only — aye, if *one honest* man, in this State of Massachusetts *ceasing to hold slaves* were actually to withdraw from this co-partnership and be locked up in the country gaol therefor, it would be the abolition of slavery in America. For it matters not how small the beginning may seem to be, what is once well done is done for ever." Again he says, " I have contemplated the imprisonment of the offender rather than seizure of his goods — though both will serve the same purpose, because they who assert the purest right and consequently are most dangerous to a corrupt State, commonly have not spent much time in accumulating property." We, therefore, congratulate Mr Patel and Dr Kanuga on the excellent example set by them in an excellent spirit and in an excellent cause.

Young India, 7-7-'20

58

NON-PAYMENT OF TAXES

I observe a desire in some places to precipitate mass civil disobedience by suspending payment of taxes. But I would urge the greatest caution before embarking upon the dangerous adventure. We must not be indifferent about violence, and we must make sure of masses exercising self-control whilst they are witnesses to the confiscation of their crops and cattle or forfeiture of their holdings. I know that withholding of payment of taxes is one of the quickest methods of overthrowing a government. I am equally sure that we have not yet evolved that degree of strength and discipline which are necessary for conducting a successful campaign of non-payment of taxes. Not a single *tahsil* in India is yet ready, except perhaps Bardoli and, to a lesser degree, Anand. More than fifty percent of the population of such *tahsil* has to rid itself of the curse of untouchability, must be dressed in *khadi* manufactured in the *tahsil*, must be non-violent in thought, word and deed, and must be living in perfect friendliness with all whether co-operators or non-co-operators. Non-payment of taxes without the necessary discipline will be an act of unpardonable madness. Instead of leading to Swaraj, it is likely to lead to no-*raj*.

Young India, 19-1-'22

59

NON-PAYMENT OF TAXES

The validity of the objection * (against non-payment of taxes) lies in the statement that the non-payment campaign will bring into the movement people, who are not as yet saturated with the principle of non-violence. This is very true, and because it is true, non-payment does 'hold out a material bait'. It follows, therefore, that we must not resort to non-payment because of the possibility of a ready response. The readiness is a fatal temptation. Such non-payment will not be civil or non-violent, but it will be criminal or fraught with the greatest possibility of violence. Let us remember the experience of Pandit Jawaharlal Nehru when the peasants, after they had taken the pledge of non-violence, told him that if he advised them to do violence, they would be certainly ready to do so. Not until the peasantry is trained to understand

---

* Reference is to apprehensions expressed by a friend " in deep sympathy with the national movement ".

the reason and the virtue of *civil* non-payment and is prepared to look with calm resignation upon the confiscation (which can only be temporary) of their holdings and the forced sale of their cattle and other belongings, may they be advised to withhold payment of taxes. They must be told what happened in holy Palestine. The Arabs who were fined were surrounded by soldiers. Aeroplanes were hovering overhead. And the sturdy men were dispossessed of their cattle. The latter were impounded and left without fodder and even water. When the Arabs, stupefied and rendered helpless, brought the fine and additional penalty, as if to mock them, they had their dead and dying cattle returned to them. Worse things can and certainly will happen in India. Are the Indian peasantry prepared to remain absolutely non-violent, and see their cattle taken away from them to die of hunger and thirst ? I know that such things have already happened in Andhra Desh. If the peasantry in general knowingly and deliberately remain peaceful even in such trying circumstances, they are nearly ready for non-payment.

I say ' nearly ready ', for non-payment is intended to transfer the power from the bureaucracy into our hands. It is, therefore, not enough that the peasantry remain non-violent. Non-violence is certainly nine-tenths of the battle, but it is not all. The peasantry may remain non-violent, but may not treat the untouchables as their brethren ; they may not regard Hindus, Mussalmans, Christians, Jews, Parsis, as the case may be, as their brethren ; they may not have learnt the economic and the moral value of the *charkha* and khaddar. If they have not, they cannot gain Swaraj. They will not do all these things after Swaraj, if they will not do them now. They must be taught to know that the practice of these national virtues means Swaraj.

Thus civil non-payment of taxes is a privilege capable of being exercised only after rigorous training. And even as *civil* disobedience is difficult in the case of a habitual offender against the laws of the State, so is *civil* non-payment difficult for those who have hitherto been in the habit of withholding payment of taxes on the slightest pretext. Civil non-payment of taxes is indeed the last stage in non-co-operation. We must not resort to it till we have tried the other forms of civil disobedience. And it will be the height of unwisdom to experiment with non-payment in large or many areas in the beginning stages.

Young India, 26-1-'22

60

BOYCOTT OF COURTS AND SCHOOLS

The Non-co-operation Committee has included, in the first stage, boycott of Law Courts by lawyers and of Government schools and colleges by parents or scholars as the case may be. I know that it is only my reputation as a worker and fighter, which has saved me from an open charge of lunacy for having given the advice about boycott of Courts and schools.

I venture, however, to claim some method about my madness. It does not require much reflection to see that it is through Courts that a Government establishes its authority and it is through schools that it manufactures clerks and other employees. They are both healthy institutions when the Government in charge of them is on the whole just. They are death-traps when the Government is unjust.

I submit that national non-co-operation requires suspension of their practice by lawyers. Perhaps no one co-operates with a Government more than lawyers through its Law Courts. Lawyers interpret laws to the people and thus support authority. It is for that reason that they are styled 'officers of the Court'. They may be called honorary office-holders. It is said that it is the lawyers who have put up the most stubborn fight against the Government. This is no doubt partly true. But that does not undo the mischief that is inherent in the profession.

So when the nation wishes to paralyze the Government, that profession, if it wishes to help the nation to bend the Government to its will, must suspend practice. But, say the critics, the Government will be too pleased, if the pleaders and barristers fell into the trap laid by me. I do not believe it. What is true in ordinary times is not true in extraordinary times. In normal times the Government resent fierce criticism of their manners and methods by lawyers, but in the face of fierce action they would be loath to part with a single lawyer's support through his practice in the Courts.

Moreover, in my scheme, suspension does not mean stagnation. The lawyers are not to suspend practice and enjoy rest. They will be expected to induce their clients to boycott Courts. They will improvise arbitration boards in order to settle disputes. A nation, that is bent on forcing justice from an unwilling Government, has little time for engaging in mutual quarrels. This truth the lawyers will be expected to bring home to their clients. The readers may not know that many of the most noted lawyers of England suspended their work during the late war. The lawyers, then, upon temporarily leaving their profession, became whole time workers instead of being workers only during their recreation hours. Real politics are not a game. The late Mr Gokhale used to deplore that we had not gone beyond treating politics as a pastime. We have no notion as to how much the country has lost by reason of amateurs having managed its battles with the serious-minded, trained and wholetime working bureaucracy.

Now for the Schools

I feel that if we do not have the courage to suspend the education of our children, we do not deserve to win the battle.

I contend that there is no sacrifice involved in emptying the schools. We must be specially unfit for non-co-operation if we are so helpless as to be unable to manage our own education in total independence of the Government. Every village should manage the education of its own children. I would not depend upon Government aid.

If there is a real awakening the schooling need not be interrupted for a single day. The very schoolmasters who are now conducting Government schools, if they are good enough to resign their office, could take charge of national schools and teach our children the things they need, and not make of the majority of them indifferent clerks. I do look to the Aligarh College to give the lead in this matter. The moral effect created by the emptying of our *madrassas* will be tremendous. I doubt not that the Hindu parents and scholars would not fail to copy their Mussalman brethren.

Indeed what could be grander education than that the parents and scholars should put religious sentiment before a knowledge of letters ? If therefore no arrangement could be immediately made for the literary instruction of youths who might be withdrawn, it would be most profitable training for them to be able to work as volunteers for the cause which may necessitate their withdrawal from Government schools. For as in the case of the lawyers, so in the case of boys, my notion of withdrawal does not mean an indolent life. The withdrawing boys will, each according to his worth, be expected to take their share in the agitation.

Young India, 11-8-'20

61

EMPIRE GOODS BOYCOTT

It is curious how the question of the Empire goods boycott continues to challenge public attention from time to time. From the standpoint of non-violent non-co-operation it seems to me to be wholly indefensible. It is retaliation pure and simple and as such punitive. So long, therefore, as the Congress holds to *non-violent* non-co-operation, so long must boycott of British, as distinguished from other foreign goods, be ruled out. And if I am the only Congressman holding the view, I must move a resolution at the next Congress repealing the resolution in the matter carried at the last Special Session.

But for the moment, I propose to discuss not the ethics but the utility of the retaliatory boycott. The knowledge that even the Liberals joined the boycott campaign cannot make one shrink from the inquiry. On the contrary, if they come to believe with me that the retaliatory boycott that they and the Congress took up was not only ineffective but was one more demonstration of our impotent rage and waste of precious energy, I would appeal to them to take up with zeal and determination the boycott of all foreign cloth and replacing same not with Indian mill-cloth but with hand-spun khaddar.

If our rage did not blind us, we should be ashamed of the boycott resolution when we realized that we depended upon British goods for some of our national requirements. When we may not do without English books and English medicines, should we boycott English watches because we can procure Geneva watches ? And if we will not do without English books because we need them, how shall we expect the importer of British watches or perfumes to sacrifice his trade ? My very English efficient nurse whom I loved to call ' tyrant ' because she insisted in all loving ways on my taking more food and more sleep than I did, with a smile curling round her lips and insidious twinkle in her eyes, gently remarked after I was safely removed to a private ward escorted by the house-surgeon and herself: " As I was shading you with my umbrella I could not help smiling that you, a fierce boy-cotter of everything British, probably owed your life to the skill of a British surgeon handling British surgical instruments, administering British drugs, and to the ministrations of a British nurse. Do you know that as we brought you here, the umbrella that shaded you was of British make ? " The gentle nurse as she finished the last triumphant sentence evidently expected my complete col-lapse under her loving sermon. But happily I was able to confound her self-assurance by saying : " When will you people begin to know things as they are ? Do you know that I do not boycott anything merely because it is British ? I simply boycott all foreign cloth because the dumping down of foreign cloth in India has reduced mil-lions of my people to pauperism." I was even able to interest her in the khaddar movement. Probably she became a convert to it. Anyway she understood the pro-priety, the necessity and the utility of khaddar, but she could only laugh (and rightly) against the wholly ineffect-ive and meaningless boycott of British goods.

If the champions of this retaliatory boycott will look at their homes and their own belongings, they will, I have no doubt, discover the ludicrousness of their position even as my nurse friend did, under the supposition that I be-longed to that boycott school.

Young India, 15-5-'24

62

SOCIAL BOYCOTT

It would be a dangerous thing if, for differences of opinion, we were to proclaim social boycott. It would be totally opposed to the doctrine of non-violence to stop the supply of water and food. This battle of non-co-operation is a programme of propaganda by reducing profession to practice, not one of compelling others to yield obedience by violence direct or indirect. We must try patiently to convert our opponents. If we wish to evolve the spirit of democracy out of slavery, we must be scrupulously exact in our dealings with opponents. We may not replace the slavery of the Government by that of the non-co-operationists. We must concede to our opponents the freedom we claim for ourselves and for which we are fighting. The stoutest co-operationist will bend to the stern realities of practice if there is real response from the people.

But there is a non-violent boycott which we shall be bound to practise if we are to make any impression. We must not compromise with what we believe to be an untruth, whether it resides in a white skin or a brown. Such boycott is political boycott. We may not receive favours from the new Councillors. The voters, if they are true to their pledge, will be bound to refrain from making use of the services of those whom they have declined to regard as their representatives. They must ratify their verdict by complete abstention from any encouragement of the so-called representatives.

The public will be bound, if they are non-co-operationists, to refrain from giving these representatives any prestige by attending their political functions or parties.

I can conceive the possibility of non-violent social ostracism under certain extreme conditions, when a defiant minority refuses to bend to the majority, not out of any regard for principle but from sheer defiance or worse. But that time has certainly not arrived. Ostracism of a violent

character, such as the denial of the use of public wells is
a species of barbarism, which I hope will never be practised by any body of men having any desire for national
self-respect and national uplift. We will free neither Islam
nor India by processes of coercion, whether among ourselves or against Englishmen.

Young India, 8-12-'20

63

SOCIAL BOYCOTT

Non-co-operation being a movement of purification is
bringing to the surface all our weaknesses as also excesses
of even our strong points. Social boycott is an age-old
institution. It is coeval with caste. It is the one terrible
sanction exercised with great effect. It is based upon the
notion that a community is not bound to extend its
hospitality or service to an excommunicate. It answered
when every village was a self-contained unit, and the
occasions of recalcitrancy were rare. But when opinion is
divided, as it is today, on the merits of non-co-operation,
when its new application is having a trial, a summary
use of social boycott in order to bend a minority to the
will of the majority is a species of unpardonable violence.
If persisted in, such boycott is bound to destroy the movement. Social boycott is applicable and effective when it
is not felt as a punishment and accepted by the object
of boycott as a measure of discipline. Moreover, social
boycott to be admissible in a campaign of non-violence
must never savour of inhumanity. It must be civilized.
It must cause pain to the party using it, if it causes inconvenience to its object. Thus, depriving a man of the
services of a medical man, as is reported to have been
done in Jhansi, is an act of inhumanity tantamount in the
moral code to an attempt to murder. I see no difference
in murdering a man and withdrawing medical aid from
a man who is on the point of dying. Even the laws of

war, I apprehend, require the giving of medical relief to the enemy in need of it. To deprive a man of the use of an only village well is notice to him to quit that village. Surely, non-co-operators have acquired no right to use that extreme pressure against those who do not see eye to eye with them. Impatience and intolerance will surely kill this great religious movement. We may not make people pure by compulsion. Much less may we compel them by violence to respect our opinion. It is utterly against the spirit of democracy we want to cultivate.

I hope, therefore, that non-co-operation workers will beware of the snares of social boycott. But the alternative to social boycott is certainly not social intercourse. A man who defies strong clear public opinion on vital matters is not entitled to social amenities and privileges. We may not take part in his social functions such as marriage feasts, we may not receive gifts from him. But we dare not deny social service. The latter is a duty. Attendance at dinner parties and the like is a privilege, which it is optional to withhold or extend. But it would be wisdom to err on the right side and to exercise the weapon even in the limited sense described by me on rare and well-defined occasions. And in every case the user of the weapon will use it at his own risk. The use of it is not as yet in any form a duty. No one is entitled to its use if there is any danger of hurting the movement.

Young India, 16-2-'21

64

SYMPATHETIC STRIKES

Any premature precipitation of sympathetic strikes will result in infinite harm to our cause. In the programme of non-violence, we must rigidly exclude the idea of gaining anything by embarrassing the Government. If our activity is pure and that of the Government impure, the latter is embarrassed by our purity, if it does not itself become pure. Thus, a movement of purification benefits both parties. Whereas a movement of mere destruction leaves the destroyer unpurified, and brings him down to the level of those whom he seeks to destroy.

Even our sympathetic strikes, therefore, have to be strikes of self-purification, i.e., non-co-operation. And so, when we declare a strike to redress a wrong, we really cease to take part in the wrong, and thus leave the wrong-doer to his own resources, in other words, enable him to see the folly of continuing the wrong. Such a strike can only succeed, when behind it is the fixed determination not to revert to service.

Speaking, therefore, as one having handled large successful strikes, I repeat the following maxims, already stated in these pages, for the guidance of all strike leaders :

1.   There should be no strike without a real grievance.

2.   There should be no strike, if the persons concerned are not able to support themselves out of their own savings or by engaging in some temporary occupation, such as carding, spinning and weaving. Strikers should never depend upon public subscriptions or other charity.

3.   Strikers must fix an unalterable minimum demand, and declare it before embarking upon their strike.

A strike may fail in spite of a just grievance and the ability of strikers to hold out indefinitely, if there are workers to replace them. A wise man, therefore, will not strike for increase of wages or other comforts, if he feels that he can be easily replaced. But a philanthropic or patriotic man will strike in spite of supply being greater than the demand, when he feels for and wishes to associate himself with his neighbour's distress. Needless to say, there is no room in a civil strike of the nature described by me for violence in the shape of intimidation, incendiarism or otherwise. I should, therefore, be extremely sorry to find, that the recent derailment near Chittagong was due to mischief done by any of the strikers. Judged by the tests suggested by me, it is clear that the friends of the strikers should never have advised them to apply for or receive Congress or any other public funds for their support. The value of the strikers' sympathy was diminished to the extent, that they received or accepted financial aid. The merit of a sympathetic strike lies in the inconvenience and the loss suffered by the sympathizers.

Young India, 22-9-'21

65

MORE OBJECTIONS ANSWERED

I do not know from where the information has been derived that I have given up the last two stages of non-co-operation. What I have said is that they are a distant goal. I abide by it. I admit that all the stages are fraught with some danger but the last two are fraught with the greatest — the last most of all. The stages have been fixed with a view to running the least possible risk. The last two stages will not be taken up unless the Committee has attained sufficient control over the people to warrant the belief that the laying down of arms or suspension of taxes will, humanly speaking be free from an outbreak of violence on the part of the people. I do entertain the belief that it is possible for the people to attain the discipline necessary for taking the two steps. When once they realize that violence is totally unnecessary to bend an unwilling Government to their will and that the result can be obtained with certainty by dignified non-co-operation, they will cease to think of violence even by way of retaliation. The fact is that hitherto we have not attempted to take concerted and disciplined action from the masses. Some day, if we are to become truly a self-governing nation, that has to be made. The present, in my opinion, is a propitious movement. Every Indian feels the insult to the Punjab as a personal wrong, every Mussalman resents the wrong done to the Khilafat. There is, therefore, a favourable atmosphere for expecting cohesive and restrained movement on the part of the masses.

So far as response is concerned, I agree with the Editor that the quickest and the largest response is to be expected in the matter of suspension of payment of taxes, but as I have said, so long as the masses are not educated to appreciate the value of non-violence even whilst their holdings are being sold, so long must it be difficult to take up the last stage into any appreciable extent.

I agree too that a sudden withdrawal of the military and the police will be a disaster if we have not acquired the ability to protect ourselves against robbers and thieves. But I suggest that when we are ready to call out the military and the police on an extensive scale, we would find ourselves in a position to defend ourselves. If the police and the military resign from patriotic motives, I would certainly expect them to perform the same duty as national volunteers, not as hirelings but as willing protectors of the life and liberty of their countrymen. The movement of non-co-operation is one of automatic adjustment. If the Government schools are emptied, I would certainly expect national schools to come into being. If the lawyers as a whole suspended practice, they would devise arbitration courts and the nation will have expeditious and cheaper method of settling private disputes and awarding punishment to the wrong-doer. I may add that the Khilafat Committee is fully alive to the difficulty of the task and is taking all the necessary steps to meet the contingencies as they arise.

Regarding the leaving of civil employment, no danger is feared, because no one will leave his employment, unless he is in a position to find support for himself and family either through friends or otherwise.

Disapproval of the proposed withdrawal of students betrays, in my humble opinion, lack of appreciation of the true nature of non-co-operation. It is true enough that we pay the money wherewith our children are educated. But when the agency imparting the education has become corrupt, we may not employ it without partaking of the agent's corruption. When students leave schools or colleges I hardly imagine that the teachers will fail to perceive the advisability of themselves resigning. But even if they do not, money can hardly be allowed to count where honour or religion are the stake.

As to the boycott of the councils, it is not the entry of the Moderates or any other persons that matters so much as the entry of those who believe in non-co-operation. You may not co-operate at the top and non-co-operate at the bottom. A councillor cannot remain in the council and ask the *gumasta* who cleans the council table to resign.

Young India, 18-8-'20

66

ANSWERS TO QUESTIONS

My experience of last year shows me that in spite of aberrations in some parts of India, the country was entirely under control, that the influence of Satyagraha was profoundly for its good and that where violence did break out, there were local causes that directly contributed to it. At the same time I admit that even the violence that did take place on the part of the people and the spirit of lawlessness that was undoubtedly shown in some parts should have remained under check. I have made ample acknowledgment of the miscalculation I then made. But all the painful experience that I then gained did not in any way shake my belief in Satyagraha or in the possibility of that matchless force being utilized in India. Ample provision is being made this time to avoid the mistakes of the past. But I must refuse to be deterred from a clear course because it may be attended by violence totally unintended and in spite of extraordinary efforts that are being made to prevent it. At the same time I must make my position clear. Nothing can possibly prevent a Satyagrahi from doing his duty because of the frown of the authorities. I would risk, if necessary, a million lives so long as they are voluntary sufferers and are innocent, spotless victims. It is the mistakes of the people that matter in a Satyagraha campaign. Mistakes, even insanity must be expected from the strong and the powerful, and the moment of victory has come when there is no resort to the mad fury of the powerful but a voluntary, dignified and quiet submission, but not submission to the will of the authority that has put itself in the wrong. The secret of success lies, therefore, in holding every English life and the life of every officer serving the Government as sacred as those of our own dear ones. All the wonderful experience I have gained now during nearly 40 years of conscious existence, has convinced me that there is no gift so precious as that of life. I make bold to say that the moment Englishmen feel that although they are in India in a hopeless minority, their lives are protected against harm not because of the matchless weapons of destruction which are at their disposal, but because Indians refuse to take the lives even of those whom they may consider to be utterly in the wrong, that moment will see a transformation in the English nature in its relation to India, and that moment will also be the moment when all the destructive cutlery that is to be had in India will begin to rust. I know that this is a far-off vision. That cannot matter to me. It is enough for me to see the light and to act up to it, and it is more than enough when I gain companions in the onward march. I have claimed in private conversations with English friends that it is because of my incessant preaching of the gospel of non-violence and my having successfully demonstrated its practical utility that so far the forces of violence, which are undoubtedly in existence in connection with the Khilafat movement, have remained under complete control.

I consider non-co-operation to be such a powerful and pure instrument, that if it is enforced in an earnest spirit, it will be like seeking first the Kingdom of God and everything else following as a matter of course. People will have then realized their true power. They would have learnt the value of discipline, self-control, joint action, non-violence, organization and everything else that goes to make a nation great and good, and not merely great.

I do not know that I have a right to arrogate greater purity for myself than for our Mussalman brethren. But I do admit that they do not believe in my doctrine of non-violence to the full extent. For them it is a weapon of the weak, an expedient. They consider non-co-operation without violence to be the only thing open to them in the way of direct action. I know that if some of them could offer successful violence, they would today. But they are convinced that humanly speaking it is an impossibility. For them, therefore, non-co-operation is a matter not merely of duty but also of revenge. Whereas I take up non-co-operation against the Government as I have actually taken it up in practice against members of my own family. I entertain very high regard for the British Constitution. I have not only no enmity against Englishmen but I regard much in English character as worthy of my emulation. I count many as my friends. It is against my religion to regard any one as an enemy. I entertain similar sentiments with respect to Mohammedans. I find their cause to be just and pure. Although therefore their view-point is different from mine I do not hesitate to associate with them and invite them to give my method a trial, for, I believe that the use of a pure weapon even from a mistaken motive does not fail to produce some good, even as the telling of truth, if only because for the time being it is the best policy, is at least so much to the good.

Young India, 2-6-'20

67

NON-CO-OPERATION EXPLAINED

A representative of this journal * called on Mr M. K. Gandhi yesterday at his temporary residence in the Pursewalkum High Road for an interview on the subject of non-co-operation. Mr Gandhi, who has come to Madras on a tour to some of the principal Muslim centres in Southern India, was busy with a number of workers discussing his programme ; but he expressed his readiness to answer questions on the chief topic which is agitating Muslims and Hindus.

" After your experience of the Satyagraha agitation last year, Mr Gandhi, are you still hopeful and convinced of the wisdom of advising non-co-operation ? "

" Certainly."

" How do you consider conditions have altered since the Satyagraha movement of last year ? "

" I consider that people are better disciplined now than they were before. In this I include even the masses whom I have had opportunities of seeing in large numbers in various parts of the country."

" And you are satisfied that the masses understand the spirit of Satyagraha ? "

" Yes."

" And that is why you are pressing on with the programme of non-co-operation ? "

" Yes. Moreover, the danger that attended the civil-disobedience part of Satyagraha does not apply to non-co-operation, because in non-co-operation we are not taking up civil disobedience of laws as a mass movement. The result hitherto has been most encouraging. For instance, people in Sindh and Delhi, in spite of the irritating restrictions upon their liberty by the authorities, have

---

* The present article is the report of a talk the representative of *The Madras Mail* had with Gandhiji. It was reproduced in the *Young India* from that paper.

carried out the Committee's instructions in regard to the
Seditious Meetings Proclamation and to the prohibition
of posting placards on the walls which we hold to be
inoffensive but which the authorities consider to be
offensive."

" What is the pressure which you expect to bring to
bear on the authorities if co-operation is withdrawn ? "

"I believe, and everybody must grant, that no Government can exist for a single moment without the co-
operation of the people, willing or forced, and if people
suddenly withdraw their co-operation in every detail, the
Government will come to a stand-still."

" But is there not a big ' If ' in it ? "

" Certainly, there is."

" And how do you propose to succeed against the big
' If ' ? "

" In my plan of campaign expediency has no room.
If the Khilafat movement has really permeated the masses
and the classes, there must be adequate response from the
people."

" But are you not begging the question ? "

" I am not begging the question, because so far as the
data before me go, I believe that the Muslims keenly feel
the Khilafat grievance. It remains to be seen whether their
feeling is intense enough to evoke in them the measure of
sacrifice adequate for successful non-co-operation."

" That is, your survey of the conditions, you think,
justifies your advising non-co-operation in the full conviction that you have behind you the support of the vast
masses of the Mussalman population ? "

" Yes."

" This non-co-operation, you are satisfied, will extend
to complete severance of co-operation with the Government ? "

" No ; nor is it at the present moment my desire that
it should. I am simply practising non-co-operation to the
extent that is necessary to make the Government realize
the depth of popular feeling in the matter and the dissatisfaction with the Government that all that could be done

has not been done either by the Government of India or by
the Imperial Government, whether on the Khilafat question or on the Punjab question."

"Do you, Mr Gandhi, realize that even amongst
Mohammedans there are sections of people who are not
enthusiastic over non-co-operation however much they
may feel the wrong that has been done to their community ? "

"Yes, but their number is smaller than those who are
prepared to adopt non-co-operation."

"And yet does not the fact that there has not been
an adequate response to your appeal for resignation of
titles and offices and for boycott of elections of the Councils
indicate that you may be placing more faith in their
strength of conviction than is warranted ? "

"I think not ; for the reason that the stage has only
just come into operation and our people are always most
cautious and slow to move. Moreover, the first stage largely
affects the uppermost strata of society, who represent a
microscopic minority though they are undoubtedly an in-
fluential body of people."

"This upper class, you think, has sufficiently responded to your appeal ? "

"I am unable to say either one way or the other at
present. I shall be able to give a definite answer at the
end of this month."

"Do you think that without one's loyalty to the King
and the Royal Family being questioned, one can advocate
non-co-operation in connection with the Royal visit ? "

"Most decidedly ; for the simple reason that if there
is any disloyalty about the proposed boycott of the
Prince's visit, it is disloyalty to the Government of the day
and not to the person of His Royal Highness."

"What do you think is to be gained by promoting this
boycott in connection with the Royal visit ? "

"I want to show that the people of India are not in
sympathy with the Government of the day and that they
strongly disapprove of the policy of the Government in
regard to the Punjab and Khilafat, and even in respect of

other important administrative measures. I consider that the visit of the Prince of Wales is a singularly good opportunity to the people to show their disapproval of the present Government. After all, the visit is calculated to have tremendous political results. It is not to be a non-political event, and seeing that the Government of India and the Imperial Government want to make the visit a political event of first-class importance, namely, for the purpose of strengthening their hold upon India, I for one consider that it is the bounden duty of the people to boycott the visit which is being engineered by the two Governments in their own interest which at the present moment is totally antagonistic to the people."

"Do you mean that you want this boycott promoted because you feel that the strengthening of the hold upon India is not desirable in the best interests of the country?"

"Yes. The strengthening of the hold of a Government so wicked as the present one is not desirable for the best interests of the people. Not that I want the bond between England and India to become loosened for the sake of loosening it, but I want that bond to become strengthened only in so far as it adds to the welfare of India."

"Do you think that non-co-operation and the non-boycott of the Legislative Councils are consistent?"

"No; because a person who takes up the programme of non-co-operation cannot consistently stand for Councils."

"Is non-co-operation, in your opinion, an end in itself or a means to an end, and if so, what is the end?"

"It is a means to an end, the end being to make the present Government just, whereas it has become mostly unjust. Co-operation with a just Government is a duty; non-co-operation with an unjust Government is equally a duty."

"Will you look with favour upon the proposal to enter the Councils and to carry on either obstructive tactics or to decline to take the oath of allegiance as consistent with your non-co-operation?"

" No ; as an accurate student of non-co-operation, I consider that such a proposal is inconsistent with the true spirit of non-co-operation. I have often said that a Government really thrives on obstruction, and so far as the proposal not to take the oath of allegiance is concerned, I can really see no meaning in it ; it amounts to a useless waste of valuable time and money."

" In other words, obstruction is no stage in non-co-operation ? "

" No."

" Are you satisfied that all efforts at constitutional agitation have been exhausted and that, non-co-operation is the only course left us ? "

" I do not consider non-co-operation to be unconstitutional, but I do believe that of all the constitutional remedies now left open to us, non-co-operation is the only one left for us."

" Do you consider it constitutional to adopt it with a view merely to paralyze Government ? "

" Certainly, it is not unconstitutional, but a prudent man will not take all the steps that are constitutional if they are otherwise undesirable, nor do I advise that course. I am resorting to non-co-operation in progressive stages because I want to evolve true order out of untrue order. I am not going to take a single step in non-co-operation unless I am satisfied that the country is ready for that step, namely, non-co-operation will not be followed by anarchy or disorder."

" How will you satisfy yourself that anarchy will not follow ? "

" For instance, if I advise the police to lay down their arms, I shall have satisfied myself that we are able by voluntary assistance to protect ourselves against thieves and robbers. That was precisely what was done in Lahore and Amritsar last year by the citizens by means of volunteers when the military and the police had withdrawn. Even where Government had not taken such measures in a place, for want of adequate force, I know people have successfully protected themselves."

" You have advised lawyers to non-co-operate by suspending their practice. What is your experience ? Has
the lawyers' response to your appeal encouraged you to
hope that you will be able to carry through all stages of
non-co-operation with the help of such people ? "

" I cannot say that a large number has yet responded
to my appeal. It is too early to say how many will respond. But I may say that I do not rely merely upon the
lawyer class or highly educated men to enable the Committee to carry out all the stages of non-co-operation. My
hope lies more with the masses so far as the later stages
of non-co-operation are concerned."

Young India, 18-8-'20

68

LOVE

I accept the interpretation of *ahimsa,* namely, that
it is not merely a negative state of harmlessness but it is
a positive state of love, of doing good even to the evil-doer.
But it does not mean helping the evil-doer to continue the
wrong or tolerating it by passive acquiescence. On the
contrary, love, the active state of *ahimsa,* requires you to
resist the wrong-doer by dissociating yourself from him
even though it may offend him or injure him physically.
Thus if my son lives a life of shame, I may not help him
to do so by continuing to support him ; on the contrary,
my love for him requires me to withdraw all support from
him although it may mean even his death. And the same
love imposes on me the obligation of welcoming him to
my bosom when he repents. But I may not by physical
force compel my son to become good. That in my opinion
is the moral of the story of the Prodigal Son.

Non-co-operation is not a passive state, it is an intensely active state — more active than physical resistance
or violence. Passive resistance is a misnomer. Non-co-
operation in the sense used by me must be non-violent

and, therefore, neither punitive nor vindictive nor based on malice, ill-will or hatred. It follows therefore that it would be sin for me to serve General Dyer and co-operate with him to shoot innocent men. But it will be an exercise of forgiveness or love for me to nurse him back to life, if he was suffering from a physical malady. I would co-operate a thousand times with this Government to wean it from its career of crime, but I will not for a single moment co-operate with it to continue that career. And I would be guilty of wrong-doing if I retained a title from it or "a service under it or supported its Law Courts or schools." Better for me a beggar's bowl than the richest possession from hands stained with the blood of the innocents of Jalianwala. Better by far a warrant of imprisonment than honeyed words from those who have wantonly wounded the religious sentiment of my seventy million brothers.

Young India, 25-8-'20

69

THE POET'S ANXIETY

The Poet of Asia, as Lord Hardinge called Dr Tagore, is fast becoming, if he has not already become, the Poet of the world. Increasing prestige has brought to him increasing responsibility. His greatest service to India must be his poetic interpretation of India's message to the world. The Poet is, therefore, sincerely anxious that India should deliver no false or feeble message in her name. He is naturally jealous of his country's reputation. He says he has striven hard to find himself in tune with the present movement. He confesses that he is baffled. He can find nothing for his lyre in the din and the bustle of non-co-operation. In three forceful letters he has endeavoured to give expression to his misgivings, and he has come to the conclusion that non-co-operation is not dignified enough for the India of his vision, that it is a doctrine of negation and despair. He fears that it is a doctrine of separation, exclusiveness, narrowness and negation.

No Indian can feel anything but pride in the Poet's exquisite jealousy of India's honour. It is good that he should have sent to us his misgivings in language at once beautiful and clear.

In all humility I shall endeavour to answer the Poet's doubts. I may fail to convince him or the reader who may have been touched by his eloquence, but I would like to assure him and India that non-co-operation in conception is not any of the things he fears, and he need have no cause to be ashamed of his country for having adopted non-co-operation. If in actual application it appears in the end to have failed, it will be no more the fault of the doctrine, than it would be of Truth if those who claim to apply it in practice do not appear to succeed. Non-co-operation may have come in advance of its time. India and the world must then wait, but there is no choice for India save between violence and non-co-operation.

Nor need the Poet fear that non-co-operation is intended to erect a Chinese wall between India and the West. On the contrary, non-co-operation is intended to pave the way to real, honourable and voluntary co-operation based on mutual respect and trust. The present struggle is being waged against compulsory co-operation, against one-sided combination, against the armed imposition of modern methods of exploitation masquerading under the name of civilization.

Non-co-operation is a protest against an unwitting and unwilling participation in evil.

The Poet's concern is largely about the students. He is of opinion that they should not have been called upon to give up Government schools before they had other schools to go to. Here I must differ from him. I have never been able to make a fetish of literary training. My experience has proved to my satisfaction that literary training by itself adds not an inch to one's moral height and that character-building is independent of literary training. I am firmly of opinion that the Government schools have unmanned us, rendered us helpless and Godless. They have filled us with discontent, and providing no remedy for the discontent, have made us despondent. They have made us what we were intended to become — clerks and interpreters. A Government builds its prestige upon the apparently voluntary association of the governed. And if it was wrong to co-operate with the Government in keeping us slaves, we were bound to begin with those institutions in which our association appeared to be most voluntary. The youth of a nation are its hope. I hold that as soon as we discovered that the system of Government was wholly, or mainly evil, it became sinful for us to associate our children with it.

It is no argument against the soundness of the proposition laid down by me, that the vast majority of the students went back after the first flush of enthusiasm. Their recantation is proof rather of the extent of our degradation than of the wrongness of the step. Experience has shown that the establishment of national schools has not resulted in drawing many more students. The strongest and the truest of them came out without any national schools to fall back upon, and I am convinced that these first withdrawals are rendering service of the highest order.

But the Poet's protest against the calling out of the boys is really a corollary to his objection to the very doctrine of non-co-operation. He has a horror of everything negative. His whole soul seems to rebel against the negative commandments of religion. I must give his objection in his own inimitable language. " R. in support of the present movement has often said to me that passion for rejection is a stronger power in the beginning than the acceptance of an ideal. Though I know it to be a fact, I cannot take it as a truth....*Brahmavidya* in India has for its object *mukti* (emancipation), while Buddhism has *nirvana* (extinction). *Mukti* draws our attention to the positive and *nirvana* to the negative side of truth. Therefore, he emphasized the fact of *duhkha* (misery) which had to be avoided and the *Brahmavidya* emphasized the fact of *ananda* (joy) which had to be attained." In these and kindred passages the reader will find the key to the Poet's mentality. In my humble opinion, rejection is as much an ideal as the acceptance of a thing. It is as necessary to reject untruth as it is to accept truth. All religions teach that two opposite forces act upon us and that the human endeavour consists in a series of eternal rejections and acceptances. Non-co-operation with evil is as much a duty as co-operation with good. I venture to suggest that the Poet has done an unconscious injustice to Buddhism in describing *nirvana* as merely a negative state. I make bold to say that *mukti* (emancipation) is as much a negative state as *nirvana*. Emancipation from or extinction of the bondage of the flesh leads to *ananda* (eternal bliss). Let me close this part of my argument by drawing attention to the fact that the final word of the *Upanishads* (*Brahmavidya*) is *Not*. *Neti* was the best description the authors of the *Upanishads* were able to find for *Brahman*.

I, therefore, think that the Poet has been unnecessarily alarmed at the negative aspect of non-co-operation. We had lost the power of saying ' no '. It had become disloyal, almost sacrilegious to say ' no ' to the Government. This deliberate refusal to co-operate is like the necessary weeding process that a cultivator has to resort to before he sows. Weeding is as necessary to agriculture as sowing. Indeed, even whilst the crops are growing, the weeding fork, as every husbandman knows, is an instrument almost of daily use. The nation's non-co-operation is an invitation to the Government to co-operate with it on its own terms as is every nation's right and every good Government's duty. Non-co-operation is the nation's notice that it is no longer satisfied to be in tutelage. The nation has taken to the harmless (for it), natural and religious doctrine of non-co-operation in the place of the unnatural and irreligious doctrine of violence. And if India is ever to attain the Swaraj of the Poet's dream, she will do so only by non-violent non-co-operation. Let him deliver his message of peace to the world, and feel confident that India through her non-co-operation, if she remains true to her pledge, will have exemplified his message. Non-co-operation is intended to give the very meaning to patriotism that the Poet is yearning after. An India prostrate at the feet of Europe can give no hope to humanity. An India awakened and free has a message of peace and goodwill to a groaning world. Non-co-operation is designed to supply her with a platform from which she will preach the message.

Young India, 1-6-'21

70

WHAT IT IS NOT

" The situation in India illustrates another curious basis of difference between us. I hold to the ' non-resistance ' idea. Gandhi, as I understand him, proclaims the Way of Love. And yet he does not see that ' Non-co-operation is a way of violence.' Suppose the milk drivers of New York had a real and just and even terrible grievance. Suppose that they should strike and cut off the milk supply from the babies of New York. They might never raise a hand in violent attack on any one and yet their way would be the way of violence. Over the dead bodies of little children they would by ' non-co-operation ' win their victory. As Bertrand Russell said of the Bolsheviki, ' such suffering makes us question the means used to arrive at a desired end.' Non-co-operation means suffering in Lancashire and is an appeal in the end to violence rather than reason.

" This is not quite to the point and yet it does illustrate in a way what I have in mind. The advocates of Home Rule in India are now in the legislative bodies and there they propose to block progress by non-co-operative methods. In England, the country in which by historical accident civil institutions got a chance to develop, as John Fiske pointed out, through absence of war, the process of growth has been by the method of co-operation."

The above is an extract from an article in *Unity* (Feb. 14, '24) sent by an unknown American friend.

The article is a letter addressed to Mr Holmes by Mr Arthur I. Weatherly. The letter is an endeavour to show that an idealist, if he will be practical, has to water his ideal down to suit given circumstances. The writer has packed his letter with illustrations in support of his argument. As I am not for the moment concerned with his main argument, I hope I am doing no violence to him by merely giving an extract from his letter. My purpose is to show that Mr Weatherly's view of Indian non-co-operation cannot fail to be of general interest to the reader.

Mr Weatherly has laid down a universal proposition that ' non-co-operation is a way of violence.' A moment's thought would have shown the falsity of the proposition. I non-co-operate when I refuse to sell liquor in a liquor-shop, or help a murderer in his plans. My non-co-operation, I hold, is not only not a way of violence, but may be an act of love, if love is the motive that has prompted my refusal. The fact is that all non-co-operation is not violent, and non-violent non-co-operation can never be an act of violence. It may not be always an act of love. For love is an active quality which cannot always be inferred from the act itself. A surgeon may perform a most successful operation and yet he may have no love for his patient.

Mr Weatherly's illustration is most unhappy and incomplete for the purpose of examination. If the milk drivers of New York have a grievance against its Municipality for criminal mismanagement of its trust and if, in order to bend it, they decided to cut off the milk supply of the babies of New York, they would be guilty of a crime against humanity. But suppose that the milk drivers were underpaid by their employers, that they were consequently starving, they would be justified, if they have tried every other available and proper method of securing better wages, in refusing to drive the milk carts even though their action resulted in the death of the babies of New York. Their refusal will certainly not be an act of violence though it will not be an act of love. They were not philanthropists. They were driving milk carts for the sake of their maintenance. It was no part of their duty as employees under every circumstance to supply milk to babies. There is no violence when there is no infraction of duty. Suppose further that the milk drivers in question knew that their employers supplied cheap but adulterated milk and another dairy company supplied better but dearer milk and they felt for the welfare of the babies of New York, their refusal to drive the milk carts will be an act of love even though some short-sighted mother of New York might be deprived of the adulterated milk and may not have bought better but dearer milk from the more honest dairy company whose existence has been assumed for the purpose of our argument.

From the imaginary heartless milk drivers and the heaps of dead bodies of New York babies, the writer in *Unity* takes us to Lancashire and pictures its ruin when Indian non-co-operation has succeeded. In his haste to prove his main argument, the writer has hardly taken the trouble to study even simple facts. Indian non-co-operation is not designed to injure Lancashire or any other part of the British Isles. It has been undertaken to vindicate India's right to administer her own affairs. Lancashire's trade with India was established at the point of the bayonet and it is sustained by similar means. It has ruined the one vital cottage-industry which supplemented the resources of millions of India's peasants and kept starvation from their doors. If India now strives to revive her cottage industry and hand-spinning and refuses to buy any foreign cloth or even cloth manufactured by Indian mills and Lancashire or Indian mills suffer thereby, non-co-operation cannot by any law of morals be held to be an act of violence. India never bound herself to maintain Lancashire. Visitors to taverns or houses of ill fame would be congratulated on their self-restraint, and will be held even as benefactors of keepers of taverns or questionable houses, if they ceased to visit those places even without notice and even if their abstention resulted in the starvation of the keepers of those houses. Similarly, if customers of money-lenders ceased to borrow and the latter starved, the former cannot be regarded as violent by reason of their withdrawal. But they might be so considered if they transferred their custom from one money-lender to another through ill-will or spite and without just cause.

Thus it is clear that non-co-operation is not violence when the refusal of the restraint is a right and a duty even though by reason of its performance some people may have to suffer. It will be an act of love when non-co-operation is resorted to solely for the good of the wrong-doer. Indian non-co-operation is a right and a duty, but cannot be regarded as an act of love because it has been undertaken by a weak people in self-defence.

Young India, 10-4-'24

71

THE NON-CO-OPERATION OF A SATYAGRAHI

Q. It has been suggested in Bombay that you went to the Governor uninvited, in fact you forced yourself upon his attention. If so, was it not co-operation even without response ? What could you have to do with the Governor, I wonder ?

A. My answer is that I am quite capable even of forcing myself upon the attention of my opponent when I have strength. I did so in South Africa. I sought interviews after interviews with General Smuts when I knew that I was ready for battle. I pleaded with him to avoid the untold hardships that the Indian settlers must suffer, if the great historic march had to be undertaken. It is true that he in his haughtiness turned a deaf ear ; but I lost nothing. I gained added strength by my humility. So would I do in India when we are strong enough to put a real fight for freedom. Remember that ours is a non-violent struggle. It pre-supposes humility. It is a truthful struggle and consciousness of truth should give us firmness. We are not out to destroy men. We own no enemy. We have no ill-will against a single soul on earth. We mean to convert by our suffering. I do not despair of converting the hardest-hearted or the most selfish Englishman. Every opportunity of meeting him is, therefore, welcome to me.

Let me distinguish. Non-violent non-co-operation means renunciation of the benefits of a system with which we non-co-operate. We, therefore, renounce the benefits of schools, courts, titles, legislatures and offices set up under the system. The most extensive and permanent part of our non-co-operation consists in the renunciation of foreign cloth which is the foundation for the vicious system that is crushing us to dust. It is possible to think of other items of non-co-operation. But owing to our weakness or want of ability, we have restricted ourselves to these items only. If then I go to any official for the purpose of seeking the benefits above-named, I co-operate. Whereas if I go to the meanest official for the purpose of converting him, say to khaddar, or weaning him from his service or persuading him to withdraw his children from Government schools, I fulfil my duty as a non-co-operator. I should fail, if I did not go to him with that definite and direct purpose.

Young India, 27-5-'26

72

CIVIL DISOBEDIENCE

Civil disobedience was on the lips of every one of the members of the All India Congress Committee. Not having really ever tried it, every one appeared to be ena- moured of it from a mistaken belief in it as a sovereign remedy for our present-day ills. I feel sure that it can be made such if we can produce the necessary atmosphere for it. For individuals there always is that atmosphere except when their civil disobedience is certain to lead to bloodshed. I discovered this exception during the Satya- graha days. But even so a call may come which one dare not neglect, cost it what it may. I can clearly see the time coming to me when I *must* refuse obedience to every single State-made law, even though there may be a certainty of bloodshed. When neglect of the call means a denial of God, civil disobedience becomes a peremptory duty.

Mass civil disobedience stands on a different footing. It can only be tried in a calm atmosphere. It must be the calmness of strength not weakness, of knowledge not ignorance. Individual civil disobedience may be and often is vicarious. Mass civil disobedience may be and often is selfish in the sense that individuals expect personal gain from their disobedience. Thus in South Africa, Kallenbach and Polak offered vicarious civil disobedience. They had nothing to gain. Thousands offered it because they expected personal gain also in the shape, say, of the removal of the annual poll-tax levied upon ex-indentured men and their wives and grown-up children. It is sufficient in mass civil disobedience if the resisters understand the working of the doctrine.

It was in a practically uninhabited tract of country that I was arrested in South Africa when I was marching into prohibited area with over two to three thousand men and some women. The company included several Pathans and others who were able-bodied men. It was the greatest testimony of merit the Government of South Africa gave to the movement. They knew that we were as harmless as we were determined. It was easy enough for that body of men to cut to pieces those who arrested me. It would have not only been a most cowardly thing to do, but it would have been a treacherous breach of their own pledge, and it would have meant ruin to the struggle for freedom and the forcible deportation of every Indian from South Africa. But the men were no rabble. They were disciplined soldiers and all the better for being unarmed. Though I was torn from them, they did not disperse, nor did they turn back. They marched on to their destination till they were, every one of them, arrested and imprisoned. So far as I am aware, this was an instance of discipline and non-violence for which there is no parallel in history. Without such restraint I see no hope of successful mass civil disobedience here.

We must dismiss the idea of overawing the Government by huge demonstrations every time some one is arrested. On the contrary, we must treat arrest as the normal condition of the life of a non-co-operator. For we must seek arrest and imprisonment, as a soldier who goes to battle seeks death. We expect to bear down the opposition of the Government by courting and not by avoiding imprisonment, even though it be by showing our supposed readiness to be arrested and imprisoned *en masse*. Civil disobedience then emphatically means our desire to surrender to a single unarmed policeman. Our triumph consists in thousands being led to the prisons like lambs to the slaughter house. If the lambs of the world had been willingly led, they would have long ago saved themselves from the butcher's knife. Our triumph consists again in being imprisoned for no wrong whatsoever. The greater our innocence, the greater our strength and the swifter our victory.

As it is, this Government is cowardly, we are afraid of imprisonment. The Government takes advantage of our fear of gaols. If only our men and women welcome gaols as health-resorts, we will cease to worry about the dear ones put in gaols which our countrymen in South Africa used to nickname His Majesty's Hotels.

We have too long been mentally disobedient to the laws of the State and have too often surreptitiously evaded them, to be fit all of a sudden for civil disobedience. Disobedience to be civil has to be open and non-violent.

Complete civil disobedience is a state of peaceful rebellion — a refusal to obey every single State-made law. It is certainly more dangerous than an armed rebellion. For it can never be put down if the civil resisters are prepared to face extreme hardships. It is based upon an implicit belief in the absolute efficiency of innocent suffering. By noiselessly going to prison a civil resister ensures a calm atmosphere. The wrong-doer wearies of wrong-doing in the absence of resistance. All pleasure is lost when the victim betrays no resistance. A full grasp of the conditions of successful civil resistance is necessary at least on the part of the representatives of the people before we can launch out on an enterprise of such magnitude. The quickest remedies are always fraught with the greatest danger and require the utmost skill in handling them. It is my firm conviction that if we bring about a successful boycott of foreign cloth, we shall have produced an atmosphere that would enable us to inaugurate civil disobedience on a scale that no Government can resist. I would, therefore, urge patience and determined concentration on Swadeshi upon those who are impatient to embark on mass civil disobedience.

Young India, 4-8-'21

73

CIVIL DISOBEDIENCE

We dare not pin our faith solely on civil disobedience. It is like the use of a knife to be used most sparingly if at all. A man who cuts away without ceasing cuts at the very root, and finds himself without the substance he was trying to reach by cutting off the superficial hard crust. The use of civil disobedience will be healthy, necessary, and effective only if we otherwise conform to the laws of all growth. We must therefore give its full and therefore greater value to the adjective ' civil ' than to ' disobedience '. Disobedience without civility, discipline, discrimination, non-violence is certain destruction. Disobedience combined with love is the living water of life. Civil disobedience is a beautiful variant to signify growth, it is not discordance which spells death.

Young India, 5-1-'22

THE RIGHT OF CIVIL DISOBEDIENCE

I wish I could persuade everybody that civil disobedience is the inherent right of a citizen. He dare not give it up without ceasing to be a man. Civil disobedience is never followed by anarchy. Criminal disobedience can lead to it. Every State puts down criminal disobedience by force. It perishes, if it does not. But to put down civil disobedience is to attempt to imprison conscience. Civil disobedience can only lead to strength and purity. A civil resister never uses arms and hence he is harmless to a State that is at all willing to listen to the voice of public opinion. He is dangerous for an autocratic State, for he brings about its fall by engaging public opinion upon the matter for which he resists the State. Civil disobedience therefore becomes a sacred duty when the State has become lawless, or which is the same thing, corrupt. And a citizen that barters with such a State shares its corruption or lawlessness.

It is therefore possible to question the wisdom of applying civil disobedience in respect of a particular act or law ; it is possible to advise delay and caution. But the right itself cannot be allowed to be questioned. It is a birthright that cannot be surrendered without surrender of one's self-respect.

At the same time that the right of civil disobedience is insisted upon, its use must be guarded by all conceivable restrictions. Every possible provision should be made against an outbreak of violence or general lawlessness. Its area as well as its scope should also be limited to the barest necessity of the case.

Young India, 5-1-'22

AGGRESSIVE *v.* DEFENSIVE

It is now necessary to understand the exact distinction between aggressive civil disobedience and defensive. Aggressive, assertive or offensive civil disobedience is non-violent, wilful disobedience of laws of the State whose breach does not involve moral turpitude and which is undertaken as a symbol of revolt against the State. Thus disregard of laws relating to revenue or regulation of personal conduct for the convenience of the State, although such laws in themselves inflict no hardship and do not require to be altered, would be assertive, aggressive or offensive civil disobedience.

Defensive civil disobedience, on the other hand, is involuntary or reluctant non-violent disobedience of such laws as are in themselves bad and obedience to which would be inconsistent with one's self-respect or human dignity. Thus formation of volunteer corps for peaceful purposes, holding of public meetings for like purposes, publication of articles not contemplating or inciting to violence in spite of prohibitory orders, is defensive civil disobedience. And so is conducting of peaceful picketing undertaken with a view to wean people from things or institutions picketed in spite of orders to the contrary. The fulfilment of the conditions mentioned above is as necessary for defensive civil disobedience as for offensive civil disobedience.

Young India, 9-2-'22

MY FAITH

[Extract from Gandhiji's Presidential Address at the 39th Session of the Indian National Congress, Belgaum, Dec. 1924.]

Non-co-operation and civil disobedience are but different branches of the same tree called Satyagraha. It is my *Kalpadruma* — my *Jam-i-Jam* — the Universal Provider. Satyagraha is search for Truth ; and God is Truth. *Ahimsa* or non-violence is the light that reveals that Truth to me. Swaraj for me is part of that Truth. This Satyagraha did not fail me in South Africa, Kheda, or Champaran and in a host of other cases I could mention. It excludes all violence or hate. Therefore, I cannot and will not hate Englishmen. Nor will I bear their yoke. I must fight unto death the unholy attempt to impose British methods and British institutions on India. But I combat the attempt with non-violence. I believe in the capacity of India to offer non-violent battle to the English rulers. The experiment has not failed. It has succeeded, but not to the extent we had hoped and desired. I do not despair. On the contrary, I believe that India will come to her own in the near future, and that only through Satyagraha. The proposed suspension is part of the experiment. Non-co-operation need never be resumed if the programme sketched by me can be fulfilled. Non-violent non-co-operation in some form or other, whether through the Congress or without it, will be resumed if the programme fails. I have repeatedly stated that Satyagraha never fails and that one perfect Satyagrahi is enough to vindicate Truth. Let us all strive to be perfect Satyagrahis. The striving does not require any quality unattainable by the lowliest among us. For Satyagraha is an attribute of the spirit within. It is latent in every one of us. Like Swaraj it is our birthright. Let us know it.

Young India, 26-12-'24

[The Vykom Satyagraha was undertaken in 1924 and 1925 to obtain permission for " untouchables " and " unapproachables " to use certain roads round about the temple in Vykom in Travancore, South India. — Ed.]

77

VYKOM

The anti-untouchability campaign at Vykom is providing an interesting study in Satyagraha, and as it is being conducted in a calm spirit, it must prove of great use for future workers along similar lines. The Travancore authorities, whilst they still remain unbending regarding the prohibition order, are carrying out their purpose in a courteous manner. The public already know how quickly the authorities tried to check violence against Satyagrahis. The treatment in the gaols too is in keeping with their conduct in the open.

Why Petition ?

Surprise has been expressed over the advice I have tendered to the Satyagrahis that whilst Satyagraha continues, the organizers should leave no stone unturned by way of petitions, public meetings, deputations, etc., in order to engage the support of the State and public opinion on their side. The critics argue that I am partial to the State authorities because they represent Indian rule, whereas I am hostile to the British authorities because they represent an alien rule. For me every ruler is alien that defies public opinion. In South Africa Indians continued to negotiate with the authorities up to the last moment even though Satyagraha was going on. In British India we are non-co-operating and we are doing so because we are bent on mending or ending the whole system of Government, and therefore the method of petition is a hopeless effort.

In Travancore the Satyagrahis are not attacking a whole system. They are not attacking it at any point at all. They are fighting sacerdotal prejudice. The Travancore State comes in by a side door as it were. Satyagrahis would therefore be deviating from their path if they did not try to court junction with the authorities and cultivate public support by means of deputations, meetings, etc. Direct action does not always preclude other consistent methods. Nor is petitioning etc. in every case a sign of weakness on the part of a Satyagrahi. Indeed he is no Satyagrahi who is not humble.

Some Implications

I have been also asked to develop the argument against sending aid apart from public sympathy from outside Travancore. I have already stated the utilitarian argument in an interview. But there is a root objection too to getting, indeed even accepting, such support. Satyagraha is either offered by a few self-sacrificing persons in the name of the many weak, or by very few in the face of enormous odds. In the former case, which is the case in Vykom, many are willing but weak, and a few are willing and capable of sacrificing their all for the cause of the " untouchables ". In such a case it is obvious they need no aid whatsoever. But suppose that they took outside aid, how would it serve the " untouchable " countrymen ? The weak Hindus in the absence of strong ones rising in their midst will not prevail against the strong opponents. The sacrifice of helpers from other parts of India will not convert the opponents and it is highly likely that the last state of the " untouchables " will be worse than the first. Let it be remembered that Satyagraha is a most powerful process of conversion. It is an appeal to the heart. Such an appeal cannot be successfully made by people from other parts of India flocking to Vykom.

Nor should a campaign conducted from within need outside monetary support. All the weak but sympathetic Hindus of Travancore may not court arrest and other suffering, but they can and should render such pecuniary assistance as may be needed. I could not understand their sympathy without such support.

In the case too of a very few offering Satyagraha against heavy odds, outside support is not permissible. Public Satyagraha is an extension of private or domestic Satyagraha. Every instance of public Satyagraha should be tested by imagining a parallel domestic case. Thus suppose in my family I wish to remove the curse of untouchability. Suppose further that my parents oppose the view, that I have the fire of the conviction of Prahlad, that my father threatens penalties, calls in even the assistance of the State to punish me. What should I do ? May I invite my friends to suffer with me the penalties my father has devised for me ? Or is it not up to me, meekly to bear all the penalties my father inflicts on me and absolutely rely on the law of suffering and love to melt his heart and open his eyes to the evil of untouchability ? It is open to me to bring in the assistance of learned men, the friends of the family, to explain to my father what he may not understand from me his child. But I may allow no one to share with me the privilege and the duty of suffering. What is true of this supposed case of domestic Satyagraha is equally true and no less of the case we have imagined of public Satyagraha. Whether therefore the Vykom Satyagrahis represent a hopeless minority or as I have been informed a majority of the Hindus concerned, it is clear that they should avoid aid from outside save that of public sympathy. That in every such case we may not be able to conform to the law, that in the present case too, we may not be able to do so may be true. Let us not however forget the law and let us conform to it as far as ever we can.

Young India, 24-4-'24

78

VYKOM SATYAGRAHA

Vykom Satyagraha has attracted such wide public attention, and though restricted to a small area, presents so many problems for solution that I offer no apology to the reader for constantly engaging his attention for it.

I have received several important and well thought-out letters protesting against my countenancing it in any way whatsoever. One such letter even urges me to use whatever influence I may have, for stopping it altogether. I am sorry that I am unable to publish all these letters. But I hope to cover all the points raised in these letters or otherwise brought to my notice.

The first may be cleared at once. Exception has been taken to Mr George Joseph — a Christian — having been allowed to replace Mr Menon as leader and organizer. In my humble opinion the exception is perfectly valid. As soon as I heard that Mr Joseph was 'invited to take the lead' and he contemplated taking it, I wrote to him as follows on 6th April :

"As to Vykom, I think that you shall let the Hindus do the work. It is they who have to purify themselves. You can help by your sympathy and by your pen, but not by organizing the movement and certainly not by offering Satyagraha. If you refer to the Congress resolution of Nagpur, it calls upon the Hindu members to remove the curse of untouchability. I was surprised to learn from Mr Andrews that the disease had infected even the Syrian Christians."

Unfortunately before the letter could reach him, Mr Menon was arrested and Mr George Joseph had taken his place. But he had nothing to expiate, as every Hindu has, in the matter of untouchability as countenanced by the Hindus. His sacrifice cannot be appropriated by the Hindus in general as expiation made, say, by Malaviyaji would be. Untouchability is the sin of the Hindus. They must suffer for it, they must purify themselves, they must pay the debt they owe to their suppressed brothers and sisters. Theirs is the shame and theirs must be the glory when they have purged themselves of the black sin. The silent loving suffering of one single pure Hindu as such will be enough to melt the hearts of millions of Hindus; but the sufferings of thousands of non-Hindus on behalf of the "untouchables" will leave the Hindus unmoved. Their blind eyes will not be opened by outside interference, however well-intentioned and generous it may be ; for it will not bring home to them the sense of guilt. On the contrary, they would probably hug the sin all the more for such interference. All reform to be sincere and lasting must come from within.

But why may the Vykom Satyagrahis not receive monetary aid from outside, especially if it be from Hindus ? So far as non-Hindu assistance is concerned, I am as clear about such pecuniary help as I am about such personal help. I may not build my Hindu temple with non-Hindu money. If I desire a place of worship I must pay for it. This removal of untouchability is much more than building a temple of brick and mortar. Hindus must bleed for it, must pay for it. *They* must be prepared to forsake wife, children and all for the sake of removing the curse. As for accepting assistance from Hindus from outside, such acceptance would betray unreadiness on the part of the local Hindus for the reform. If the Satyagrahis have the sympathy of the local Hindus, they must get locally all the money they may need. If they have not, the very few who may offer Satyagraha must be content to starve. If they are not, it is clear that they will evoke no sympathy among the local Hindus whom they want to convert. Satyagraha is a process of conversion. The reformers, I am sure, do not seek to force their views upon the community ; they strive to touch its heart. Outside pecuniary help must interfere with the love process if I may so describe the method of Satyagraha. Thus viewed the proposed Sikh free kitchen, I can only regard, as a menace to the frightened Hindus of Vykom.

There is no doubt in my mind about it that the orthodox Hindus who still think that worship of God is inconsistent with .touching a portion of their own co-religionists, and that a religious life is summed up in ablutions and avoidance of physical pollutions merely, are alarmed at the developments of the movement at Vykom. They believe that their religion is in danger. It behoves the organizers, therefore, to set even the most orthodox and the most bigoted at ease and to assure them that they do not seek to bring about the reform by compulsion. The Vykom Satyagrahis must stoop to conquer. They must submit to insults and worse at the hands of the bigoted and yet love them, if they will change their hearts.

But a telegram says in effect, ' the authorities are barricading the roads ; may we not break or scale the fences ? May we not fast ? For we find that fasting is effective.'

My answer is : If we are Satyagrahis, we dare not scale or break fences. Breaking or scaling fences will certainly bring about imprisonment but the breaking will not be civil disobedience. It will be essentially incivil and criminal. Nor may we fast. I observe that my letter to Mr Joseph with reference to fasting has been misunderstood. For the sake of ready reference I reproduce below the relevant part :

" ' Omit fasting but stand or squat in relays with quiet submission till arrested.'

" The above is the wire sent to you in reply to yours. Fasting in Satyagraha has well-defined limits. You cannot fast against a tyrant, for it will be a species of violence done to him. You invite penalty from him for disobedience of his orders but you cannot inflict on yourselves penalties when he refuses to punish and renders it impossible for you to disobey his orders so as to compel infliction of penalty. Fasting can only be resorted to against a lover, not to extort rights but to reform him, as when a son fasts for a father who drinks. My fast at Bombay and then at Bardoli was of that character. I fasted to reform those who loved me. But I will not fast to reform, say, General Dyer, who not only does not love me but who regards himself as my enemy. Am I quite clear ? "

It need not be pointed out that the above remarks are of a general character. The words *tyrant* and *lover* have also a general application. The one who does an injustice is styled ' tyrant '. The one who is in sympathy with you is the ' lover '. In my opinion, in the Vykom movement opponents of the reform are the ' tyrant '. The State may or may not be that. In this connection I have considered the State as merely the police striving to keep the peace. In no case is the State or the opponents in the position of ' lover '. The supporters of Vykom Satyagrahis enjoy that status. There are two conditions attached to a Satyagrahi fast. It should be against the lover and for his reform, not for extorting rights from him. The only possible case in the Vykom movement when a fast will be justified, would be when the local supporters go back upon their promise to suffer. I can fast against my father to cure him of a vice, but I may not in order to get from him an inheritance. The beggars of India who sometimes fast against those who do not satisfy them are no more Satyagrahis than children who fast against a parent for a fine dress. The former are impudent, the latter are childish. My Bardoli fast was against fellow-workers who ignited the Chauri-chaura spark and for the sake of reforming them. If the Vykom Satyagrahis fast because the authorities will not arrest them, it will be, I must say in all humility, the beggar's fast described above. If it proves effective, it shows the goodness of the authorities, not that of the cause or of the actors. A Satyagrahi's first concern is not the effect of his action. It must always be its propriety. He must have faith enough in his cause and his means, and know that success will be achieved in the end.

Some of my correspondents object altogether to Satyagraha in an Indian State. In this matter too, let me quote the remaining portion of my foregoing letter to Mr Joseph :

"You must be patient. You are in an Indian State. Therefore, you may wait in deputation on the Dewan and the Maharaja. Get up a monster petition by the orthodox Hindus who may be well-disposed towards the movement. See also those who are opposing. You can support the gentle direct action in a variety of ways. You have already drawn public attention to the matter by preliminary Satyagraha. Above all see to it that it neither dies nor by impatience becomes violent."

Satyagraha in an Indian State by the Congress for the attainment of its object is, I think, clearly forbidden. But Satyagraha in an Indian State in connection with local abuses may be legitimately taken up at any time provided the other necessary conditions are fulfilled. As in an Indian State there can be no question of non-co-operation, the way of petitions and deputations is not only always open, but it is obligatory. But, say some of my correspondents, the conditions for lawful Satyagraha do not exist in Vykom. They ask :

1. Is unapproachability exclusively observed at Vykom or is it general throughout Kerala ?

2. If it is general, then what is the special reason for selecting Vykom in preference to places within the British territory in Kerala ?

3. Did the Satyagrahis petition the Maharaja, the local Assembly etc. ?

4. Did they consult the orthodox sections ?

5. Is not the use of the road the thin end of the wedge, is it not a step towards the abolition of caste altogether ?

6. Is not the road a private road ?

The first two questions are irrelevant. Unapproachability and untouchability have to be tackled wherever they exist. Wherever the workers consider a place or time suitable, it is their duty to start work whether by Satyagraha or other legitimate means.

My information goes to show that the method of petition etc. was tried not once but often.

They did consult the orthodox people and thought that they had the latter's support.

I am assured that the use of the road is the final goal of the Satyagrahis. It is however not to be denied that the present movement throughout India is to throw open to the suppressed classes all the *public* roads, *public* schools, *public* wells and *public* temples which are accessible to non-Brahmins.

It is in fact a movement to purify caste by ridding it of its most pernicious result. I personally believe in Varnashrama, though it is true that I have my own meaning for it. Any way, anti-untouchability movement does not aim at inter-dining or inter-marrying. Those who mix up the touch and the last two things together are doing harm to the cause of the suppressed classes as also to that of inter-dining and inter-marriage.

I have letters which protest that the road in question is a public road. In fact my informants tell me it was some years ago even accessible to the " unapproachables " as to other non-Brahmins.

In my opinion, therefore, there is a just cause for the Vykom Satyagraha and so far as it is kept within proper limits and conducted with the strictest regard to non-violence and truth, it deserves full public sympathy.

Young India, 1-5-'24

79

VYKOM SATYAGRAHA

His Holiness Shri Narayan Guru, spiritual leader of the Tiyas, is reported to have disapproved of the present methods of Satyagraha at Vykom. He suggests that volunteers should advance along barricaded roads and scale the barricades. They should enter temples and sit with others to dine. Though I have compressed the interview I have reproduced almost the exact words. Now the action proposed is not Satyagraha. For scaling barricades is open violence. If you may scale barricades, why not break open temple doors and even pierce through temple walls ? How are volunteers to pierce through a row of policemen except by using physical force ? I do not for one moment suggest that by the methods proposed the Tiyas if they are strong and are willing to die in sufficient numbers cannot gain their point. All I submit is that they will have gained it by something the reverse of Satyagraha ; and then too they would not have converted the orthodox to their view but would have imposed it on them by force. A friend who has sent me the press cutting recording the interview suggests that by reason of the violent advice of the *Guru* I should ask the local Congress committee to call off Satyagraha. I feel that would mean want of faith in one's means and surrender to violence. So long as the organizers strictly keep within the limits which they have prescribed for themselves there is no cause for calling off Satyagraha. The friend cites Chaurichaura as an illustration. In doing so, he has betrayed confusion of thought or ignorance of facts. The Bardoli Satyagraha was suspended because Congress and Khilafat men were implicated in the Chaurichaura outrage. If Congressmen connected with the Vykom movement entertain the suggestions said to be favoured by the Tiya spiritual leader, there would be a case for penance and therefore suspension but not otherwise. I would therefore urge the organizers at Vykom to make redoubled efforts and at the same time keep stricter watch on the conduct of those who take part in the movement. Whether it takes long or short to reach the goal, the way is the way of peaceful conversion of the orthodox by self-suffering and self-purification and no other.

Young India, 19-6-'24

VYKOM

The Vykom Satyagraha has entered upon probably the last stage. The newspapers report — and the report is confirmed by private advice — that the Travancore authorities have now practically abandoned the Satyagrahis to the tender mercies of *goondas*. This is euphemistically called the organized opposition of the orthodox section. Every one knows that orthodoxy is often unscrupulous. It has as a rule prestige and public opinion behind it in comparison with the reformer. It, therefore, does things with impunity which the poor reformer dare not. But what baffles one is the attitude of the Travancore authorities. Are they conniving at this open violence against the innocent Satyagrahis ? Has such an advanced State like Travancore abdicated its elementary function of protection of life and property ? The violence of the *goondas* is said to be of a particularly barbarous type. They blind the eyes of volunteers by throwing lime into them.

The challenge of the *goondas* must be taken up. But the Satyagrahis must not lose their heads. The khaddar dress of the volunteers is said to have been torn from them and burnt. This is all most provoking. They must remain cool under every provocation and courageous under the hottest fire. Loss even of a few hundred lives will not be too great a price to pay for the freedom of the " unapproachables ". Only the martyrs must die clean. Satyagrahis like Caesar's wife must be above suspicion.

Young India, 3-7-'24

VYKOM SATYAGRAHA

The Vykom Satyagraha has perhaps a meaning deeper than is generally realized. The young men who have organized it are stern in discipline and gentle in their dealings with the orthodox section. But this is the least part of their trials. Some of them are suffering too the persecution of social boycott. We of the western presidency have no idea of what this persecution can mean. These young men who are taking part in the movement are not only being denied social amenities but are threatened even with the deprivation of their share in the family property. If they would go to law, probably they would get their due. But a Satyagrahi cannot go to law for a personal wrong. He sets out with the idea of suffering persecution. In a reform that the Vykom struggle seeks to achieve, the Satyagrahi seeks to convert his opponent by sheer force of character and suffering. The purer he is and the more he suffers, the quicker the progress. He must therefore resign himself to being excommunicated, debarred from the family privileges and deprived of his share in the family property. He must not only bear such hardships cheerfully but he must actively love his persecutors. The latter honestly believe that the reformer is doing something sinful and, therefore, resort to the only means they know to be effective to wean him from his supposed error. The Satyagrahi on the other hand does not seek to carry out his reform by a system of punishments but by penance, self-purification and suffering. Any resentment of the persecution, therefore, would be an interruption of the course of discipline he has imposed upon himself. It may be a prolonged course, it may even seem to be never-ending. A little bullying or even moral suasion or coercion may appear more expeditious. What, however, I am showing here is not the greater efficacy of Satyagraha but the implications of the method the Satyagrahi has deliberately chosen for himself. Indeed I have often shown in these pages that Satyagraha is, as a matter of fact and in the long run, the most expeditious course. But my purpose here is merely to show what the young Satyagrahis of Vykom are doing. The public know much of what they are doing in the shape of picketing, but they know nothing of the silent suffering some of them are undergoing at the hands of their families and caste-men. But I know that it is this silent and loving suffering which will finally break the wall of prejudice. I am anxious therefore that the reformers should realize their responsibility to the full and not swerve by a hair's breadth from their self-imposed discipline.

Young India, 18-9-'24

82

VYKOM SATYAGRAHA

[Extract from Gandhiji's reply to a letter from a Vykom Satyagrahi.]

Satyagrahis must not be dejected. They dare not give way to despair. Of all my Tamil lessons one proverb at least abides with me as an evergreen. Its literal meaning is, " God is the only Help for the helpless." The grand theory of Satyagraha is built upon a belief in that truth. Hindu religious literature, indeed all religious literature, is full of illustrations to prove the truth. The Travancore Durbar may have failed them. I may fail them. But God will never fail them, if they have faith in Him. Let them know that they are leaning on a broken reed if they are relying on me. I am living at a safe distance from them. I may wipe their tears, but suffering is their sole privilege. And victory will surely come out of their sufferings provided they are pure. God tries His votaries through and through, but never beyond endurance. He gives them strength enough to go through the ordeal He prescribes for them. For the Satyagrahis of Vykom their Satyagraha is not a mere experiment to be given up if it does not succeed within a prescribed time or after a prescribed force of suffering. There is no time limit for a Satyagrahi nor is there a limit to his capacity for suffering. Hence there is no such thing as defeat in Satyagraha. Their so-called defeat may be the dawn of victory. It may be the agony of birth.

The Vykom Satyagrahis are fighting a battle of no less consequence than that of Swaraj. They are fighting against an age-long wrong and prejudice. It is supported by orthodoxy, superstition, custom and authority. Theirs is only one among the many battles that must be fought in the holy war against irreligion masquerading as religion, ignorance appearing in the guise of learning. If their battle is to be bloodless, they must be patient under the severest trials. They must not quail before a raging fire.

The Congress Committee may give them no help. They may get no pecuniary help, they may have to starve. Their faith must shine through all these dark trials.

Theirs is ' direct action '. They dare not be irritated against their opponents. They know no better. They are not all dishonest men as Satyagrahis are not all honest men. They are resisting what they honestly believe to be an encroachment upon their religion. The Vykom Satyagraha is the argument of suffering. The hardest heart and the grossest ignorance must disappear before the rising sun of suffering without anger and without malice.

Young India, 19-2-'25

VYKOM SATYAGRAHA

I cannot help endorsing the remark of Dewan Bahadur T. Raghaviah that "there is a world of difference between Satyagraha meant to be an educative force and Satyagraha intended as an instrument for the coercion of the Government and through them of the orthodox Hindu. What the Satyagrahis should aim at is the conversion of the orthodox to whom untouchability is part of their faith." I make bold to state that from the very outset Satyagraha at Vykom was intended to be an educative force and never an instrument of coercion of the orthodox. It was for that reason that the fast against the orthodox was abandoned. It was to avoid coercion of the Government by embarrassment that the barricades have been scrupulously respected. It was for that reason that no attempt was made to dodge the Police. It has been recognized that what appears to the reformers as a gross and sinful superstition is to the orthodox a part of their faith. The Satyagrahi's appeal has therefore been to the reason of the orthodox. But experience has shown that mere appeal to the reason produces no effect upon those who have settled convictions. The eyes of their understanding are opened not by argument but by the suffering of the Satyagrahi. The Satyagrahi strives to reach the reason through the heart. The method of reaching the heart is to awaken public opinion. Public opinion for which one cares is a mightier force than that of gunpowder. The Vykom Satyagraha has vindicated itself in that it has drawn the attention of the whole of India to the cause and it has been instrumental in the Travancore Assembly considering in a remarkable debate a resolution favouring the reform sought for and lastly in eliciting a considered reply from the Dewan of Travancore. I am sure that victory is a certainty if only the Satyagrahis will retain their patience and their spirit of suffering.

Young India, 19-3-'25

SATYAGRAHI'S DUTY

[The following is almost a verbatim report of the quiet talk I gave to the inmates of the Satyagraha Ashram at Vykom. The Ashram has at the present moment over fifty volunteers who stand or squat in front of the four barricades which are put up to guard the four entrances to the Vykom temple. They spin whilst they are stationed there and remain there at a stretch for six hours. They are sent in two relays. I reproduce the talk as being of general interest and applicable to all Satyagrahis.   —M. K. G.]

I want to tell you as briefly as I can what I expect of you. I would ask you to forget the political aspect of the programme. Political consequences of this struggle there are, but you are not to concern yourself with them. If you do, you will miss the true result and also miss the political consequences, and when the real heat of the struggle is touched you will be found wanting. I am therefore anxious, even if it frightens you, to explain to you the true nature of the struggle. It is a struggle deeply religious for the Hindus. We are endeavouring to rid Hinduism of its greatest blot. The prejudice we have to fight against is an age-long prejudice. The struggle for the opening of the roads round the temple which we hold to be public to the "unapproachables" is but a small skirmish in the big battle. If our struggle was to end with the opening of the roads in Vykom you may be sure I would not have bothered my head about it. If, therefore, you think that the struggle is to end with opening of the roads in Vykom to the "unapproachables" you are mistaken. The road must be opened. It has got to be opened. But that will be the beginning of the end. The end is to get all such roads throughout Travancore to be opened to the "unapproachables"; and not only that, but we expect that our efforts may result in amelioration of the general condition of the "untouchables" and "unapproachables". That will require tremendous sacrifice. For our aim is not to do things by violence to opponents. That will be conversion by violence or compulsion ; and if we import compulsion in matters of religion, there is no doubt that we shall be committing suicide. We should carry on this struggle on the lines of strict non-violence, i.e. by suffering in our own persons. That is the meaning of Satyagraha. The question is whether you are capable of every suffering that may be imposed upon you or may be your lot in the journey towards the goal. Even whilst you are suffering you may have no bitterness — no trace of it — against your opponents. And I tell you it is not a mechanical act at all. On the contrary I want you to feel like loving your opponents, and the way to do it is to give them the same credit for honesty of purpose which you would claim for yourself. I know that it is a difficult task. I confess that it was a difficult task for me yesterday whilst I was talking to those friends who insisted on their right to exclude the " unapproachables " from the temple roads. I confess there was selfishness behind their talk. How then was I to credit them with honesty of purpose ? I was thinking of this thing yesterday and also this morning, and this is what I did. I asked myself : ' Wherein was their selfishness or self-interest ? It is true that they have their ends to serve. But so have we our ends to serve. Only we consider our ends to be pure and, therefore, selfless. But who is to determine where selflessness ends and selfishness begins ? Selflessness may be the purest form of selfishness.' I do not say this for the sake of argument. But that is what I really feel. I am considering their condition of mind from their point of view and not my own. Had they not been Hindu they would not have talked as they did yesterday. And immediately we begin to think of things as our opponents think of them, we shall be able to do them full justice. I know that this requires a detached state of mind, and it is a state very difficult to reach. Nevertheless for a Satyagrahi it is absolutely essential. Three-fourths of the miseries and misunderstandings in the world will disappear, if we step into the shoes of our adversaries and understand their standpoint. We will then agree with our adversaries quickly or think of them charitably. In our case there is no question of our agreeing with them quickly as our ideals are radically different. But we may be charitable to them and believe that they actually mean what they say. They do not want to open the roads to the "unapproachables". Now whether it is their self-interest or ignorance that tells them to say so, we really believe that it is wrong of them to say so. Our business, therefore, is to show them that they are in the wrong and we should do so by *our* suffering. I have found that mere appeal to reason does not answer where prejudices are age-long and based on supposed religious authority. Reason has to be strengthened by suffering and suffering opens the eyes of understanding. Therefore, there must be no trace of compulsion in our acts. We must not be impatient, and we must have an undying faith in the means we are adopting. The means we are adopting just now are that we approach the four barricades, and as we are stopped, there we sit down and spin away from day to day, and we must believe that through it the roads must be opened. I know that it is a difficult and slow process. But if you believe in the efficacy of Satyagraha, you will rejoice in this slow torture and suffering, and you will not feel the discomfort of your position as you go and sit in the boiling sun from day to day. If you have faith in the cause and the means and in God the hot sun will be cool for you. You must not be tired and say, 'how long', and never get irritated. That is only a small portion of your penance for the sin for which Hinduism is responsible.

I regard you as soldiers in this campaign. It is not possible for you to reason out things for yourselves. You have come to the Ashram because you have faith in the management. That does not mean faith in me. For I am not manager. I am directing the movement, so far as ideals and general direction are concerned. Your faith therefore must be in those who are managers for the time being. The choice before coming to the Ashram was yours. But having made your choice and come to the

Ashram it is not for you to reason why. If we are to become a powerful nation you must obey all directions that may be given to you from time to time. That is the only way in which either political or religious life can be built up. You must have determined for yourselves certain principles and you must have joined the struggle in obedience to these principles. Those who remain in the Ashram are taking as much part in the struggle as those who go and offer Satyagraha at the barricades. Every piece of work in connection with the struggle is just as important as any other piece, and, therefore, the work of sanitation in the Ashram is just as important as spinning away at the barricades. And if in this place the work of cleaning the closets and compound is more distasteful than spinning it should be considered far more important and profitable. Not a single minute should be wasted in idle conversation, but we must be absorbed in the work before us, and if every one of us works in that spirit you will see that there is pleasure in the work itself. Every bit of property, any thing in the Ashram should be regarded by you as your own property and not property that can be wasted at pleasure. You may not waste a grain of rice or a scrap of paper, and similarly a minute of your time. It is not ours. It belongs to the nation and we are trustees for the use of it.

I know that all this will sound hard and difficult for you. My presentation may be hard, but it has not been possible for me to present the thing in any other way. For it will be wrong on my part if I deceive you or myself in believing that this is an easy thing.

Much corruption has crept into our religion. We have become lazy as a nation, we have lost the time sense. Selfishness dominates our action. There is mutual jealousy amongst the tallest of us. We are uncharitable to one another. And if I did not draw your attention to the things I have, it will not be possible for us to rid ourselves of all these evils. Satyagraha is a relentless search for truth and a determination to reach truth. I can only hope you will realize the import of what you are doing. And

if you do, your path will be easy — easy because you will
take delight in difficulties and you will laugh in hope when
everybody is in despair. I believe in the illustrations the
rishis or poets have given in religious books. For example,
I literally believe in the possibility of a Sudhanva smiling
away whilst he was being drowned in the boiling oil. For
to him it was greater torture to forget his Maker than
to be in boiling oil. And so it can be in a lesser measure
here, if we have a spark of Sudhanva's faith in this
struggle.

Young India, 19-3-'25

85

VYKOM

And now for the "unapproachables" miscalled. I
understand that they are getting restive. They have a
right to do so. I am further told that they are losing faith
in Satyagraha. If so, their want of faith betrays ignorance
of the working of Satyagraha. It is a force that works
silently and apparently slowly. In reality, there is no force
in the world that is so direct or so swift in working. But
sometimes apparent success is more quickly attained by
brute force. To earn one's living by body-labour is a
method of earning it by Satyagraha. A gamble on the
stock-exchange or house-breaking, either of which is the
reverse of Satyagraha, may apparently lead to an instantaneous acquisition of wealth. But the world has by now,
I presume, realized that gambling and house-breaking are
no methods of earning one's livelihood, and that they
do harm rather than good to the gambler or the thief. The
"unapproachables" may force their way by engaging in
a free fight with the superstitious *savarnas* but they will
not have reformed Hinduism. Theirs will be a method of
forcible conversion. But I am further told that some of
them even threaten to seek shelter in Christianity, Islam
or Buddhism if relief is not coming soon. Those who use

the threat do not, in my humble opinion, know the meaning of religion. Religion is a matter of life and death. A man does not change religion as he changes his garments. He takes it with him beyond the grave. Nor does a man profess his religion to oblige others. He professes a religion because he cannot do otherwise. A faithful husband loves his wife as he would love no other woman. Even her faithlessness would not wean him from his faith. The bond is more than blood-relationship. So is the religious bond if it is worth anything. It is a matter of the heart. An " untouchable " who loves his Hinduism in the face of persecution at the hands of those Hindus who arrogate to themselves a superior status is a better Hindu than the self-styled superior Hindu, who by the very act of claiming superiority denies his Hinduism. Therefore, those who threaten to renounce Hinduism are in my opinion betraying their faith.

But the Satyagrahi's course is plain. He must stand unmoved in the midst of all these cross-currents. He may not be impatient with blind orthodoxy, nor be irritated over the unbelief of the suppressed people. He must know that his suffering will melt the stoniest heart of the stoniest fanatic and that it will also be a wall of protection for the wavering *panchama* brother who has been held under suppression for ages. He must know that relief will come when there is the least hope for it. For such is the way of that cruelly kind Deity who insists upon testing His devotees through a fiery furnace and delights in humbling him to the dust. In his hour of distress let the Satyagrahi recall to his mind the prayer of the fabled godly Elephant King who was saved only when he thought he was at his last gasp.

Young India, 4-6-'25

86

TRUE SATYAGRAHA

For a long time I have purposely refrained from writing anything in these columns about Vykom and its struggle against unapproachability. Nor do I want as yet to say anything directly bearing on it. But I do want to tell the reader how the Satyagrahis at Vykom are passing their time.

A letter was received at Calcutta from Vykom dated the 1st of August. It has remained unpublished through oversight. But the substance of it is as fresh today as it was when it was received. I reproduce it below :

"Now there are only ten volunteers including myself. One of us daily does the kitchen-work while others except one offer Satyagraha for three hours each. Including the time taken to go and return the time for Satyagraha comes to four hours. We regularly get up at 4-30 a.m. and prayer takes half an hour. From 5 to 6 we have sweeping, drawing water and cleaning vessels. By seven all of us except two (who go for Satyagraha at 5-45 after bath) return after bath and spin or card till it is time for going to the barricade. Most of us regularly give 1,000 yards each per day and some of us even more. The average output is over 10,000 yards per day. I do not insist on our doing any work on Sundays when each does according to his will. Some of us card and spin for two or three more hours on Sundays too. Anyhow no yarn is returned on Sundays. Those who are Congress members spin for the Congress franchise on Sundays. Some of us are now spinning on Sundays and other spare hours for our humble gift towards All India Deshabandhu Memorial Fund which you have instituted. We wish to pack a small bundle of yarn to you on the 4th September (G. O. M. Centenary Day). I hope you will be glad to receive it. This we shall spin apart from our routine work. We mean either to beg or to spin the whole of that auspicious day and to send whatever is obtained. We have not yet settled what we should do."

This shows that the Satyagrahis of Vykom have understood the spirit of their work. There is no bluster, there is no fireworks display ; but there is here a simple determination to conquer by exact conduct. A Satyagrahi should be able to give a good account of every minute at his disposal. This the Vykom Satyagrahis are doing. The reader cannot fail to notice the honesty in spinning Congress yarn, and the yarn for the G. O. M. Centenary during their off day. The idea too of spinning for the All India Deshabandhu Memorial is in keeping with the rest of their doings. The letter before me gives me details of each member's spinning during the preceding week omitting Sunday. The largest quantity spun by a single inmate is 6,895 yards of 17 counts. The lowest is 2,936 yards of 18 counts. The remark against his name is that he was absent on leave for three days. The average per man per day during that week was 866.6 yards. I have also before me the figures for the week ending 26th August. The highest during that week was 7,700 for a single individual, and the lowest was 2,000, the spinner having spun only two days during the week. The reader may ask what connection is there between the removal of untouchability and spinning. Apparently nothing. In reality much. It is not any single isolated act which can be called Satyagraha apart from the spirit behind. Here, there is the spirit behind the spinning which is bound to tell in the long run ; for, spinning to these young men is a sacrificial national act calculated unconsciously to exhibit true humility, patience and pertinacity — qualities indispensable for clean success.

Young India, 24-9-'25

87

VYKOM SATYAGRAHA

Hindu reformers who are intent on removal of untouchability should understand the implications of Vykom Satyagraha and its results. The immediate goal of the Satyagrahis was the opening of the roads surrounding the temple, not their entry into the latter. Their contention was that the roads should be opened to the so-called untouchables as they were to all other Hindus and even non-Hindus. That point has been completely gained. But whilst Satyagraha was directed to the opening of roads, the ultimate aim of reformers is undoubtedly removal of every disability that "the untouchables" are labouring under and which the other Hindus are not. It, therefore, includes access to temples, wells, schools etc. to which other non-Brahmins are freely admitted. But for achieving these reforms much remains to be done before the method of direct action can be adopted. Satyagraha is never adopted abruptly and never till all other and milder methods have been tried. The reformers of the South have to cultivate public opinion in the matter of temple-entry etc. This is, moreover, a disability not peculiar to the South but unfortunately and, to our shame, it must be admitted, common, to more or less extent, to Hinduism throughout India. I, thereore, welcome the decision of Sjt. Kellappen Nayar who was in charge of the camp at Vykom to concentrate his effort on working among the unhappiest and the most suppressed among " the untouchables ", i.e., Puliyas whose very shadow defiles. It is a golden rule to follow out every direct action with constructive work, i.e., work of conservation. Reform has to be undertaken at both ends to make *savarnas* do their duty by the "untouchables" whom they have so cruelly suppressed and to help the latter to become more presentable and to shed habits for which they can in no way be held accountable but which nevertheless have to be given up if they are to occupy their proper place in the social scale.

Young India, 14-1-'26

88

SATYAGRAHA *v.* COMPULSION

An earnest but impatient worker has been trying to have temples and public places thrown open to Harijans. He had some success but nothing to be proud of. In his impatience, therefore, he writes :

> "It is no use waiting for these orthodox men to make a beginning. They will never move unless compelled to do so. Drastic steps are required to wipe off untouchability. I therefore beg you to kindly favour me with your opinion if Satyagraha at the entrance of the temples, by workers and Harijans preventing orthodox persons from entering the temples, will be an effective method. Appeals and entreaties have produced no effect, and to lose more time on these will, in my humble opinion, be sheer waste of valuable time."

Such blocking the way will be sheer compulsion. And there should be no compulsion in religion or in matters of any reform. The movement for the removal of untouchability is one of self-purification. No man can be purified against his will. Therefore, there can be no force directly or indirectly used against the orthodox. It should be remembered that many of us were like the orthodox people before our recognition of the necessity of the removal of untouchability. We would not then have liked anybody to block our way to the temples, because we in those days believed, no doubt wrongly as we now think, that Harijans should not be allowed to enter temples. Even so may we not block the way of the orthodox to the temples.

I should also remind correspondents that the word Satyagraha is often most loosely used and is made to cover veiled violence. But as the author of the word I may be allowed to say that it excludes every form of violence, direct or indirect, veiled or unveiled, and whether in thought, word or deed. It is breach of Satyagraha to wish ill to an opponent or to say a harsh word to him or of him with the intention of harming him. And often the evil thought or the evil word may, in terms of Satyagraha, be more dangerous than actual violence used in the heat of the moment and perhaps repented and forgotten the next moment. Satyagraha is gentle, it never wounds. It must not be the result of anger or malice. It is never fussy, never impatient, never vociferous. It is the direct opposite of compulsion. It was conceived as a complete substitute for violence.

Nevertheless, I fully agree with the correspondent that 'most drastic steps are required to wipe off untouchability'. But these steps have to be taken against ourselves. The orthodox people sincerely believe that untouchability, as they practise it, is enjoined by the *Shastras* and that great evil will befall them and Hinduism if it was removed. How is one to cope with this belief ? It is clear that they will never change their belief by being compelled to admit Harijans to their temples. What is required is not so much the entry of Harijans to the temples as the conversion of the orthodox to the belief that it is wrong to prevent Harijans from entering the temples. This conversion can only be brought about by an appeal to their hearts, i.e. by evoking the best that is in them. Such an appeal can be made by the appellants' prayers, fasting and other suffering in their own persons, in other words, by their ever increasing purity. It has never yet been known to fail. For it is its own end. The reformer must have consciousness of the truth of his cause. He will not then be impatient with the opponent, he will be impatient with himself. He must be prepared even to fast unto death. Not every one has the right or the capacity to do so. God is most exacting. He exacts humility from His votaries. Even fasts may take the form of coercion. But there is nothing in the world that in human hands does not lend itself to abuse. The human being is a mixture of good and evil, Jekyll and Hyde. But there is the least likelihood of abuse when it is a matter of self-suffering.

89

RELIGIOUS SATYAGRAHA

Mixing up of motives is damaging in any species of Satyagraha ; but in religious Satyagraha it is altogether inadmissible. It is fatal to use or allow religious Satyagraha to be used as a cloak or a device for advancing an ulterior political or mundane objective.

As with regard to the goal so with the means, unadulterated purity is of the very essence in this species of Satyagraha. The leader in such a movement must be a man of deeply spiritual life, preferably a *brahmachari* — whether married or unmarried. He must be a believer in — as in fact everybody participating in such a movement must be — and practiser of the particular religious observance for which the movement is launched. The leader must be versed in the science of Satyagraha. Truth and *ahimsa* should shine through his speech. All his actions must be transparent through and through. Diplomacy and intrigue can have no place in his armoury.

Absolute belief in *ahimsa* and in God is an indispensable condition in such Satyagraha.

In religious Satyagraha there can be no room for aggressiveness, demonstrativeness, show. Those who take part in it must have equal respect and regard for the religious convictions and susceptibilities of those who profess a different faith from theirs. The slightest narrowness in their outlook is likely to be reflected magnified multifold in the opponent.

Religious Satyagraha is, above all, a process of self-purification. It disdains mere numbers and external aids since these cannot add to the Satyagrahi's self-purification. Instead, it relies utterly on God who is the fountainhead of all strength. Religious Satyagraha, therefore, best succeeds under the leadership of a true man of God who will compel reverence and love even of the opponent by the purity of his life, the utter selflessness of his mission and the breadth of his outlook.

Harijan, 27-5-'39

SECTION FIFTH: KHEDA AND BARDOLI

SATYAGRAHAS

[Owing to failure of crops, conditions approaching famine prevailed in the Kheda District in Gujarat in 1918. The Gujarat Sabha,
of which Gandhiji was President, sent petitions and telegrams to
Government, but these had no effect. Thereupon Gandhiji after consulting co-workers advised the Patidars of the area to resort to Satyagraha and withhold payment of land revenue. This campaign soon
came to a successful termination, Government granting remission to
the poorer peasants.

Bardoli, an area in Gujarat, was where Gandhiji wanted to
experiment with mass civil disobedience, as the people there were
well disciplined. The idea, however, was given up in February 1922
owing to outbreaks of violence in other parts of the country. But
Bardoli had its opportunity in 1928, when it was to have its periodical
settlement of land revenue, and the Government wished to raise
the revenue by about 25 per cent. The people insisted that there
should be a public enquiry into conditions before the revenue was
enhanced. On the Government refusing, a No-tax campaign was
organized and successfully carried through by the people till the
Government yielded to their wishes.   — Ed.]

90

THE KHEDA SATYAGRAHA

A condition approaching famine had arisen in the
Kheda District owing to a widespread failure of crops, and
the Patidars of Kheda were considering the question of
getting the revenue assessment for the year suspended.

Sjt. Amritlal Thakkar had already inquired into and
reported on the situation, and personally discussed the
question with the Commissioner, before I gave any definite
advice to the cultivators. Sjt. Mohanlal Pandya and
Shankarlal Parikh had also thrown themselves into the
fight, and had set up an agitation in the Bombay Legislative Council through Sjt. Viththalbhai Patel and the late
Sir Gokuldas Kahandas Parekh. More than one deputation
had waited upon the Governor in that connection.

I was at this time President of the Gujarat Sabha. The Sabha sent petitions and telegrams to the Government and even patiently swallowed the insults and threats of the Commissioner. The conduct of the officials on this occasion was so ridiculous and undignified as to be almost incredible now.

The cultivators' demand was as clear as daylight, and so moderate as to make out a strong case for its acceptance. Under the Land Revenue Rules, if the crop was four annas * or under, the cultivators could claim full suspension of the revenue assessment for the year. According to the official figures the crop was said to be over four annas. The contention of the cultivator, on the other hand, was that it was less than four annas. But the Government was in no mood to listen, and regarded the popular demand for arbitration as *lese majeste*. At last all petitioning and prayer having failed, after taking counsel with co-workers, I advised the Patidars to resort to Satyagraha.

Besides the volunteers of Kheda, my principal comrades in this struggle were Sjt. Vallabhbhai Patel, Shankarlal Banker, Shrimati Anasuyabehn, Sjts. Indulal Yajnik, Mahadev Desai and others. Sjt. Vallabhbhai, in joining the struggle, had to suspend a splendid and growing practice at the bar, which for all practical purposes he was never able to resume.

We fixed up our headquarters at the Nadiad Anathashram, no other place being available which would have been large enough to accommodate all of us.

The following pledge was signed by the Satyagrahis :

" Knowing that the crops of our villages are less than four annas, we requested the Government to suspend the collection of revenue assessment till the ensuing year, but the Government has not acceded to our prayer. Therefore, we, the undersigned, hereby solemnly declare that we shall not, of our own accord, pay to the Government the full or the remaining revenue for the year. We shall let the Government take whatever legal steps it may think fit and gladly suffer the consequences of our non-payment. We shall rather let our lands be forfeited than

* i.e. 4 annas in the rupee meaning 25 per cent of the normal crop.

that by voluntary payment we should allow our case to be considered false or should compromise our self-respect. Should the Government, however, agree to suspend collection of the second instalment of the assessment throughout the district, such among us as are in a position to pay will pay up the whole or the balance of the revenue that may be due. The reason why those who are able to pay still withold payment is that, if they pay up, the poorer ryots may in a panic sell their chattels or incur debts to pay their dues, and thereby bring suffering upon themselves. In these circumstances we feel that, for the sake of the poor, it is the duty even of those who can afford to pay to withhold payment of their assessment."

I cannot devote many chapters to this struggle. So a number of sweet recollections in this connection will have to be crowded out. Those who want to make a fuller and deeper study of this important fight would do well to read the full and authentic history of the Kheda Satyagraha by Sjt. Shankarlal Parikh of Kathlal, Kheda.

' The Onion Thief '

The Gujaratis were deeply interested in the fight, which was for them a novel experiment. They were ready to pour forth their riches for the success of the cause. It was not easy for them to see that Satyagraha could not be conducted simply by means of money. Money is a thing that it least needs. In spite of my remonstrance, the Bombay merchants sent us more money than necessary, so that we had some balance left at the end of the campaign.

At the same time the Satyagrahi volunteers had to learn the new lesson of simplicity. I cannot say that they imbibed it fully, but they considerably changed their ways of life.

For the Patidar farmers, too, the fight was quite a new thing. We had, therefore, to go about from village to village explaining the principles of Satyagraha.

The main thing was to rid the agriculturists of their fear by making them realize that the officials were not the masters but the servants of the people, inasmuch as they received their salaries from the taxpayer. And then it seemed well nigh impossible to make them realize the duty of combining civility with fearlessness. Once they had shed the fear of the officials, how could they be stopped from returning their insults? And yet if they resorted to incivility it would spoil their Satyagraha, like a drop of arsenic in milk. I realized later that they had less fully learnt the lesson of civility than I had expected. Experience has taught me that civility is the most difficult part of Satyagraha. Civility does not here mean the mere outward gentleness of speech cultivated for the occasion, but an inborn gentleness and desire to do the opponent good. These should show themselves in every act of a Satyagrahi.

In the initial stages, though the people exhibited much courage, the Government did not seem inclined to take strong action. But as the people's firmness showed no signs of wavering, the Government began coercion. The attachment officers sold people's cattle and seized whatever movables they could lay hands on. Penalty notices were served, and in some cases standing crops were attached. This unnerved the peasants, some of whom paid up their dues, while others desired to place safe movables in the way of the officials so that they might attach them to realize the dues. On the other hand some were prepared to fight to the bitter end.

While these things were going on, one of Sjt. Shankarlal Parikh's tenants paid up the assessment in respect of his land. This created a sensation. Sjt. Shankarlal Parikh immediately made amends for his tenant's mistake by giving away for charitable purposes the land for which the assessment had been paid. He thus saved his honour and set a good example to others.

With a view to steeling the hearts of those who were frightened, I advised the people, under the leadership of Sjt. Mohanlal Pandya, to remove the crop of onion, from a field which had been, in my opinion, wrongly attached. I did not regard this as civil disobedience, but even if it was, I suggested that this attachment of standing crops, though it might be in accordance with law, was morally wrong, and was nothing short of looting, and that therefore it was the people's duty to remove the onion in spite of the order of attachment. This was a good opportunity for the people to learn a lesson in courting fines or imprisonment, which was the necessary consequence of such disobedience. For Sjt. Mohanlal Pandya it was a thing after his heart. He did not like the campaign to end without some one undergoing suffering in the shape of imprisonment for something done consistently with the principles of Satyagraha. So he volunteered to remove the onion crop from the field, and in this seven or eight friends joined him.

It was impossible for the Government to leave them free. The arrest of Sjt. Mohanlal and his companions added to the people's enthusiasm. When the fear of jail disappears, repression puts heart into the people. Crowds of them besieged the court-house on the day of the hearing. Pandya and his companions were convicted and sentenced to a brief term of imprisonment. I was of opinion that the conviction was wrong, because the act of removing the onion could not come under the definition of ' theft ' in the Penal Code. But no appeal was filed as the policy was to avoid the law courts.

A procession escorted the ' convicts ' to jail, and on that day Sjt. Mohanlal Pandya earned from the people the honoured title of *dungli chor* (onion thief) which he enjoys to this day.

Autobiography, pt. v, ch. xxiii, xxiv.

(*Young India*, 20-9-'28 and 27-9-'28)

91

BARDOLI'S DECISION

30th January, 1922

Bardoli has come to a momentous decision. It has made its final and irrevocable choice. Viththalbhai Patel, the President, addressed a conference of the representatives of the Taluka in a speech impressive for its warning. He certainly did not mince matters. There was an audience of khaddar-clad representatives numbering 4,000. There were five hundred women, a large majority of whom were also in khaddar. They were interested and interesting listeners. It was an audience of sober, responsible men and women with a stake.

I followed Viththalbhai and went through every one of the conditions of mass civil disobedience laid down by the Congress. I took the sense of the meeting on every one of the conditions separately. They understood the implications of Hindu-Muslim-Parsi-Christian unity. They realized the significance and the truth of non-violence. They saw what the removal of untouchability meant ; they were prepared, not merely to take into national schools, but to induce ' untouchable ' children to join them ; they have had no objection to the 'untouchable' drawing water from the village wells. They knew that they were to nurse the 'untouchable' sick as they would nurse their ailing neighbours. They knew that they could not exercise the privilege of non-payment of revenue and other forms of civil disobedience until they had purified themselves in the manner described by me. They knew too that they had to become industrious and spin their own yarn and weave their own khaddar. And lastly, they were ready to face forfeiture of their movables, their cattle and their land. They were ready to face imprisonment and even death, if necessary, and they would do all this without resentment.

There was an old dissentient voice on the question of untouchability. He said that what I said was right in theory, but it was difficult in practice to break down the custom all of a sudden. I drove the point home but the audience had made up its mind.

Before the larger meeting, I had met the real workers about fifty in number. Before that meeting, Viththalbhai Patel, some workers and I conferred together and felt that we would pass a resolution postponing the decision for about a fortnight, to make the Swadeshi preparation more complete and removal of untouchability more certain, by actually having ' untouchable ' children in all the sixty national schools. The brave and earnest workers of Bardoli would not listen to the postponement. They were certain that more than 50 per cent of the Hindu population were quite ready about untouchability and they were sure of being able to manufacture enough khaddar for their future wants. They were bent on trying conclusions with the Government. They bore down every objection raised by Viththalbhai Patel ; and Abbas Tyabji, with his hoary beard and ever smiling face, was there to utter the warning. But they would not budge an inch from their position and so the resolution which I give below was unanimously passed.

" After having fully understood and considered the conditions essential for the starting of mass civil disobedience, this Conference of the inhabitants of the Bardoli Taluka resolves that this Taluka is fit for mass civil disobedience.

" This Conference is of opinion —

(a) That for the redress of India's grievances, unity among Hindus, Mohammedans, Parsis, Christians and other communities of India is absolutely necessary.

(b) That non-violence, patience and endurance are the only remedy for the redress of the said grievances.

(c) That the use of the spinning wheel in every home, and the adoption of hand-spun and hand-woven garments to the exclusion of all other cloth by every individual are indispensable for India's freedom.

(d) That Swaraj is impossible without complete removal of untouchability by the Hindus.

(e) That for the people's progress and for the attainment of freedom, readiness to sacrifice movable and immovable property, to suffer imprisonment and, if necessary, to lay down one's life, is indispensable.

"This Conference hopes that the Bardoli Taluka will have the privilege to be the first for the aforesaid sacrifices, and this Conference hereby respectfully informs the Working Committee that unless the Working Committee otherwise decides or unless the proposed Round Table Conference is held, this Taluka will immediately commence mass civil disobedience under the advice and guidance of Mr Gandhi and the President of the Conference.

"This Conference recommends that those tax-payers of the Taluka who are ready and willing to abide by the conditions laid down by the Congress for mass civil disobedience, will refrain, till further instruction, from paying land revenue and other taxes due to the Government."

Who knows the issue ? Who knows whether the men and women of Bardoli will stand the repression that the Government may resort to ? God only knows. In His name has the battle been undertaken. He must finish it.

The Government have acted hitherto in a most exemplary manner. They might have prohibited the Conference. They did not. They know the workers. They would have removed them long ago. They have not done so. They have not interfered with any of the activities of the people. They have permitted them to make all preparations. I have watched their conduct with wonder and admiration. Both sides have up to the time of writing behaved in a manner worthy of chivalrous warriors of old. In this battle of peace it ought not to be otherwise. If the battle continues in this fashion, it will end only in one way. Whoever has the ear of 85,000 men and women of Bardoli will gain the day.

The Working Committee has to sit and pass its judgment upon Bardoli's decision. The Viceroy has still choice and will have yet another choice given to him. No charge of hurry, want of preparation or thought, no charge of discourtesy will it be possible to bring against the people of Bardoli.

Therefore,

> Lead, kindly Light, amid the encircling gloom,
> Lead Thou me on :
> The night is dark and I am far from home,
> Lead Thou me on.

92

BARDOLI ON TRIAL

One may hastily think that the Government is on its trial in Bardoli. But that would be a wrong opinion. The Government has been tried and found wanting scores of times. "Frightfulness" is its code of conduct when its vital parts are affected. If its prestige or its revenue is in danger, it seeks to sustain it by means either fair or foul. It does not hesitate to resort to terrorism and cover it with unblushing untruths. The latest information that Pathans are now being posted in villages with instructions to surround the houses of the villagers day and night need not cause either surprise or anger. The surprise is that they have not yet let loose in Bardoli a punitive police and declared martial law. We ought by this time to know what a punitive police or martial law means. It is evident that by the latest form of " frightfulness " the Government is seeking to goad people into some act of violence, be it ever so slight, to justify their enactment of the last act in the tragedy.

Will the people of Bardoli stand this last trial ? They have already staggered Indian humanity. They have shown heroic patience in the midst of great provocation. Will they stand the greatest provocation that can be offered ? If they will, they will have gained everything. Imprisonments, forfeitures, deportations, death must all be taken in the ordinary course by those who count honour before everything else. When the terror becomes unbearable, let the people leave the land they have hitherto believed to be theirs. It is wisdom to vacate houses or places that are plague-infected. Tyranny is a kind of plague and when it is likely to make us angry or weak it is wisdom to leave the scene of such temptation. History is full of instances of brave people having sought exile in preference to surrender to *zoolum*.

Let me hope however that such a step will not be

necessary. One hears rumours of intercessions by well-meaning friends. They have the right, it may be even their duty, to intercede. But let these friends realize the significance of the movement. They are not to represent a weak cause or a weak people. The people of Bardoli stand for an absolutely just cause. They ask no favour, they seek only justice. They do not ask any one to consider their case to be true. Their cause is to seek an independent, open, judicial inquiry, and they undertake to abide by the verdict of such a tribunal. To deny the tribunal is to deny justice which the Government have hitherto done. The means at the disposal of the people are self-suffering. In such a cause then minimum and maximum are almost convertible terms. Those who rely upon self-suffering for redress of a grievance cannot afford to rate it higher than it actually is. Those therefore who will intervene will harm the people and their cause, if they do not appreciate the implications of the struggle which cannot be lightly given up or compromised.

The public have a duty to perform by the Satyagrahis. The response is already being made to Vallabhbhai's appeal for funds. It will be remembered that he refused to make the appeal as long as it was possible to refrain. The imprisonments have made the appeal imperative. I have no doubt that the response will be quick and generous. Equally necessary is the expression of enlightened public opinion. Let the public study the facts carefully and then cover the whole of the land with public meetings. I like the suggestion made by Sjt. Jairamdas that June 12th or any other suitable date should be proclaimed as Bardoli Day when meetings representing all parties may be held to pass resolutions and make collections in aid of the sufferers of Bardoli.

Young India, 31-5-'28

93

NON-CO-OPERATION OR CIVIL RESISTANCE ?

Fear has been entertained in Government circles that the movement going on in Bardoli is one of non-co-operation. It is necessary, therefore, to distinguish between non-co-operation and civil resistance. Both are included in the wider term Satyagraha which covers any and every effort based on truth and non-violence. The term non-co-operation was designed to include among other things the items named in the programme of 1920 at the special session of the Congress at Calcutta and reaffirmed the same year at Nagpur with the object of attaining Swaraj. Under it no negotiation with or petition to the Government of the day was possible except for the purpose of attaining Swaraj. Whatever the Bardoli struggle may be, it clearly is not a struggle for the direct attainment of Swaraj. That every such awakening, every such effort as that of Bardoli brings Swaraj nearer and may bring it nearer even than any direct effort is undoubtedly true. But the struggle of Bardoli is to seek redress of a specific grievance. It ceases the moment the grievance is redressed. The method adopted in the first instance was through conventional prayer and petition. And when the conventional method failed utterly, the people of Bardoli invited Sjt. Vallabhbhai Patel to lead them in civil resistance. The civil resistance does not mean even civil disobedience of the laws and rules promulgated by constituted authority. It simply means non-payment of a portion of a tax which former, the aggrieved ryots contend, has been improperly and unjustly imposed on them. This is tantamount to the repudiation by a private debtor of a part of the debt claimed by his creditor as due to him. If it is the right of a private person to refuse payment of a debt he does not admit, it is equally the right of the ryot to refuse to pay an imposition which he believes to be unjust. But it is not the purpose here to prove the correctness of the action of the people of Bardoli. My purpose is to distinguish between non-co-operation with attainment of Swaraj as its object and civil resistance as that of Bardoli with the redress of a specific grievance as its object. This I hope is now made clear beyond doubt. That Sjt. Vallabhbhai and the majority of the workers under his command are confirmed non-co-operators is beside the point. The majority of those whom they represent are not. National non-co-operation is suspended. The personal creed of a non-co-operator does not preclude him from representing the cause of those who are helplessly co-operators.

Young India, 19-7-'28

94

LIMITATIONS OF SATYAGRAHA

Sardar Sardul Singh is an esteemed worker. His open letter advising me to invite sympathetic civil disobedience for Bardoli demands a reply especially because it enables me to clear my own position. If Bardoli Satyagraha were a campaign of lawlessness as the Government paint it, nothing would be more tempting or more natural than sympathetic Satyagraha and that too without the limits prescribed in the Sardar's letter. But the Sardar rightly says : ' I find in prominent Gujarat workers a tendency to allow Bardoli peasants to be kept isolated. This impression has been created in my mind by the reports of Sjt. Vallabhbhai's speeches and your writings. Friends think that any more scruples on this point go beyond the limits of practical politics.'

The Sardar's impression is correct. In order strictly to limit the scope of the struggle to the purely local and economic issue and to keep it non-political Sjt. Vallabhbhai would not let Sjt. Rajagopalachari and other leaders to go to Bardoli. It was only when the Government gave it a political character and made it an all-India issue by their coercive measures that the reins were loosened and

Vallabhbhai could no longer prevent public men from going to Bardoli, though where his advice or permission was sought, he said, 'Not yet.'

I do not know what Sjt. Vallabhbhai Patel would say to the Sardar's suggestion ; but I can say, 'Not yet.' Time has not come even for limited sympathetic Satyagraha. Bardoli has still to prove its mettle. If it can stand the last heat and if the Government go to the farthest limit, nothing that I or Sjt. Vallabhbhai can do will stop the spread of Satyagraha or limit the issue to a bona fide re-inquiry and its logical consequences. The limit will then be prescribed by the capacity of India as a whole for self-sacrifice and self-suffering. If that manifestation is to come it will be natural and incapable of being stayed by any agency no matter how powerful. But so far as I understand the spirit of Satyagraha and its working, it is the duty of Sjt. Vallabhbhai and myself to keep to the original limits in spite of the Government provocations which are strong enough even as they are to warrant the crossing of the original boundary.

The fact is that Satyagraha presupposes the living presence and guidance of God. The leader depends not on his own strength but on that of God. He acts as the Voice within guides him. Very often, therefore, what are practical politics so called are unrealities to him, though in the end his prove to be the most practical politics. All this may sound foolish and visionary on the eve of what bids fair to become the toughest battle that India has hitherto had to face. But I would be untrue to the nation and myself if I failed to say what I feel to be the deepest truth. If the people of Bardoli are what Vallabhbhai believes them to be, all will be well, in spite of the use of all the weapons that the Government may have at its command. Let us wait and see. Only let the M. L. C.'s and others who are interested in compromises not take a single weak step in the hope of saving the people of Bardoli. They are safe in the hands of God.

Young India, 2-8-'28

95

ALL'S WELL

It is a matter for sincere joy that the settlement has at last been reached over the Bardoli Satyagraha. All's well that ends well. I tender my congratulations both to the Government of Bombay and the people of Bardoli and Valod and Sjt. Vallabhbhai without whose firmness as well as gentleness the settlement would have been impossible. The reader will note that the Satyagrahis have achieved practically all that they had asked for. The terms of reference to the Committee of Enquiry are all that could be desired. True, there is to be no inquiry into the allegations about the coercive measures adopted by the Government to enforce payment. But it was generous on the part of Sjt. Vallabhbhai to waive the condition, seeing that the lands forfeited including lands sold are to be restored, the *talatis* are to be reinstated, and other minor matters are to be attended to. It is well not to rake up old wrongs for which beyond the reparation made there can be no other remedy. The inquiry into the assessment question will be carried in a calmer atmosphere for the waiver of the clause about the coercive processes.

Let not the Satyagrahis sleep over their well-deserved victory. They have to collect and collate material to prove their allegations about the assessment.

And above all, if they are to consolidate their position, they must proceed with constructive work with redoubled vigour. Their strength lies in their ability and willingness to handle this difficult, slow and unpretentious work of construction. They have to rid themselves of many social abuses. They must better their economic condition by attention to the *charkha*. It was the *charkha* that led to the awakening among them. They must remove the reproach of drink from their midst. They must attend to village sanitation and have a properly managed school in every village. The so-called higher classes must befriend the depressed and the suppressed classes. The greater the attention given to these matters, the greater will be their ability to face crises like the one they have just gone through.

Young India, 9-8-'28

96

A SIGN OF THE TIMES

Bardoli is a sign of the times. It has a lesson both for the Government and the people — for the Government if they will recognize the power of the people when they have truth on their side and when they can form a non-violent combination to vindicate it. By such recognition a wise Government consolidates its power which is then built upon people's goodwill and co-operation not merely in act enforced by brute power but in speech and thought as well. Non-violent energy properly stored up sets free a force that becomes irresistible.

Let us then turn to the people of Bardoli. The lesson that they have to learn is that so long as they remain united in non-violence they have nothing to fear, not even unwilling officials. But have they learnt that lesson, have they recognized the unseen power of non-violence, have they realized that if they had committed one single act of violence, they would have lost their cause ? If they have, then they will know from day to day that they will not become a non-violent organization unless they undergo a process of what may be called continuous corporate cleansing. This they can only do by engaging in carrying out a well thought out constructive programme requiring combined effort and promoting common good. In other words before they can claim to have become a non-violent organization, they must receive education in non-violence not through speeches or writings, necessary as both may be, but through an unbroken series of corporate acts, each evoking the spirit of non-violence. Sjt. Vallabhbhai

Patel knows what he is about. He has set for himself this more difficult task of constructive effort or internal reform. May God grant him therein the same measure of success that has attended the struggle against the Government.

Young India, 16-8-'28

SECTION SIXTH: SALT SATYAGRAHA

[Gandhiji launched civil disobedience in 1930 to rectify some of the evils of British rule, and symbolically singled out the Salt Laws for violation. He regarded these laws as iniquitous as they taxed salt which was the only flavouring to a bowlful of rice or other grain which the poorest in the land could afford. — Ed.]

97

" NEVER FAILETH "

अहिंसाप्रतिष्ठायां तत्सन्निधौ वैरत्यागः ।

' Hate dissolves in the presence of Love.'

" In the opinion of the Working Committee civil disobedience should be initiated and controlled by those who believe in non-violence for the purpose of achieving *Purna Swaraj* as an article of faith, and as the Congress contains in its organization not merely such men and women, but also those who accept non-violence as a policy essential in the existing circumstances in the country, the Working Committee welcomes the proposal of Mahatma Gandhi and authorizes him and those working with him who believe in non-violence as an article of faith to the extent above indicated to start civil disobedience as and when they desire and in the manner and to the extent they decide. The Working Committee trusts that when the campaign is actually in action all Congressmen and others will extend to the civil resisters their full co-operation in every way possible, and that they will observe and preserve complete non-violence notwithstanding any provocation that may be offered. The Working Committee further hopes that in the event of a mass movement taking place, all those who are rendering voluntary co-operation to the Government, such as lawyers, and those who are receiving so-called benefits from it, such as students, will withdraw their co-operation or renounce benefits as the case may be, and throw themselves into the final struggle for freedom. The Working Committee trusts, that in the event of the leaders being arrested and imprisoned, those, who are left behind and have the spirit of sacrifice and service in them, will carry on the Congress organization, and guide the movement to the best of their ability."

This resolution of the Working Committee gives me my charter of freedom if it also binds me in the tightest chains. It is the formula of which I have been in search

220

these long and weary months. For me the resolution is not so much a political as a religious effort. My difficulty was fundamental. I saw that I could not work out *ahimsa* through an organization holding a variety of mentalities. It could not be subject to the decision of majorities. To be consistent with itself, it might have to be inconsistent with the whole world.

A person who has a choice before him is ever exposed to temptation. The instinct of those, therefore, with whom non-violence is a policy, when tempted by violence, may fail them. That of those who have no remedy but non-violence open to them can never fail them if they have non-violence in them in reality. Hence the necessity for freedom from Congress control. And I was thankful that the members of the Working Committee saw the utter correctness of my position.

It is to be hoped that no one will misunderstand the position. Here there is no question of superiority. Those, who hold non-violence for the attainment of freedom as an article of faith, are in no way superior to those with whom it is a mere policy, even as there is no such inequality between brown men and yellow men. Each acts according to his lights.

The responsibility devolving on me is the greatest I have ever undertaken. It was irresistible. But all will be well, if it is *ahimsa* that is guiding me. For the seer who knew what he gave to the world said, ' Hate dissolves in the presence of *ahimsa*.' The true rendering of the word in English is love or charity. And does not the Bible say :

"Love worketh no ill to his neighbour,
" Believeth all things,
" Hopeth all things,
" Never faileth."

Civil disobedience is sometimes a peremptory demand of love. Dangerous it undoubtedly is, but no more than the encircling violence. Civil disobedience is the only non-violent escape from its soul-destroying heat. The danger lies only in one direction, in the outbreak of

violence side by side with civil disobedience. If it does
I know now the way; not the retracing as at the time of
Bardoli. The struggle, in freedom's battle, of non-violence
against violence, no matter from what quarter the latter
comes, must continue till a single representative is left
alive. More no man can do, to do less would be tantamount
to want of faith.

Young India, 20-2-'30

98

TO ENGLISH FRIENDS

[On the eve of starting Civil Disobedience. An extract.]

Hatred and ill-will there undoubtedly are in the air.
They are bound sooner or later to burst into acts of fury
if they are not anticipated in time. The conviction has
deepened in me that civil disobedience alone can stop the
bursting of that fury. The nation wants to feel its power
more even than to have independence. Possession of such
power *is* independence.

That civil disobedience may resolve itself into violent
disobedience is, I am sorry to have to confess, not an
unlikely event. But I know that it will not be the cause
of it. Violence is there already corroding the whole body
politic. Civil Disobedience will be but a purifying process
and may bring to the surface what is burrowing under and
into the whole body. And British officials, if they choose,
may regulate civil disobedience so as to sterilize the forces
of violence. But whether they do so, or whether, as many
of us fear, they will, directly or indirectly, consciously or
unconsciously, provoke violence, my course is clear. With
the evidence I have of the condition of the country and
with the unquenchable faith I have in the method of civil
resistance, I must not be deterred from the course the
Inward Voice seems to be leading me to.

But whatever I do and whatever happens, my English
friends will accept my word, that whilst I am impatient
to break the British bondage, I am no enemy of Britain.

Young India, 23-1-'30

99

WHEN I AM ARRESTED

It must be taken for granted, that when civil disobedience is started, my arrest is a certainty. It is, therefore, necessary to consider what should be done when the event takes place.

On the eve of my arrest in 1922 I had warned co-workers against any demonstration of any kind save that of mute, complete non-violence, and had insisted that constructive work, which alone could organize the country for civil disobedience, should be prosecuted with the utmost zeal. The first part of the instructions was, thanks be to God, literally and completely carried out — so completely that it has enabled an English noble contemptuously to say, ' Not a dog barked.' For me when I learnt in the jail that the country had remained absolutely non-violent, it was a demonstration that the preaching of non-violence had had its effect and that the Bardoli decision was the wisest thing to do. It would be foolish to speculate what might have happened if ' dogs ' had barked and violence had been let loose on my arrest. One thing, however, I can say, that in that event there would have been no Independence Resolution at Lahore, and no Gandhi with his confidence in the power of non-violence left to contemplate taking the boldest risks imaginable.

Let us, however, think of the immediate future. This time on my arrest there is to be no mute, passive non-violence, but non-violence of the activest type should be set in motion, so that not a single believer in non-violence as an article of faith for the purpose of achieving India's goal should find himself free or alive at the end of the effort to submit any longer to the existing slavery. It would be, therefore, the duty of every one to take up such civil disobedience or civil resistance as may be advised and conducted by my successor, or as might be taken up by the Congress. I must confess, that at the present moment, I have no all-India successor in view. But I have sufficient faith in the co-workers and in the mission itself to know that circumstances will give the successor. This peremptory condition must be patent to all that he must be an out-and-out believer in the efficacy of non-violence for the purpose intended. For without that living faith in it he will not be able at the crucial moment to discover a non-violent method.

It must be parenthetically understood that what is being said here in no way fetters the discretion and full authority of the Congress. The Congress will adopt only such things said here that may commend themselves to Congressmen in general. If the nature of these instructions is to be properly understood, the organic value of the charter of full liberty given to me by the Working Committee should be adequately appreciated. Non-violence, if it does not submit to any restrictions upon its liberty, subjects no one and no institution to any restriction whatsoever, save what may be self-imposed or voluntarily adopted. So long as the vast body of Congressmen continue to believe in non-violence as the only policy in the existing circumstances and have confidence not only in the bona fides of my successor and those who claim to believe in non-violence as an article of faith to the extent indicated but also in the ability of the successor wisely to guide the movement, the Congress will give him and them its blessings and even give effect to these instructions and his.

So far as I am concerned, my intention is to start the movement only through the inmates of the Ashram and those who have submitted to its discipline and assimilated the spirit of its methods. Those, therefore, who will offer battle at the very commencement will be unknown to fame. Hitherto the Ashram has been deliberately kept in reserve in order that by a fairly long course of discipline it might acquire stability. I feel, that if the Satyagraha Ashram is to deserve the great confidence that has been reposed in it and the affection lavished upon it by friends, the time has arrived for it to demonstrate the qualities implied in the word *satyagraha*. I feel that our self-imposed restraints have become subtle indulgences, and the prestige acquired has provided us with privileges and conveniences of which we may be utterly unworthy. These have been thankfully accepted in the hope that some day we would be able to give a good account of ourselves in terms of Satyagraha. And if at the end of nearly 15 years of its existence, the Ashram cannot give such a demonstration, it and I should disappear, and it would be well for the nation, the Ashram and me.

When the beginning is well and truly made I expect the response from all over the country. It will be the duty then of every one who wants to make the movement a success to keep it non-violent and under discipline. Every one will be expected to stand at his post except when called by his chief. If there is a spontaneous mass response, as I hope there will be, and if previous experience is any guide, it will largely be self-regulated. But every one who accepts non-violence whether as an article of faith or policy would assist the mass movement. Mass movements have, all over the world, thrown up unexpected leaders. This should be no exception to the rule. Whilst, therefore, every effort imaginable and possible should be made to restrain the forces of violence, civil disobedience once begun this time cannot be stopped and must not be stopped so long as there is a single civil· resister left free or alive. A votary of Satyagraha should find himself in one of the following states :

1. In prison or in an analogous state ; or
2. Engaged in civil disobedience ; or
3. Under orders at the spinning wheel, or at some constructive work advancing Swaraj.

Young India, 27-2-'30

100

LETTER TO THE VICEROY

[On the eve of launching on Civil Disobedience Gandhiji wrote
a letter on 2-3-'30 to the Viceroy stating the evils which required to be
removed immediately from the British Government of India. He ended
it by pointing out the method of Satyagraha he would adopt in case
there was no adequate response. We reproduce below the concluding
part of his letter. — Ed.]

Sinful to Wait Any Longer

It is common cause that, however disorganized, and,
for the time being, insignificant, it may be, the party of
violence is gaining ground and making itself felt. Its
end is the same as mine. But I am convinced that it cannot
bring the desired relief to the dumb millions. And the
conviction is growing deeper and deeper in me that
nothing but unadulterated non-violence can check the
organized violence of the British Government. Many
think that non-violence is not an active force. My
experience, limited though it undoubtedly is, shows
that non-violence can be an intensely active force. It is
my purpose to set in motion that force as well against
the organized violent force of the British rule as
the unorganized violent force of the growing party of
violence. To sit still would be to give rein to
both the forces above mentioned. Having an unquestion-
ing and immovable faith in the efficacy of non-violence,
as I know it, it would be sinful on my part to wait any
longer.

This non-violence will be expressed through civil disobedience, for the moment confined to the inmates of the
Satyagraha Ashram, but ultimately designed to cover all
those who choose to join the movement with its obvious
limitations.

My Ambition — Conversion of British People

I know that in embarking on non-violence I shall be
running what might fairly be termed a mad risk. But the
victories of truth have never been won without risks, often

of the gravest character. Conversion of a nation that has consciously or unconsciously preyed upon another, far more numerous, far more ancient and no less cultured than itself, is worth any amount of risk.

I have deliberately used the word *conversion*. For my ambition is no less than to convert the British people through non-violence, and thus make them see the wrong they have done to India. I do not seek to harm your people. I want to serve them even as I want to serve my own. I believe that I have always served them. I served them up to 1919 blindly. But when my eyes were opened and I conceived non-co-operation, the object still was to serve them. I employed the same weapon that I have in all humility successfully used against the dearest members of my family. If I have equal love for your people with mine it will not long remain hidden. It will be acknowledged by them even as the members of my family acknowledged it after they had tried me for several years. If the people join me, as I expect they will, the sufferings they will undergo, unless the British nation sooner retraces its steps, will be enough to melt the stoniest hearts.

If You Cannot See Your Way

The plan through Civil Disobedience will be to combat such evils as I have sampled out. If we want to sever the British connection it is because of such evils. When they are removed the path becomes easy. Then the way to friendly negotiation will be open. If the British commerce with India is purified of greed, you will have no difficulty in recognizing our independence. I respectfully invite you then to pave the way for immediate removal of those evils, and thus open a way for a real conference between equals, interested only in promoting the common good of mankind through voluntary fellowship and in arranging terms of mutual help and commerce equally suited to both. You have unnecessarily laid stress upon the communal problems that unhappily affect this land. Important though they undoubtedly are for the consideration of any scheme of Government, they have little bearing on the greater problems which are above communities and which affect

them all equally. But if you cannot see your way to deal
with these evils and my letter makes no appeal to your
heart, on the 11th day of this month, I shall proceed with
such co-workers of the Ashram as I can take, to disregard
the provisions of the Salt laws. I regard this tax to be the
most iniquitous of all from the poor man's standpoint. As
the Independence movement is essentially for the poorest
in the land the beginning will be made with this evil. The
wonder is that we have submitted to the cruel monopoly
for so long. It is, I know, open to you to frustrate my
design by arresting me. I hope that there will be tens of
thousands ready, in a disciplined manner, to take up the
work after me, and, in the act of disobeying the Salt Act,
to lay themselves open to the penalties of a law that should
never have disfigured the Statute Book.

No Threat but a Sacred Duty

I have no desire to cause you unnecessary embarrassment, or any at all, so far as I can help. If you think that
there is any substance in my letter, and if you will care to
discuss matters with me, and if to that end you would like
me to postpone publication of this letter, I shall gladly
refrain on receipt of a telegram to that effect soon after
this reaches you. You will, however, do me the favour not
to deflect me from my course unless you can see your way
to conform to the substance of this letter.

This letter is not in any way intended as a threat but
is a simple and sacred duty peremptory on a civil resister.
Therefore, I am having it specially delivered by a young
English friend who believes in the Indian cause and is a
full believer in non-violence and whom Providence seems
to have sent to me, as it were, for the very purpose.

Young India, 12-3-'30

101

SOME QUESTIONS & ANSWERS

The Risk of Violence

Q. Will not your movement lead to violence ?

A. It may, though I am trying my best to prevent any outbreak of violence. Today there is a greater risk of violence, in the absence of any safety-valve in the shape of a movement of non-violence like the one I am contemplating.

Q. Yes, I have heard you say that you are launching this campaign for the very purpose of stopping violence.

A. It is one argument, but that is not the most conclusive argument. The other and most conclusive argument for me is that if non-violence has to prove its worth, it must prove its worth today. It must cease to be the passive or even impotent instrument that it has come to be looked upon in certain quarters. And when it is exercised in the most effective way, it must act in spite of the most fatal *outward* obstructions. In fact non-violence by its very nature must neutralize all *outward* obstruction. On the contrary, inward obstacles in the shape of fraud, hatred, and ill-will would be fatal to the movement. Up to now I used to say, ' Let me get control over the forces of violence.' It is growing upon me now that it is only by setting the force of non-violence in motion that I can get those elements under control.

But I hear people say, ' History will have to repeat itself in India.' Let it repeat itself, if it must. I for one must not postpone the movement unless I am to be guilty of the charge of cowardice. I must fight unto death the system based on violence and thus bring under control the force of political violence. When real organic non-violence is set to work, the masses also will react manfully.

A Miracle

Q. But after you are removed the movement will no longer be in your control ?

A. In South Africa the movement was not in my control during the latter part of it, when it gained considerable momentum without any action on my part. Thousands joined the movement instinctively. I had not even seen the faces of them, much less known them. They joined because they felt that they must. They had possibly only heard my name, but they saw in the twinkling of an eye that it was a movement for their liberation ; they knew that there was a man prepared to fight the £ 3 tax and they took the plunge. And against what odds ? Their mines were converted into jails ; the men who oppressed them day and night were appointed warders over them. They knew that there would be hell let loose on them. And yet they did not waver or falter. It was a perfect miracle.

The Opportunity of a Lifetime

Q. But would not the movement add to the already numerous divisions existing in the country ?

A. I have no such fear. The forces of disunion can be kept under control, even as the forces of violence. You may say that there is fear elsewhere. The party of violence may not respond to my advances and the masses might behave unthinkingly. I am an optimist and have an abiding faith in human nature. The party of violence will give me fair play and the masses will act rightly by instinct. It is possible that I may be living in a fool's paradise. But no general can possibly provide for all contingencies. For me it is the opportunity of a lifetime. The movement is none of my seeking. Almost in spite of myself I was irresistibly drawn to Calcutta. I entered into a compromise to which I was driven. The period of two years I changed to one, simply because it did not involve any moral principle. In Lahore I had to conceive and frame practically every resolution. There I saw the forces of violence and non-violence in full play, acting side by side ; and I found that non-violence ultimately triumphed over violence.

How is the Time Ripe Now ?

Q. You said some time ago that the time was not ripe for civil disobedience. What has happened between that time and today that has helped you to alter your view ?

A. I am quite positive that it is fully ripe. The reason I will tell you. Nothing has happened externally, but the internal conflict in me, which was the only barrier, has ceased ; and I am absolutely certain now that the campaign had been long overdue. I might have started it long before this.

Q. And what was that internal conflict ?

A. You know I have always been guided solely by my attitude towards non-violence, but I did not know then how to translate that attitude into action in the face of growing violence. But now I see as clearly as daylight that, pursuing the course that I have adopted, I minimize the risk I am taking.

Q. Are you sure that the salt campaign will lead you to jail ?

A. I have not a shadow of doubt that it will. How long exactly it will take is more than I can say, but I feel that it will be much sooner than most people would be inclined to think. I expect a crisis to be soon reached which would lead to a proper Conference — not a Round Table Conference, but a Square Table one where everybody attending it would know his bearings. The exact lineaments of that Conference I cannot at present depict, but it will be a Conference between equals met to lay their heads together to devise ways and means for the establishment of an Independent Constitution in India.

About the Interview

Q. Were you not responsible for allowing the Vice-regal negotiations to come to an abrupt end ?

A. I know that is the impression in certain quarters ; the public blamed me for a time, but now it has come to understand the true position.

Q. Are you quite sure that in the position you took, the influence of the younger generation did not weigh with you ?

A. No. Not a bit. I had never been sanguine about the Round Table Conference. I went of course as far as I could. But the central thing I always insisted on was that the Conference should apply itself to a scheme of Dominion Status suited to the needs of India. If the Viceroy had said ' Yes,' I should gladly have asked him to proceed to the other points.

Q. Then you had no objection to the scheme coming into operation some years hence ?

A. If the scheme was such as to come into operation at a future time, I should rule it out. But I may not talk about our interview with the Viceroy. The public might know more about it some day. I can assure you, however, that there was no question of a real Dominion Status scheme being framed.

The Eleven Points

Q. Just a question about your now famous eleven points. If some of them are conceded, would there be room for a compromise ?

A. If they were to concede a few main points and couple the concession with a promise that the rest would be conceded as soon as possible, I would be prepared to consider a proposition for a Conference. But the justice of all those demands must be admitted. You will agree that there is nothing new about them. Most have been handed down to us from Dadabhai Naoroji's time.

Q. Supposing they conceded your demand about the reduction of civil and military expenditure, would you not regard it as a sufficient proof of their bona fides ?

A. I should seriously reconsider my position, but it would all depend on the spirit in which the concession was made.

Young India, 20-3-'30

102

ON THE EVE OF THE MARCH

[Gandhiji addressed these words to the vast audience assembled on the sands of the Sabarmati near the Sabarmati Ashram after prayer on the eve of his Salt Satyagraha March to Dandi:]

In all probability this will be my last speech to you. Even if the Government allow me to march tomorrow morning, this will be my last speech on the sacred banks of the Sabarmati. Possibly these may be the last words of my life here.

I have already told you yesterday what I had to say. Today I shall confine myself to what you should do after my companions and I are arrested. The programme of the march to Jalalpur must be fulfilled as originally settled. The enlistment of volunteers for this purpose should be confined to Gujarat. From what I have seen and heard during the last fortnight, I am inclined to believe that the stream of civil resisters will flow unbroken.

But let there be not a semblance of breach of peace even after all of us have been arrested. We have resolved to utilize all our resources in the pursuit of an exclusively non-violent struggle. Let no one commit a wrong in anger. This is my hope and prayer. I wish these words of mine reached every nook and corner of the land. My task shall be done if I perish and so do my comrades. It will then be for the Working Committee of the Congress to show you the way and it will be up to you to follow its lead. That is the only meaning of the Working Committee's resolution. The reins of the movement will still remain in the hands of those of my associates who believe in non-violence as an article of faith. Of course, the Congress will be free to chalk out what course of action commends itself to it. So long as I have not reached Jalalpur, let nothing be done in contravention to the authority vested in me by the Congress. But once I am arrested, the whole general responsibility shifts to the Congress. No one who believes in non-violence, as a creed, need therefore sit still. My compact with the Congress ends as soon as I am arrested. In that case there should be no slackness in the enrolment of volunteers. Wherever possible, civil disobedience of Salt laws should be started. These laws can be violated in three ways. It is an offence to manufacture salt wherever there are facilities for doing so. The possession and sale of contraband salt (which includes natural salt or salt earth) is also an offence. The purchasers of such salt will be equally guilty. To carry away the natural salt deposits on the sea-shore is likewise a violation of law. So is the hawking of such salt. In short, you may choose any one or all of these devices to break the salt monopoly.

We are, however, not to be content with this alone. Wherever there are Congress Committees, wherever there is no ban by the Congress and wherever the local workers have self-confidence, other suitable measures may be adopted. I prescribe only one condition, viz., let our pledge of truth and non-violence as the only means for the attainment of Swaraj be faithfully kept. For the rest, every one has a free hand. But that does not give a licence to all and sundry to carry on on their individual responsibility. Wherever there are local leaders, their orders should be obeyed by the people. Where there are no leaders and only a handful of men have faith in the programme, they may do what they can, if they have enough self-confidence. They have a right, nay it is their duty, to do so. The history of the world is full of instances of men who rose to leadership by sheer force of self-confidence, bravery and tenacity. We too, if we sincerely aspire to Swaraj and are impatient to attain it, should have similar self-confidence. Our ranks will swell and our hearts strengthen as the number of our arrests by Government increases.

Let nobody assume that after I am arrested there will be no one left to guide you. It is not I but Pandit Jawaharlal who is your guide. He has the capacity to lead. Though the fact is that those who have learnt the lesson of fearlessness and self-effacement need no leader. If we lack these virtues, not even Jawaharlal will be able to produce them in us.

Much can be done in other ways besides these. Liquor and foreign cloth shops can be picketed. We can refuse to pay taxes if we have the requisite strength. The lawyers can give up practice. The public can boycott the Courts by refraining from litigation. Government servants can resign their posts. In the midst of the despair reigning all round people quake with fear of losing employment. Such men are unfit for Swaraj. But why this despair ? The number of Government servants in the country does not exceed a few hundred thousand. What about the rest ? Where are they to go ? Even free India will not be able to accommodate a greater number of public servants. A Collector then will not need the number of servants he has got today. He will be his own servant. How can a poor country like India afford to provide a Collector with separate servants for performing the duties of carrying his papers, sweeping, cooking, latrine cleaning and letter carrying ? Our starving millions can by no means afford this enormous expenditure. If, therefore, we are sensible enough, let us bid good-bye to Government employment, no matter if it is the post of a judge or a peon. It may be difficult for a judge to leave his job, but where is the difficulty in the case of a peon ? He can earn his bread everywhere by honest manual labour. This is the easiest solution of the problem of freedom : Let all who are co-operating with the Government in one way or another, be it by paying taxes, keeping titles, or sending children to official schools etc., withdraw their co-operation in all or as many ways as possible. One can devise other methods too of non-co-operating with the Government. And then there are women who can stand shoulder to shoulder with men in this struggle.

You may take it as my will. It was the only message that I desired to impart to you before starting on the march or for the jail. I wish that there should be no suspension or abandonment of the war that commences tomorrow morning, or earlier if I am arrested before that time. I shall eagerly await the news that ten batches are ready as soon as my batch is arrested. I believe there are men in India to complete the work begun by me today. I have faith in the righteousness of our cause and the purity of our weapons. And where the means are clean, there God is undoubtedly present with His blessings. And where these three combine, there defeat is an impossibility. A Satyagrahi, whether free or incarcerated, is ever victorious. He is vanquished only when he forsakes truth and non-violence and turns a deaf ear to the Inner Voice. If, therefore, there is such a thing as defeat for even a Satyagrahi, he alone is the cause of it. God bless you all and keep off all obstacles from the path in the struggle that begins tomorrow. Let this be our prayer.

Young India, 20-3-'30

103

ASHRAM DISCIPLINE DURING THE MARCH

It may be mentioned in passing that in spite of the weary marches Gandhiji has insisted on the Ashram routine being followed by every one of the pilgrims, especially in the three essentials, viz., prayer, spinning and writing up the daily diary. It is easy enough to attend the prayers, inasmuch as the hours of march depend on the due observance of the hours of prayer, but the other two items are often difficult of achievement. One often feels dead tired and falls off to sleep before writing up the diary ; in some places it is difficult to get the spinning wheel, or, at any rate, a sufficient number of spinning wheels, and for a slow spinner it is difficult to do the quota of 212 yards on the *takli* in anything less than three hours. But Gandhiji would listen to no such excuse. " Ours is a sacred pilgrimage," he said, " and we should be able to account for every minute of our time. Let those who cannot finish their quota or do not find time to spin or to write up their diaries see me. I shall discuss the thing with them. There must be something wrong about their time-table and I should help them to readjust it. We should be resourceful enough to do all our daily duties without the march coming in our way. I dare say we are not hardy enough for a strenuous trek, and I am therefore providing for a weekly day of rest. But I should listen to no proposal for the relaxation of the regular discipline of the Ashram. I repeat that ours is a sacred pilgrimage, and self-examination and self-purification are essentials without which we cannot do. The diary is a great help in this matter. This regular spinning, counting the yards spun each day, the daily diary — all these things were thought out by me in the Yeravda Jail, and for us whose ambition it is to lay the foundation of the edifice of Swaraj, inasmuch as ours will be the first sacrificial offering, it should be as unsullied as possible. Those who follow us may dispense with the rigid discipline we are going through, but for us there is no escape. That rigorous self-discipline will generate in us a force which will enable us to retain what we have won. It is the natural result of active non-violence and should stand us in good stead after Swaraj. It is hardly likely that when we are imprisoned, we shall all be kept together. Therefore if our life is well regulated from now, we should not have the slightest difficulty in going regularly through our daily task."

Young India, 20-3-'30

104

DUTY OF DISLOYALTY

The spectacle of three hundred million people being cowed down by living in the dread of three hundred men is demoralizing alike for the despots as for the victims. It is the duty of those who have realized the evil nature of the system, however attractive some of its features, torn from their context, may appear to be, to destroy it without delay. It is their clear duty to run any risk to achieve the end.

But it must be equally clear that it would be cowardly for three hundred million people to seek to destroy the three hundred authors or administrators of the system. It is a sign of gross ignorance to devise means of destroying these administrators or their hirelings. Moreover, they are but creatures of circumstances. The purest man entering the system will be affected by it and will be instrumental in propagating tne evil. The remedy therefore naturally is, not being enraged against the administrators and therefore hurting them, but to non-co-operate with the system by withdrawing all the voluntary assistance possible and refusing all its so-called benefits. A little reflection will show that civil disobedience is a necessary part of non-co-operation. You assist an administration most effectively by obeying its orders and decrees. An evil administration never deserves such allegiance. Allegiance to it means partaking of the evil. A good man will therefore resist an evil system or administration with his whole soul. Disobedience of the laws of an evil State is therefore a duty. Violent disobedience deals with men who can be replaced. It leaves the evil itself untouched and often accentuates it. Non-violent, i.e. civil, disobedience is the only and the most successful remedy and is obligatory upon him who would dissociate himself from evil.

There is danger in civil disobedience only because it is still only a partially tried remedy and has always to be tried in an atmosphere surcharged with violence. For when tyranny is rampant much rage is generated among the victims. It remains latent because of their weakness and bursts in all its fury on the slightest pretext. Civil disobedience is a sovereign method of transmitting this undisciplined life-destroying latent energy into disciplined life-saving energy whose use ensures absolute success. The attendant risk is nothing compared to the result promised. When the world has become familiar with its use and when it has had a series of demonstrations of its successful working, there will be less risk in civil disobedience than there is in aviation, in spite of that science having reached a high stage of development.

Young India, 27-3-'30

105

SOME SUGGESTIONS

The resolution passed by the A. I. C. C. at its Ahmedabad meeting throws the burden on me of giving the signal for starting civil disobedience all over the country, assuming that I am kept free till I reach Dandi. The reason is obvious. The A. I. C. C. wishes to take every reasonable precaution against mishaps. In the event of my arrest, it would be dangerous to stop the movement. Before my arrest, the A. I. C. C. will not anticipate me. So far as I can judge now, the workers may assume that the date for making an all-India start will be the 6th of April. It is the day of commencement of the national week. It is the day of Satyagraha that in 1919 witnessed a mass awakening unknown before. The seven days that followed witnessed some dark deeds on our part and culminated in the inhuman Jalianwala massacre. If all goes well I should reach Dandi on April 5th. April 6th therefore appears to me to be the most natural day for commencing Satyagraha. But the workers, while they may make preparations, must await the final word.

The release of the embargo however does not mean that every province or every district is bound at once to commence civil disobedience although it may not be ready and although its First Servant does not feel the inner urge. He will refuse to be hustled into action if he has no confidence in himself or in his immediate surroundings. No one will be blamed for inaction, but blame will most decidedly descend upon the shoulders of him who instead of controlling the surroundings is carried away by them.

What we all are after is mass civil disobedience. It cannot be made. It must be spontaneous, if it is to deserve the name and if it is to be successful. And there certainly will be no mass response where the ground has not been previously tilled, manured and watered. The greatest precaution has to be taken everywhere against an outbreak of violence. Whilst it is true, as I have said, that civil resistance this time will continue even though violence may break out, it is equally true that violence on our part will harm the struggle and retard its progress. Two opposite forces can never work concurrently so as to help each other. The plan of civil disobedience has been conceived to neutralize and ultimately entirely to displace violence and enthrone non-violence in its stead, to replace hatred by love, to replace strife by concord.

The meaning then of not suspending the fight in spite of any outbreak of violence simply is that votaries of non-violence will allow themselves, will even seek, to be consumed in the flames if any should rise. They will not care to remain helpless witnesses either of the organized violence of the Government or of the sporadic violence of an enraged group or nation. The workers will therefore take, in each province, all precautions humanly possible and then plunge into the fight even though in so doing they run the greatest risks imaginable. It follows that everywhere there will be willing submission to the judgment of those who may be in their own provinces known for their belief in non-violence as an article of faith for the purpose of gaining *Purna Swaraj*.

There has been talk of disobeying other laws. The proposal has not attracted me. I believe in concentrating attention upon the Salt laws. Salt mines are to be found almost everywhere. The idea is not to manufacture salt in saleable quantities but through manufacture and otherwise to commit a deliberate and open breach of Salt laws.

The *chaukidari* tax laws have been suggested for possible disobedience. This tax does not in my opinion comply with the conditions that the Salt tax fulfils. The idea is to disobey such laws as are bad for all time as far as can be seen today. We do not want the Salt tax even under Swaraj. *Chaukidari* tax is perhaps not such a tax. We may need *chaukidars* even under Swaraj. If such is the case, it may be wise not to touch that tax so long as we have other taxes or other laws to combat.

Then there are the forest laws. I have not studied them. I must therefore write with reserve. There can be no doubt that we do not want our forests to be destroyed altogether or wood to be cut uneconomically. There is a need, I have little doubt, for mending these laws. There is greater need perhaps for humaner administration of these laws. The reform may well await the establishment of Swaraj. Nor so far as I am aware has there been any popular education about the grievances arising out of these laws or their administration.

Closely allied to the forests are grazing areas. I do not know that regulations governing their use are so irksome as to be a just grievance.

Much better from my standpoint is the picketing of liquor shops, opium dens and foreign cloth shops. Though picketing is not by itself illegal, past experience shows that the Government will want to suppress all effective picketing. That does not much matter. We are out to resist it wherever we can, consistently with our creed. But I fear the unscrupulous behaviour of liquor dealers and the ignorant wrath of foreign cloth dealers. I should like public opinion to consolidate itself more fully around these two evils and would like workers to undertake more systematic education of the dealers as also of their customers.

We have to eradicate both the evils some day or other. Wherever, therefore, workers have confidence in their ability to carry on picketing without taking undue risks of the type I have mentioned, they should start the campaign, but in no case because they must be doing something when the word is given for action and because they do not see their way to take up the Salt laws. It seems to me to be the safest thing to take up the latter for the time being ; what I have said above is merely by way of caution. Wherever workers feel that they have the real inner call for action and are themselves free from violence, they are at liberty, as soon as the word is given, to take up such civil disobedience as they may consider necessary and desirable, subject of course to the A. I. C. C. control.

Meanwhile between now and the 6th of April the provinces should lose no time in making their preparation for mobilization.

Young India, 27-3-'30

106

TURNING THE SEARCHLIGHT INWARD

[Condensed translation by Gandhiji himself of an introspective speech he delivered at Bhatgam (Dist. Surat) on 29-3-'30 during the Dandi March.   — Ed.]

Only this morning at the prayer time I was telling my companions that as we had entered the district in which we were to offer civil disobedience, we should insist on greater purification and intenser dedication. I warned them that as the district was more organized and contained many intimate co-workers, there was every likelihood of our being pampered. I warned them against succumbing to their pampering. We are not angels. We are very weak, easily tempted. There are many lapses to our debit. God is great. Even today some were discovered. One defaulter confessed his lapse himself whilst I was brooding over the lapses of the pilgrims. I discovered that my warning was given none too soon. The local workers had ordered milk from Surat to be brought in a motor lorry and they had incurred other expenses which I could not justify. I therefore spoke strongly about them. But that did not allay my grief. On the contrary it increased with the contemplation of the wrongs done.

The Right to Criticize

In the light of these discoveries, what right had I to write to the Viceroy the letter in which I have severely criticized his salary which is more than 5,000 times our average income ? How could he possibly do justice to that salary ? And how can we tolerate his getting a salary out of all proportion to our income ? But he is individually not to be blamed for it. He has no need for it. God has made him a wealthy man. I have suggested in my letter that probably the whole of his salary is spent in charity. I have since learnt that my guess is largely likely to be true. Even so, of course, I should resist the giving of such a large salary. I could not vote Rs 21,000 per month, not perhaps even Rs 2,100 per month. But when could I offer such resistance ? Certainly not if I was myself taking from the people an unconscionable toll. I could resist it only if my living bore some correspondence with the average income of the people. We are marching in the name of God. We profess to act on behalf of the hungry, the naked and the unemployed. I have no right to criticize the Viceregal salary, if we are costing the country say fifty times seven pice, the average daily income of our people. I have asked the workers to furnish me with an account of the expenses. And the way things are going, I should not be surprised if each of us is costing something near fifty times seven pice. What else can be the result if they will fetch for me from whatever source possible, the choicest oranges and grapes, if they will bring 120 when I should want 12 oranges, if when I need one pound of milk, they will produce three ? What else can be the result if we would take all the dainties you may place before us under the excuse that we would hurt your feeling, if we did not take them. You give us guavas and grapes and we eat them because they are a free gift from a princely farmer. And then imagine me with an easy conscience writing the Viceregal letter on costly glazed paper with a fountain pen, a free gift from some accommodating friend ! ! ! Will this behove you and me ? Can a letter so written produce the slightest effect ?

Trustees of the Dumb Millions

To live thus would be to illustrate the immortal verse of Akho Bhagat who says, " stolen food is like eating unprocessed mercury." And to live above the means befitting a poor country is to live on stolen food. This battle can never be won by living on stolen food. Nor did I bargain to set out on this march for living above our means. We expect thousands of volunteers to respond to the call. It will be impossible to keep them on extravagant terms. My life has become so busy that I get little time to come in close touch even with the eighty companions so as to be able to identify them individually. There was therefore no course open to me but to unburden my soul in public. I expect you to understand the central point of my message. If you have not, there is no hope of Swaraj through the present effort. We must become real trustees of the dumb millions.

I have exposed our weaknesses to the public gaze. I have not yet given you all the details, but I have told you enough to enable you to realize our unworthiness to write the letter to the Viceroy.

Now the local co-workers will understand my agony. Weak, ever exposed to temptations, ever failing, why will you tempt us and pamper us ? We may not introduce these incandescent burners in our villages. It is enough that one hundred thousand men prey upon three hundred million. But how will it be when we begin to prey upon one another ? In that event dogs will lick our corpses.

Account for Every Pice

These lights are merely a sample of the extravagance I have in mind. My purpose is to wake you up from torpor. Let the volunteers account for every pice spent.

I am more capable of offering Satyagraha against our-selves than against the Government. I have taken many years before embarking upon civil resistance against the Government. But I should not take as many days for offering it against ourselves. The risk to be incurred is nothing compared to what has to be incurred in the present Satyagraha.

Therefore in your hospitality towards servants like us, I would have you to be miserly rather than lavish. I shall not complain of unavoidable absence of things. In order to procure goat's milk for me you may not deprive poor women of milk for their children. It would be like poison if you did. Nor may milk and vegetables be brought from Surat. We can do without them if necessary. Do not resort to motor cars on the slightest pretext. The rule is, do not ride, if you can walk. This is not a battle to be conducted with money. It will be impossible to sustain a mass movement with money. Any way it is beyond me to conduct the campaign with a lavish display of money.

Extravagance has no room in this campagin. If we cannot gather crowds unless we carry on a hurricane expensive propaganda, I would be satisfied to address half a dozen men and women. Success depends not upon our high skill. It depends solely upon God. And He only helps the vigilant and the humble.

A Humiliating Sight

We may not consider anybody as low. I observed that you had provided for the night journey a heavy kitson burner mounted on a stool which a poor labourer carried on his head. This was a humiliating sight. This man was being goaded to walk fast. I could not bear the sight. I therefore put on speed and outraced the whole company. But it was no use. The man was made to run after me. The humiliation was complete. If the weight had to be carried, I should have loved to see some one among ourselves carrying it. We would then soon dispense both with the stool and the burner. No labourer would carry such a load on his head. We rightly object to

begar (forced labour). But what was this if it was not
begar? Remember that in Swaraj we would expect one
drawn from the so-called lower class to preside over India's
destiny. If then we do not quickly mend our ways, there
is no Swaraj such as you and I have put before the people.

From my outpouring you may not infer that I shall
weaken in my resolve to carry on the struggle. It will
continue no matter how co-workers or others act. For
me there is no turning back whether I am alone or joined
by thousands. I would rather die a dog's death and have
my bones licked by dogs than that I should return to the
Ashram a broken man.

(Turning to the women I concluded and nearly broke
down as I finished the last sentences.)

I admit that I have not well used the money you have
given out of the abundance of your love. You are entitled
to regard me as one of those wretches described in the
verses sung in the beginning. Shun me.

Young India, 3-4-'30

107

NOTES ON THE WAY TO DANDI

Dog in the Manger

The volume of information being gained daily shows
how wickedly the Salt tax has been designed. In order
to prevent the use of salt that has not paid the tax which
is at times even fourteen times its value, the Government
destroys the salt it cannot sell profitably. Thus it taxes
the nation's vital necessity, it prevents the public from
manufacturing it and destroys what nature manufactures
without effort. No adjective is strong enough for charac-
terizing this wicked dog-in-the-manger policy. From
various sources I hear tales of such wanton destruction
of nation's property in all parts of India. Maunds if not
tons of salt are said to be destroyed on the Konkan coast.
The same tale comes from Dandi. Wherever there is

likelihood of natural salt being taken away by the people living in the neighbourhood of such areas for their personal use, salt officers are posted for the sole purpose of carrying on destruction. Thus valuable national property is destroyed at national expense and salt taken out of the mouths of the people.

Nor is this all. I was told on entering the Olpad Taluka that through the poor people being prevented from collecting the salt that was prepared by nature or from manufacturing it they were deprived of the supplementary village industry they had in addition to the spinning wheel.

The salt monopoly is thus a fourfold curse. It deprives the people of a valuable easy village industry, involves wanton destruction of property that nature produces in abundance, the destruction itself means more national expenditure, and fourthly, to crown this folly, an unheard of tax of more than 1,000 per cent is exacted from a starving people.

I cannot help recalling in this connection the hue and cry that was raised when I first proposed the burning of foreign cloth. It was considered to be an inhuman, wasteful proposal. It is generally admitted that foreign cloth is harmful to the people. Salt on the other hand is a vital necessity. Yet it has been and is daily being wantonly destroyed in the interest of wicked exaction.

This tax has remained so long because of the apathy of the general public. Now that it is sufficiently roused, the tax has to go. How soon it will be abolished depends upon the strength the people are able to put forth. Happily the test will not be long delayed.

Exaggerated Statements

Paragraphs have appeared in the press to the effect that 18 of my companions have become ill and incapacitated. This is a gross exaggeration. It is quite true that that number had to take a two days' rest at the Broach Sevashram. But that was because they were fatigued and footsore. With the exception of the case of smallpox which proved to be quite mild, there was no illness worth the name. One of the companions certainly had high fever. But that fever too proved to be due to overzeal in marching. He had a wiry constitution and was over-confident about his ability to pull through without resting. He would not therefore rest till nature absolutely compelled him. But both are quite well now though being weak they are still being made to rest a few days. They expect to join the company at Surat. A third, though still a little footsore, insisted on walking, but had to rest at Ankleshvar. All the others are fit and marching daily. It has become necessary to make this statement in order to prevent anxiety on the part of guardians and friends. It would be ungrateful not to mention here the great attention the villagers are paying to the Satyagrahis and the exceptional care that was bestowed upon the smallpox patient by the Charotar Education Society at Anand and on the footsore men by Dr Chandulal's staff at Sevashram.

A moral may also be drawn from these accidents. The modern generation is delicate, weak and much pampered. If they will take part in national work, they must take ample exercise and become hardy. And exercise is as good and as effective as long vigorous marches. Gymnastics and the like are good and may be added to walking. They are no substitute for walking, justly called the prince of exercises. Our march is in reality child's play. Less than twelve miles per day in two stages with not much luggage should cause no strain. Those who have not been footsore have gained in weight. I may add too that the hot Condy's fluid, baths and wet-sheet packs are proving a most efficient remedy for smallpox.

The True Spirit

Shrimati Khorshedbai Naoroji came the other day to Sandhiar, a halting station during the march. She was accompanied by Mridulabehn, the daughter of Sjt. Ambalal Sarabhai, Madalasa the little daughter of Jamnalalji, Shrimati Vasumatibehn and Radhabehn from the Ashram. They had to await a lift for Sandhiar. They wanted to turn to national account the time at their disposal. They saw that the surroundings of the place were not over clean.

They therefore decided to clean up the rubbish and so asked for brooms from the surprised villagers. As soon as the villagers realized what had happened, they also joined these national scavengers some of whom were drawn from aristocratic families and the village of Sayan perhaps never looked as clean as when these sisters utilized their spare time for scavenging. I commend this true service, this mute speech of the sisters to the army of young men who are pining to serve and free the country. Freedom will come only when we deliver a simultaneous attack on all the weak points. Let it be known that all these sisters have enlisted as civil resisters and are eagerly, even impatiently, awaiting marching orders. In this campaign of Swaraj by self-purification, it will be nothing surprising if the women outdo the men.

Young India, 3-4-'30

108

REMEMBER 6TH APRIL

This will be in the readers' hands on Thursday 3rd instant. If there is no previous cancelling, they all may regard this as the word from me that all are free, and those who are ready are expected to start mass civil disobedience regarding the Salt laws, as from 6th April.

Let me gather up what has been said in these pages at various times.

The only stipulation for civil disobedience is perfect observance of non-violence in the fullest sense of the term.

Mass civil disobedience means spontaneous action. The workers will merely guide the masses in the beginning stages. Later the masses will regulate the movement themselves.

Congress volunteers will watch developments and render aid wherever needed. They will be expected to be in the forefront.

Volnteers may not take sides in any communal quarrels.

Wherever there is a violent eruption, volunteers are expected to die in the attempt to quell violence.

Perfect discipline and perfect co-operation among the different units are indispensable for success.

If there is true mass awakening, those who are not engaged in civil disobedience are expected to occupy themselves and induce others to be engaged in some national service such as *khadi* work, liquor and opium picketing, foreign cloth exclusion, village sanitation, assisting the families of civil resistance prisoners in a variety of ways.

Indeed if there is a real response about civil resistance regarding the Salt tax, we should by proper organization secure boycott of foreign cloth through *khadi* and secure total prohibition. This should mean a saving of 91 crores per year, and supplementary work for the millions of unemployed. If we secure these things, we cannot be far from independence. And not one of these things is beyond our capacity.

Young India, 3-4-'30

109

HINDU-MUSLIM QUESTION

[Summary of a speech delivered at Broach on 26th March, 1930, on the communal question.]

A Muslim youth has sent me questions on the Hindu-Muslim problem. One of them is : ' Do you expect to win Swaraj through your own single effort or assisted merely by the Hindus ? ' I have never dreamt that I could win Swaraj merely through my effort or assisted only by the Hindus. I stand in need of the assistance of Mussalmans, Parsis, Christians, Sikhs, Jews and all other Indians. I need the assistance even of Englishmen. But I know too that all this combined assistance is worthless if I have not one other assistance, that is from God. All is vain without

His help. And if He is with this struggle no other help is necessary.

But to realize His help and guidance in this struggle, I need your blessings, the blessings of all communities. The blessings of thousands of men and women belonging to all communities that have attended this march are to me a visible sign of the hand of God in this struggle.

Now is the Time

I know that there are occasions when the hand of God has to be traced in the curses of men. But this is not such an occasion. Today I am doing what the nation has been yearning for during the past ten years. Have I not been rebuked for delaying civil resistance? Have not friends angrily said, " You are stopping the progress of the nation towards its goal. You have only to say, ' Let there be civil resistance, behold! there is Swaraj.' " ? There is some truth in the taunt. Full civil resistance does mean Swaraj. But I was staying my hand. I had no confidence in myself. I was straining my ear to listen to the still small voice within, but only up to yesterday there was no response. It was in Lahore I had told a journalist that I saw nothing on the horizon to warrant civil resistance. But suddenly, as in a flash, I saw the light in the Ashram. Self-confidence returned. Englishmen and some Indian critics have been warning me against the hazard. But the voice within is clear. I must put forth all my effort or retire altogether and for all time from public life. I feel that now is the time or it will be never.

And so I am out for battle and am seeking help on bended knee from this white beard (pointing to Sjt. Abbas Tyabji) as also the little girls. For in this battle even they can help; and thank God, they are eager to do so. I have insistent letters from them demanding enlistment.

The Satyagrahi's Strength

Thus the answer to the Muslim youth's question is complete. I need the help of all races and from all climes.

A Satyagrahi has no power he can call his own. All the power he may seem to possess is from and of God. He therefore moves towards his goal carrying the world's opinion with him. Without the help of God he is lame, blind, groping.

Ever since 1921 I have been reiterating two words, *self-purification* and *self-sacrifice*. God will not assist him without these two. The world is touched by sacrifice. It does not then discriminate about the merits of a cause. Not so God. He is all seeing. He insists on the purity of the cause and on adequate sacrifice therefor.

The question was put by a Mussalman representing a powerful interest. But had a little Parsi girl representing but a hundred thousand Parsis asked the question, I should have given the same answer and said, 'Without the help of Parsis there is no Swaraj.' I am thankful to be able to say that I have had during the march abundant proof of the blessings of these communities. I have read friendliness in the eyes and in the speech of the Mussalmans who along with the rest have lined our route or attended the meetings. They have even given material aid.

Yet I know that I have not the Ali Brothers with me. Maulana Shaukat Ali will no longer have me in his pocket. Do not think, I do not miss him. I hold no distinction between him and a blood brother. His resistance therefore can only be short-lived. If truth is in me, the brothers must capitulate. They cannot long keep out of the battle. I crave too the assistance of Englishmen. It was neither empty formula nor a touch of vanity that prompted me to send an English friend with my letter to the Viceroy. By choosing Reginald Reynolds as my messenger, I sealed the bond between them and me. For my enmity is not against them, it is against their rule. I seem to be born to be an instrument to compass the end of that rule. But if a hair of an English head was touched I should feel the same grief as I should over such a mishap to my brother. I say to them as a friend, 'Why will you not understand that your rule is ruining this country? It has got to be destroyed even though you may pound us to powder or drown us. We must declare what we feel.'

The Congress Pledge

The second question is 'Under Swaraj how many

seats will Mussalmans have in the legislatures ? ' What answer can I return to such a question ? If I were Viceroy of India I should say to the Mussalmans, Sikhs, Christians, Parsis &c., ' Take what you like, the balance will go to the Hindus.' It is true that the *Sanatani* Hindu will never let me become Viceroy. The fact is that I am unfit to do such accounting. But it should be sufficient to know that the Congress has pledged itself not to accept any communal solution that does not satisfy the parties concerned. I am bound by that pledge. For the Congress all are one. They are all Indians and therefore their freedom is guaranteed. No more can be expected by any community.

Civil resistance will merely give the power to the nation to assert her will. But when the time comes for its assertion, the document embodying the will will have to be sealed by all the communities. Thus without the co-operation of all communities, there is no independence.

But what should we do meanwhile ? We must at least be true to the salt we eat. Her starving millions are the salt of India's earth. To be true to them we must free the salt from a tax which they have to pay equally with the rich and in the same proportion as the rich. In our ignorance we have been paying this inhuman imposition. Having realized our folly we will be traitors to the starving millions, if we submit to the exaction any longer.

Who can help liking this poor man's battle ? The cruel tax is no respecter of persons. It is therefore as much the interest of the Mussalman as of the Hindu to secure its abolition. This is a fight undertaken in the name of God and for the sake of the millions of paupers of this country.

Young India, 3-4-'30

110

BARBAROUS

The threatened has after all happened. I congratulate the Government on having commenced arrests in right earnest of Salt tax resisters at least in Gujarat. They have arrested Sjt. Manilal Kothari and all his companions, so also Sjt. Amritlal Sheth and his companions, Dr Chandulal Desai of Broach Sevashram and his companions. They have arrested Darbar Gopaldas, Sjt. Fulchand, Sjt. Ravishankar the intrepid reformer who has weaned the brave but ignorant Rajputs of Kheda from many an error. They have arrested Ramdas Gandhi, Keshavbhai Ganeshji, Chimanlal Pranshankar and others. All this the Government had the right to do. But they had no right to do what they did today at the village Aat four miles from Dandi. The police tried by force to snatch salt from the civil resisters. This they had no right to do, if they were representing a civilized Government. There was no provocation offered. The resisters were not running away. Their names could have been taken. But they insulted these brave men and through them the nation by touching their sacred persons without warrant and without just cause. One of the resisters by name Ukabhai Rama of Bardoli was slightly injured on the wrist. I admit that the police went unarmed to the scene of action. They will probably admit that there never was the slightest occasion for carrying arms, for the people were obviously and absolutely peaceful. Nevertheless this laying hands on the people for the purpose of seizing the salt they were carrying was morally wrong, and even wrong I fancy according to English common law. But I do not know what powers are given by a statute that makes a crime of undefined cowardice.

This first drawing of blood, however little, brought down practically the whole of the village to the scene. Women were just yet to take no part in the act of civil

disobedience, nor were the men of the village expected as
yet to do so. But they, men and women (some with babies
in arms), immediately they heard that salt was being forcibly seized and that one of the volunteers was injured,
rushed out, and men on one side and women on the other
descended to the channel and began to dig out the salt.
As soon as I heard of the attempt at forcible seizure from
the persons of the resisters, Monday being my day of
silence, I wrote on a piece of paper that Shrimati Sarojini
Devi and Sjt. Abbas Tyabji should go, and if the police
did not desist they should also dig out salt and challenge
them to seize it from their hands. But I charitably assume
that the police had seen their mistake before these friends
reached the scene and had not the heart to touch a whole
villageful of people including women. The Satyagrahis,
however, would not be satisfied without my presence
although I might not speak. They wanted me evidently
to see with my own eyes how they had behaved and with
what zest the whole village was participating in the
struggle. Ukabhai Rama was brought to me with the salt
rescued. I went. For me it was a soul-stirring sight. The
forcible seizure served a good purpose. It brought life
to the whole village. Nevertheless, for the sake of the
Government and for the sake of keeping the salt war on
the gentlemanly plane, I wish this ugly incident had not
happened.

Legal procedure may be a cumbersome business for
the Government. But since they have begun well let them
not end ill. Let it be a pure trial of strength between them
and the people. If they will resort to terrorism and if I
am not mistaken, they will find the people, men as well
as women, ready for any ordeal they may prepare for
them. Salt in the hands of Satyagrahis represents the
honour of the nation. It cannot be yielded up except to
force that will break the hand to pieces. Ukabhai as he
was describing the action of the police said, ' God gives
strength to a Satyagrahi to defend what is entrusted to
him.' Let the people defend the salt in their possession till
they break in the attempt, but they should do so without

malice, without anger, without an angry word. The police
have the easiest way open to them of taking possession
of the salt. Let them arrest the civil resisters, and they
can take possession of the salt for they have possession
of their persons. But it can become forfeit only after conviction, not before.

Young India, 10-4-'30

111

THE INHUMAN TAX

Every new experience gained of the incidence of the
Salt tax shows it to be more inhuman than it appeared
at first. Living and moving as I am in the midst of the
salt area in Gujarat, I find that villages have been ruined
because of the prohibition of salt manufacture by the
villagers. The only use the people can make of the land
is to extract salt from it which nature deposits in abundance from month to month. This was the poor man's
staple industry in these parts. Now all this land lies fallow.
Dandi itself has a tragic history. It is a beautiful seaside
place. It takes its name from the fact that it was a place
for a *diva dandi,* i.e. a lighthouse. Now it is a deserted
village. A European and then Indians tried against nature
to reclaim the soil for cultivation. As I walk about the
otherwise beautiful peace-giving shore and listen for the
heavenly music of the gentle waves, I see about me wasted
human effort in the shape of dilapidated embanked fields
without a patch of vegetation. These very fields immediately the hateful salt monopoly is gone, will be valuable
salt pans from which villagers will extract fresh, white
sparkling salt without much labour, and it will give them
a living as it did their ancestors.

Mahadev Desai has already shown that the Government communique that this salt is injurious to health is
a wicked falsehood. In spite of the inhuman regulations,
the people round about this area have used none but the

salt that nature provides here in abundance. They do not seem to have felt any the worse for it. Thousands all over this area have been during the past week eating this salt with impunity. I hear that in Konkan people have all these years used what they regard as Swadeshi salt in contradistinction to the taxed salt which they regard as *sarkari* or 'foreign', although in the first instance it was yielded by India's earth and seas. The recipe which I publish in this issue has been prepared by two careful men who have graduated in science. According to it every household can prepare its own salt without any expense whatsoever. One boy has merely to fetch a *lota*ful of salt water and it has merely to be strained or filtered and put near the fire in a shallow pan and treated in accordance with the recipe, and the householders have every day's supply of salt much cleaner and healthier than the *sarkari* or 'foreign' dirty salt to be had in the bazars. Let the salt Satyagrahis (and they are to be counted in their tens of thousands now) not waste a single grain of Swadeshi salt. Law or no law there is now no excuse for any one to eat the bazar salt. Swadeshi salt must be introduced even where there are no salt beds. It can be easily transported in small quantities from place to place. Let the Government prosecute tens of thousands of men and women or if they dare, send their officials to search their persons and brutally force it from them. Let them say: 'The Salt law allows it.' I have already shown that the Salt regulations are as inhuman as the tax itself. If the history of the administration in the early stages of these regulations were known, it would be found that these inhuman regulations were as inhumanly administered in order to deprive the people of their natural calling and compel them to take the blood-stained *sarkari* salt. Let the reader know that even palanquins bearing *pardanashin* women were searched in order to prevent the transport of illicit salt. If today we have to bear hardships in the attempt to have this iniquitous tax removed, we are but doing a modicum of penance for our past neglect and shameful submission to the impost. The reader will thus see that it is not merely the tax, heavy as it is, that is offensive. It has not one redeeming feature about it. The revenue it brings is not the only cost to the nation. The cost to the nation is probably twenty crores per year besides the loss of an equal amount of salt which is wantonly destroyed or prevented from being gathered.

Young India, 17-4-'30

112

A SURVEY

The mass manifestation in Gujarat has exceeded all expectations. Bombay and its suburbs have done no less. And the reports slowly coming to me at this out of the way place from all over India are fully encouraging. It is the matter of the keenest joy to me to see Maharashtra united once more and Sjt. N. C. Kelkar and his friends joining the struggle. Sjt. Kelkar's and Sjt. Aney's resignations are events of great importance in the struggle. Bengal is the most tempestuous province in all India. It is pulsating with life. Its very factions are symptomatic of its great awakening. If Bengal responds in the right style it is likely to overshadow every other province. I do not know that any province, even Maharashtra, can claim the credit that Bengal can for voluntary sacrifice. If its emotional side is its weakness, it is also its greatest strength. It has the capacity for reckless abandon to non-violence, if such use of language is permissible. Sjt. Sen Gupta's action in response to the wanton assault on the students' meeting has evoked the sentiment above expressed. The sentence of Dr Suresh Bannerji and others pales into insignificance before the possibilities of the move on the part of the Bengal students and the savage counter move on the part of the police. I know what the Calcutta Commissioner of Police will say, if he sees these lines. I hear him saying 'But you do not know my Bengal.' Well, I know his Bengal more than he ever will. His Bengal is the creation of the Government. If the Government will cease to molest Bengal and not keep India from her cherished goal, Bengal will be as gentle as the greatest province of India. If Bengal is seething with the violent spirit, it is because of her sufferings.

But I expect Bengal's imagination to come to her assistance and to realize that non-violence is the trump-card. All the suffering must be dedicated to the Goddess of *Ahimsa*.

Soon after the Jalianwala massacre, I used to express and reiterate the hope that next time in no part of India must people run away on bullets being discharged against them, and that they must receive them in their chests with arms folded and with courageous resignation. That testing time seems to be coming faster than I had expected. And if we are to train ourselves to receive the bullet wounds or bayonet charges in our bare chests, we must accustom ourselves to standing unmoved in the face of cavalry or baton charges. I know that it is easier said than done. Nevertheless, I must say it if we are ever to complete our training in mass non-violence. That mass non-violence is a perfect possibility has been sufficiently demonstrated during the past eight days. Mahadev Desai has given a realistic account of the brutal treatment of volunteers in the Dholera salt bed and the volunteers suffering the brutality with meek heroism. What thousands in Bombay did when the police acted with rashness and harshness if also with comparative considerateness can be studied from a condensed translation published in this issue of a graphic description sent to me by Pt. Mukund Malaviya. His report is in the main corroborated by Dahyabhai, Sardar Vallabhbhai's son, who was also an eyewitness.

Perinbai and her companions as also Kamaladevi acted with rare courage and calmness. But they would allow me to say that they would have done better to remain outside the venue of the men's fight. For women to be in the midst of such danger as they put themselves in was against the rule of chivalry. Any way that time is not yet. Let them by all means manufacture salt in their thousands. But they may not remain deliberately in crowds which they know are likely to be charged. I have in all humility suggested to them an exclusive field in which they are at liberty and are expected to show their best qualities. There is in that field enough scope for adventure and heroism.

To revert, if then we are to stand the final heat of the battle, we must learn to stand our ground in the face of cavalry or baton charges and allow ourselves to be trampled under horses' hoofs or bruised with baton charges. An armed crowd could stand firm and retaliate if there were such charges. We, if we would learn the lesson of non-violence, should show greater courage by standing our ground without anger, without retaliation. Then a reincarnation of Dyer will find us ready for receiving bullets in the bare breast.

People have already begun to defend their salt pans. If we have evolved that sufficient amount of courage, it must be done methodically and regularly. As soon as the police come to charge us and break through the living wall, women should, if the police give the opportunity, stand aside and let their men be wounded. They do so all the world over in armed conflict ; let them do so in a conflict in which one party deliberately chooses to remain unarmed.

When there are no men left to fight the battle of free salt, if they have courage let them take up the work deserted by men. But I have no doubt that men will give a good account of themselves in this struggle.

I have already examined elsewhere the argument that the police must use force if people will not surrender the contraband salt in their possession. Here I would only remind these critics that even from confirmed thieves they do not take stolen property by force except after they are brought under arrest and then too never if they are not to be brought to trial. The property still remains the thief's until he is convicted and the court adjudges the property not to be his. That the salt regulations make the policeman the arresting officer, prosecutor and judge all rolled

into one is no answer to my charge of barbarity in respect
of the procedure adopted by the authorities.

Young India, 17-4-'30

113

THE BLACK REGIME

The past week has not been one of unmixed joy. It has
seen the disturbances in Calcutta and Karachi. And now
comes the sad news from Chittagong. It shows that in
spite of the striking demonstration of non-violence all over
the country, there is still violence in the air and cities
are the storehouses of it. Calcutta and Karachi can be
distinguished from Chittagong. The first two appear to
have been mad outbursts of the moment. Chittagong
seems to be a deliberate planning. Whatever they were,
they are most regrettable and interfere with the growth
of the movement which is otherwise shaping itself marve-
llously well and gaining fresh momentum from day to day.
I can only appeal to those who believe in violence not to
disturb the free flow of the non-violent demonstration.
Whether they listen or not, this movement will go on.
Violence is bound to impede the progress towards
independence. I am unable to demonstrate how it will
impede. Those who survive the struggle will know how.

Meanwhile Satyagrahis must continue their activity
with redoubled vigour. We must deal with the double-
edged violence ranged against us. For me popular violence
is as much an obstruction in our path as the Government
violence. Indeed I can combat the Government violence
more successfully than the popular. For one thing, in
combating the latter, I should not have the same support
as in the former. Then again one motive in the latter being
as honourable as that of the Satyagrahis, the method to be
employed has to be somewhat different from that employed
in regard to Government violence.

I hope that as in Karachi, so in Calcutta and Chittagong,

there were Satyagrahis attempting to check mob violence. Brave young Dattatreya Mane who is said to have known nothing of Satyagraha and being an athlete had merely gone to assist in keeping order, received a fatal bullet wound, Meghraj Revachand, 18 years old, has also succumbed to a bullet wound. Thus did seven men, including Jairamdas, receive bullet wounds. Jairamdas's injury gave me unmixed joy. It is the injury to leaders that would bring relief. The law of sacrifice is uniform throughout the world. To be effective it demands the sacrifice of the bravest and the most spotless. And Jairamdas is of the bravest and the cleanest. I therefore could not help wiring when I heard of Jairamdas's wound that a wound in the thigh was better than prison and wound in the heart better still.

Whilst therefore I tender my sympathy to the parents of the two brave lads who lost their lives, my inmost desire is to congratulate them for the finished sacrifices of their sons, if they would accept my congratulations. A warrior's death is never a matter for sorrow, still less that of a Satyagrahi warrior. One of the lessons that a nation yearning for freedom needs to learn is to shed several fears of losing title, wealth, position, fear of imprisonment, of bodily injury and lastly death.

Accounts from all over India tell the same tale of growing fearlessness. The Bihar letter published elsewhere in this issue makes soul-stirring reading.

One thing we must get rid of quickly. Lawless physical violence must be stopped even if it is to be through forcing the Government to use its guns. And this can be done non-violently.

I give only one out of several samples of indecent assaults by the police at Viramgam :

Statement of Aniruddha Vyas, a student of Dakshinamurti Vidyarthi Bhavan, Volunteer No. 35/3.

" I with a number of my companions got down from the 6-30 evening mail with bags of salt at the Viramgam Railway Station, when from 8 to 10 policemen surrounded us. To save the salt from being seized, I sat down with the bag of salt on the ground, clinging to it with all my might.

" All efforts of the police to make me get up having failed, one of them thrust apart my legs and squeezed my private parts with his hands so as to compel me to get up. But the weight of my body and the push and the pull of the surrounding police disengaged the parts and I fell down. I was then pulled up again. But I bent double and held the salt bag tight under my crossed arms. A policeman thereupon straightened my back by poking it with his foot which caused me intense pain. Then two police-men gave a violent jerk, twisted my fingers as they liked and loosened my arms and wrested the bag from me. I was then let go, one officer taking my name and number.'

Mahadev Desai tells me that those assaults have stop-ped for the time being. But there is no knowing that they have stopped for ever and there certainly is not the slightest ground for supposing that they will not occur in other parts of Gujarat or of other provinces. In Broach things are growing from bad to worse. A bullet wound is any day better than these barbarous, unnecessary, un-provoked assaults. The person of a citizen must be held inviolate. It can only be touched to arrest or to prevent violence, never in the manner being done now. It is a prostitution even of the Salt laws to use them against civil resisters. The provisions were designed to deal (even then unjustly as I hold) with surreptitious breaches of its new provisions, never to deal with masses of men openly defy-ing them. If the Government do not stop this brutal violation of the body, they will find the Satyagrahis pre-sently compelling them to use the guns against them. I do not want this to happen. But if the Government will have it, I should have no hesitation whatsoever in giving them the opportunity. They must not physically interfere with the bands of civil resisters manufacturing or vending salt, they may arrest every man, woman and child if they wish. If they will neither arrest nor declare salt free, they will find people marching to be shot rather than be tortured.

It is true that the barbarous interference with the body and the indecent assaults are a heritage of the past. This Government by its tacit approval has given it a currency which it never had before.

As I am writing these notes two volunteers have brought me salt said to have been poisoned. Not only do the authorities wantonly destroy salt and salt pans now, they are said to poison the sources of salt manufacture. If the report is true the blackness of the regime becomes blacker still. And all this against a people who without hurting anybody are seeking to gain freedom through self-suffering !

Young India, 24-4-'30

114

PURITY IN ACCOUNT KEEPING

Simple people are in pure faith pouring in their copper, silver and paper coins into the bowls of volunteers who sell salt or otherwise collect money. No unauthorized volunteers should make collections or sell salt at fancy prices. Accounts should be accurately kept and frequently published. Books should be weekly examined by auditors. It will be well if moneyed men of proved honesty were to constitute themselves treasurers to take charge of and collect funds and work in full co-operation with Congress volunteers. Active workers are being quickly picked up and it may be difficult before long for local organizations to hold funds and keep proper accounts. As it is, the public have everywhere taken over the financing of the movement. Let it be done responsibly and methodically.

Young India, 24-4-'30

115

CALM HEROISM

Sjt. Shriprakash writes from Banaras :

"I felt I must convey to you the story of volunteer Hiralal who seems to me to have got nearest to your instructions regarding our conduct when the police seize our salt. We started our salt campaign here on the 8th, and every day batches of 10 manufacture salt for 24 hours when they are relieved by the next batch.

"On the third day in the afternoon about 60 constables with their officers suddenly invaded the site and demanded the delivery of the salt and pan. The volunteers clung to the burning pan desperately and it could only be forcibly snatched from them after fully 20 minutes of resistance. Volunteer Hiralal caught hold of the ring of the burning pan and clung to it desperately. The result was that his right hand was completely burnt and it will be many weeks before he is able to recover the use of his fingers. Almost all other volunteers were injured, but this volunteers' conduct deserves mention and convey to you his name with pride."

Young men like Hiralal will be the makers of Swaraj.

Young India, 24-4-'30

116

MAHADEV DESAI AND HIS SUCCESSOR

In the midst of chaos going under the false name of Government, Mahadev's arrest was a courteous and reluctant business on the part of the authorities. Though he set ablaze the whole of Gujarat from Viramgam and Dholera to Ahmedabad, the authorities recognized that it was a life-giving fire, that they were safer under Mahadev's rule than their own and that he was well able to control the forces he had brought into being.

But Mahadev made it impossible for the authorities to keep him free. He had managed to 'smuggle in' a lorry load of salt from Dholera. The authorities were wide awake. They intercepted the lorry. They had hoped not to find Mahadev in it. But when he saw that the lorry was to be arrested together with its precious load, he got out of the car in which he was following and jumped into the lorry. And so if they were to arrest the lorry they could not help arresting him. Nor could Mahadev help jumping into the lorry in the circumstances. With him was a youth who was to have appeared for his final LL.B. the following day, two were young men from the Gujarat College and two were sons of wealthy men. The lorry was given by Sjt. Ranchhodlal, a mill-owner who when warned what might befall the lorry said, ' What fear about the loss of the lorry, when I am prepared to lose all for Swaraj ? '

Mahadev has got his well-deserved rest. For hundreds of strenuous workers the jail has become a resting house. Mahadev yearned as he says after ' a better fate but evidently had not yet deserved it.'

He had appointed as his successor Imamsaheb Abdul Kadir Bavazeer, a comrade from South Africa and Vice Chairman of the Ashram committee and one of its trustees. Imamsaheb is an elderly man hardly capable of strenuous labour. He may be said to be illiterate. But he is a seasoned soldier and son of a devoted Muslim who was till the time of his death muezzin of the Juma Musjid of Bombay. He is himself styled Imam because he officiated as priest in several mosques in South Africa. He is an orthodox Mussalman in the sense that he never misses his prayers or his fasts. But he is also most liberal-minded or he could not have lived with me in the closest contact in the midst of all sorts of people for an unbroken period of nearly twenty years.

But the Swaraj of my — our — dream recognizes no race or religious distinctions. Nor is it to be the monopoly of lettered persons nor yet of moneyed men. Swaraj is to be for all, including the former, but emphatically including the maimed, the blind, the starving toiling millions. A stout-hearted, honest, sane, illiterate man may well be the first servant of the nation as Imamsaheb has become in

Gujarat, and another still less known friend, by name Abdullabhai, has become one in Vile Parle. He is the successor of Swami Anand who by his inexhaustible energy and amazing self-denial made Navajivan Karyalaya, though a purely philanthropic institution, also a sound business proposition which has been bringing to the doors of the Gujaratis the truest gems of Gujarati literature understandable by the masses. But these are not rare instances. These are typical of what the struggle has thrown up all over India.

Young India, 1-5-'30

117

GOONDA RAJ

If what is going on in Gujarat is any indication of what is going on in other parts of India, even Dyerism pales into insignificance. This may appear to be an exaggerated statement. But it is meant to be literally true. The massacre of Jalianwala was a clean sweep. It created an impression both in the intended and the unintended sense.

The death by inches that is being dealt out in Gujarat is unimpressive either way, and may, if care is not taken, prove utterly demoralizing. It may weaken the victims and decidedly debases the tyrants.

If I have the time I shall summarize the events of the past week for these columns. In any case the reader will find the whole of the evidence in the daily press.

Mahadev Desai had hugged the belief that after the efforts he made by going there himself and sending lawyer friends, the barbarous torture had ceased at Viramgam. But it was not to be. A volunteer was for a few minutes isolated from his company, and this gave the representatives of law and order an opportunity of falling upon their victim and treating him as his predecessors had been treated at Viramgam.

That is what Dr Narsinbhai Mehta, a retired Chief

Medical Officer of Junagadh, who at the age of 66, was enthused with the spirit of Satyagraha, saw with his own eyes :

"I brought a party of about 120 Satyagrahis, each with a bag of ten lb. of contraband salt from Wadhwan Camp this evening.

"As I led the party, I was the first to meet the inspecting party consisting of one European officer, two Indian officers and about 4 or 5 police constables. Over and above this there were about fifty spare constables watching the entrance of the staircase.

"I was asked what I had got in the bag under my armpit. I replied, 'Ten lb. of contraband salt.' 'All right, old doctor, you can go,' they said. I said, 'I am leading a party of about 120 Satyagrahis, each with a bag of such salt. So I want to see personally how you deal with them, or whether you allow them to go freely just like other passengers.' He said, 'All right, you stand apart on one side, and watch.' One by one the Satyagrahis were made to pass through the said inspecting party and immediately all the seven or eight of them, including the European officer, caught hold of each resister and snatched the bag from the hands of the Satyagrahi, handling the resister most roughly. Almost every Satyagrahi was treated likewise. It was a disgraceful proceeding. I had a very high opinion of Englishmen throughout my life. This was my first experience of the kind during sixty-six years.

"When I could bear the treatment no longer and expostulated, the officer said: 'Speak to the public outside about this and write to the papers!' And the whole performance went on as before."

Mark the callousness with which Dr Mehta's entreaty was met. It was a jolly performance for the British officer and his fellow loyalists to indulge in the sport of dispossessing young men of their precious possession. It was no use telling them that the victims were not running away nor hiding anything. The law had to be respected without any waiting for the law's delay on the part of its administrators.

But even this was nothing compared to the scenes enacted in the Kheda district. I own that the brave sons and daughters of Kheda have carried out fairly successfully the legitimate boycott of officials who are no longer able to impose their will upon the people. They have brutally struck a graduate and professor of the Gujarat Vidyapith who had committed no offence, but who had gone simply to see what was happening when he heard the beating. In the same district near Borsad a few police supported by a local Thakore and his minions armed with long-armed sickles without notice put out the lights at a meeting and mercilessly fell upon their victims. The audience consisted of Patidars and Rajputs who were fully able to defend themselves. But not a stone was thrown, not a word was uttered. For the sake of discipline they suffered. One man narrowly escaped death. Seven are still lying in a hospital. Altogether thirty-five have been traced as having been injured. This was a cowardly edition of Jalianwala.

Then take Ahmedabad. A liquor dealer finding his till empty from day to day got so exasperated that he savagely attacked the pickets one of whom lay senseless. The picketing was of the most peaceful as acknowledged by everybody. There was not even any demonstration. Only the names of those who visited this were taken down by the pickets who knew them. The success of the picketing lies in this case in moving the caste machinery which still works fairly among the labouring classes.

Have the administrators of law and order done anything to prevent this savagery ? No. They have secretly enjoyed it. They are welcome to the joy of it. Only let this be not called 'law and order'. Let it be called *Goonda Raj*.

The duty before the people is clear. They must answer this organized hooliganism with great suffering. If they have the will and the power, freedom is assured. Freedom is a fruit of suffering, licence is born of violence. What we are all pining for is freedom that imposes restraints upon itself for the sake of society. Licence imposes suffering upon society so that it may enjoy exclusive privileges. This is a Government of unbridled licence because it is a Government whose chief, if not sole, aim is to exploit Indian society.

Young India, 1-5-'30

118

MESSAGE TO THE NATION

[The following is an English translation of a message dictated by Gandhiji at Dandi on April 9th, when there was a strong rumour of his impending arrest.]

At last the long expected hour seems to have come.

In the dead of night my colleagues and companions have roused me from deep slumber and requested me to give them a message. I am therefore dictating this message, although I have not the slightest inclination to give any.

Messages I have given enough already. Of what avail would this message be if none of the previous messages evoked a proper response? But information received until this midnight leads me to the belief that my message did not fall flat, but was taken up by the people in right earnest.

The people of Gujarat seem to have risen in a body as it were. I have seen with my own eyes thousands of men and women at Aat and Bhimrad, fearlessly breaking the Salt Act. Not a sign of mischief, not a sign of violence have I seen, despite the presence of people in such large numbers. They have remained perfectly peaceful and non-violent, although Government officers have transgressed all bounds.

Here in Gujarat well-tried and popular public servants have been arrested one after another, and yet the people have been perfectly non-violent. They have refused to give way to panic, and have celebrated the arrests, by offering civil disobedience in ever increasing numbers. This is just as it should be.

If the struggle auspiciously begun is continued in the same spirit of non-violence to the end, not only shall we see *Purna Swaraj* established in our country before long, but we shall have given to the world an object lesson worthy of India and her glorious past.

Swaraj won without sacrifice cannot last long. I would therefore like our people to get ready to make the highest sacrifice that they are capable of. In true sacrifice all the suffering is on one side — one is required to master the art of getting killed without killing, of gaining life by losing it. May India live up to this *mantra*.

At present India's self-respect, in fact her all, is symbolized as it were in a handful of salt in the Satyagrahi's hand. Let the fist holding it, therefore, be broken, but let there be no voluntary surrender of the salt.

Let the Government, if it claims to be a civilized Government, jail those who help themselves to contraband salt. After their arrest the civil resisters will gladly surrender the salt, as they will their bodies into the custody of their jailors.

But by main force to snatch the salt from the poor, harmless Satyagrahis' hands is barbarism pure and simple and an insult to India. Such insult can be answered only by allowing our hand to be fractured without loosening the grasp. Even then the actual sufferer or his comrades may not harbour in their hearts anger against the wrongdoer. Incivility should be answered not by incivility but by a dignified and calm endurance of all suffering in the name of God.

Let not my companions or the people at large be perturbed over my arrest, for it is not I, but God who is guiding this movement. He ever dwells in the hearts of all and He will vouchsafe to us the right guidance if only we have faith in Him. Our path has already been chalked out for us. Let every village fetch or manufacture contraband salt. Sisters should picket liquor shops, opium dens and foreign-cloth dealers' shops. Young and old in every home should ply the *takli* and spin and get woven heaps of yarn every day. Foreign cloth should be burnt. Hindus should eschew untouchability. Hindus, Mussalmans, Sikhs, Parsis, and Christians should all achieve heart unity. Let the majority rest content with what remains after the minorities have been satisfied. Let students leave Government schools and colleges, and Government

servants resign their service and devote themselves to service of the people, and we shall find that *Purna Swaraj*
will come knocking at our doors.

Young India, 8-5-'30

119

THE SECOND LETTER

[The following is the text of Gandhiji's letter to the Viceroy
drafted on the eve of his arrest.]

Dear Friend,

God willing, it is my intention on.... to set out for
Dharasana and reach there with my companions on....
and demand possession of the Salt Works. The public
have been told that Dharasana is private property. This
is mere camouflage. It is as effectively under Government
control as the Viceroy's House. Not a pinch of salt can be
removed without the previous sanction of the authorities.

It is possible for you to prevent this raid, as it has
been playfully and mischievously called, in three ways :

1. by removing the Salt tax ;

2. by arresting me and my party unless the country
can, as I hope it will, replace every one taken away ;

3. by sheer *goondaism* unless every head broken is
replaced, as I hope it will.

It is not without hesitation that the step has been
decided upon. I had hoped that the Government would
fight the civil resister in a civilized manner. I could have
had nothing to say if in dealing with the civil resisters the
Government had satisfied itself with applying the ordinary
processes of law. Instead, whilst the known leaders have
been dealt with more or less according to the legal
formality, the rank and file has been often savagely and
in some cases even indecently assaulted. Had these been
isolated cases, they might have been overlooked. But
accounts have come to me from Bengal, Bihar, Utkal, U.P.,
Delhi and Bombay, confirming the experiences of Gujarat
of which I have ample evidence at my disposal. In Karachi,

Peshawar and Madras, the firing would appear to have been unprovoked and unnecessary. Bones have been broken, private parts have been squeezed, for the purpose of making volunteers give up, to the Government valueless, to the volunteers precious, salt. At Mathura an Assistant Magistrate is said to have snatched the national flag from a ten-year old boy. The crowd that demanded restoration of the flag thus illegally seized, is said to have been mercilessly beaten back. That the flag was subsequently restored betrayed a guilty conscience. In Bengal there seem to have been only a few prosecutions and assaults about salt, but unthinkable cruelties are said to have been practised in the act of snatching flags from volunteers. Paddy fields are reported to have been burnt, eatables forcibly taken. A vegetable market in Gujarat has been raided because the dealers would not sell vegetables to officials. These acts have taken place in front of crowds who, for the sake of Congress mandate, have submitted without retaliation. I ask you to believe the accounts given by men pledged to truth. Repudiation even by high officials has, as in the Bardoli case, often proved false. The officials, I regret to have to say, have not hesitated to publish falsehoods to the people even during the past five weeks. I take the following samples from Government notices issued from Collectors' offices in Gujarat :

"1. Adults use five pounds of salt per year, therefore, pay three annas per year as tax.........If Government removed the monopoly people will have to pay higher prices and in addition make good to the Government the loss sustained by the removal of the monopoly......The salt you take from the seashore is not eatable therefore, the Government destroys it."

" 2. Mr Gandhi says that Government has destroyed handspinning in this country, whereas everybody knows that this is not true, because throughout the country, there is not a village where hand-spinning of cotton is not going on. Moreover, in every province cotton spinners are shown superior methods and are provided with better instruments at less price and are thus helped by Government."

" 3. Out of every five rupees of the debt that the Government has incurred rupees four have been beneficially spent."

I have taken these three sets of statements from three different leaflets. I venture to suggest that every one of these statements is demonstrably false. The daily consumption of salt by an adult is three times the amount stated and therefore the poll tax, that the Salt tax undoubtedly is, is at least 9 as. per head per year. And this tax is levied from man, woman, child and domestic cattle irrespective of age and health.

It is a wicked falsehood to say that every village has a spinning wheel, and that the spinning movement is in any shape or form encouraged or supported by the Government. Financiers can better dispose of the falsehood, that four out of every five rupees of the public debt is used for the benefit of the public. But those falsehoods are mere samples of what people know is going on in everyday contact with the Government. Only the other day a Gujarati poet, a brave man, was convicted on perjured official evidence, in spite of his emphatic statement that at the time mentioned he was sleeping soundly in another place.

Now for instances of official inactivities. Liquor dealers have assaulted pickets admitted by officials to have been peaceful and sold liquor in contravention of regulations. The officials have taken no notice either of the assaults or the illegal sales of liquor. As to the assaults, though they are known to everybody, they may take shelter under the plea that they have received no complaints.

And now you have sprung upon the country a Press Ordinance surpassing any hitherto known in India. You have found a short cut through the law's delay in the matter of the trial of Bhagatsingh and others by doing away with the ordinary procedure. Is it any wonder if I call all these official activities and inactivities a veiled form of Martial Law ? Yet this is only the fifth week of the struggle !

Before then the reign of terrorism that has just begun overwhelms India, I feel that I must take a bolder step, and if possible divert your wrath in a cleaner if more drastic channel. You may not know the things that I have described. You may not even now believe in these. I can but invite your serious attention to them.

Any way I feel that it would be cowardly on my part not to invite you to disclose to the full the leonine paws of authority so that the people who are suffering tortures and destruction of their property may not feel that I, who had perhaps been the chief party inspiring them to action that has brought to right light the Government in its true colours, had left any stone unturned to work out the Satyagraha programme as fully as it was possible under given circumstances.

For, according to the science of Satyagraha, the greater the repression and lawlessness on the part of authority, the greater should be the suffering courted by the victims. Success is the certain result of suffering of the extremest character, voluntarily undergone.

I know the dangers attendant upon the methods adopted by me. But the country is not likely to mistake my meaning. I say what I mean and think. And I have been saying for the last fifteen years in India and outside for twenty years more and repeat now that the only way to conquer violence is through non-violence pure and undefiled. I have said also that every violent act, word and thought interferes with the progress of non-violent action. If in spite of such repeated warnings people will resort to violence, I must disown responsibility save such as inevitably attaches to every human being for the acts of every other human being. But the question of responsibility apart, I dare not postpone action on any cause whatsoever, if non-violence is the force the seers of the world have claimed it to be and if I am not to belie my own extensive experience of its working.

But I would fain avoid the further step. I would therefore ask you to remove the tax which many of your illustrious countrymen have condemned in unmeasured terms and which, as you could not have failed to observe, has evoked universal protest and resentment expressed in civil disobedience. You may condemn civil disobedience as much as you like. Will you prefer violent revolt to civil disobedience ? If you say, as you have said, that the civil disobedience must end in violence, history will pronounce the verdict that the British Government, not bearing because not understanding non-violence, goaded human nature to violence, which it could understand, and deal with. But in spite of the goading I shall hope that God will give the people of India wisdom and strength to withstand every temptation and provocation to violence.

If, therefore, you cannot see your way to remove the Salt tax, and remove the prohibition on private salt-making, I must reluctantly commence the march adumbrated in the opening paragraph of my letter.

I am,

Your sincere friend,

M. K. Gandhi

Young India, 8-5-'30

120

THE GREAT ARREST

[The following is the account of Gandhiji's arrest at Karadi Camp (Dist. Surat) on the morning of 12th May, 1930, as given by Mirabehn.]

At dead of night, like thieves they came, to steal him away. For, " when they sought to lay hold on him, they feared the multitudes, because they took him for a prophet."

At twelve forty-five at night the District Magistrate of Surat, two Indian police officers, armed with pistols, and some thirty policemen, armed with rifles, silently and suddenly came into the peaceful little compound where Gandhiji and his Satyagrahis were sleeping. They immediately surrounded the party, and the English officer going up to the bed and turning a torch-light on to Gandhiji's face, said :

" Are you Mohandas Karamchand Gandhi ? "

" You want me ? " enquired Gandhiji gently, and added, " Please give me time for my ablutions."

He commenced to clean his teeth and the officers, time-piece in hand, stood watching him. Gandhiji here asked if there was a warrant and the Magistrate forthwith read out the following order :

> "Whereas the Governor-in-Council views with alarm the activities of Mohandas Karamchand Gandhi, he directs that the said Mohandas Karamchand Gandhi should be placed under restraint under Regulation xxv of 1827, and suffer imprisonment during the pleasure of the Government; and that he be immediately removed to the Yeravda Central Jail."

The ablutions finished, his few little necessities packed up, and his papers handed over to one of his party, Gandhiji again turned to the officers and said, " Please give me a few minutes more for prayer." This was granted, and he forthwith stood and prayed with his companions, surrounded by the ring of police.

As soon as the prayer was over, they hurried him away, put him into a motor-lorry and drove him off accompanied by the three officers and some eight policemen.

All telephonic and telegraphic communications were cut off, and the police guarded the roads.

Swift, silent secrecy.

No trial, no justice.

The Government is making its own statements and the accused lies buried in the silence of the prison cell.

They may take his frail body and cast it into jail. They may stifle his pure voice with the heavy prison walls. But they cannot stifle the Great Soul. Its radiance will penetrate all earthly barriers. The more they strive to smother it, the brighter and brighter will it shine, filling not only India, but the whole world.

Ah India, India, now is thy hour of greatest trial. May God lead thee on the path to Victory and Peace.

He who loves and knows thee with a love and knowledge surpassing all mortal words, has told thee that Freedom is now within thy reach if thou hast the strength and courage to stick to the Pure Path — the Path which he has shown thee of Truth and Non-violence. May God give thee that strength and fill thee with that courage.

Young India, 8-5-'30

121

MORE ABOUT THE SETTLEMENT

[The Civil Disobedience Movement continued unabated till early in 1931, when Gandhiji was released to negotiate a settlement with the Viceroy. After the settlement had been made Gandhiji addressed a mammoth meeting on the 17th March, 1931 in Bombay. Extracts from that speech relating to Satyagraha are given below : — Ed.]

For full twelve months we have developed a war mentality : we thought of war, we talked of war and nothing but war. Now we have to sing a completely different tune. We are in the midst of truce. With some of us, I know the very mention of the word *truce* sends a shiver through their bodies. That is because we had thought of nothing but war and had believed that there could be no compromise. But that was not a position becoming a true Satyagrahi. The Satyagrahi whilst he is ever ready for fight must be equally eager for peace. He must welcome any honourable opportunity for peace. The Working Committee of the Congress saw such an opportunity and availed itself of it. The essential condition of a compromise is that there should be nothing humiliating, nothing panicky about it. You may be sure that whilst I was being inundated with telegrams to make peace at any price, I was absolutely unmoved by them. I am inured to such things and I was absolutely firm that I must not allow any of these telegrams to make me flinch from whatever decision my inner voice gave me. Whilst however a Satyagrahi never yields to panic or hesitancy, neither does he think of humiliating the other party, of reducing it to an abject surrender. He may not swerve from the path of justice and may not dictate impossible terms. He may not pitch his demands too high, neither may he pitch them too low. The present settlement, I submit, satisfies all these conditions. One of the terms of the settlement seems to have caused some disappointment in certain quarters and some have rushed in to condemn the settlement on that account. They complain that we ought not to have entered into the settlement until we had secured the release of *all* political prisoners. I may tell you that we could not in justice make this demand. Not that there was any lack of will on our part, but the power to make the demand irresistible was lacking. That power will come as soon as we fulfil in letter and in spirit all the terms of the settlement that apply to us.

I may inform you that local Governments have been remiss in fulfilling their part of the contract. Some prisoners who ought to have been released are still in jail, some prosecutions — like the Chirner firing case — that ought to have been withdrawn are still going on. It is a matter for sorrow. If the remissness or failure is deliberate it would be culpable. But it would add to *our* power and make our case for Swaraj more irresistible than ever. One would like to think however that such remissness would not be deliberate in view of the stupendous machinery of Government. There is likely to be unintentional delay and inadvertance. But if there is deliberate breach of faith, we have our sovereign remedy. If you look at the settlement the last clause empowers Government to set its machinery of law and order in motion in the event of failure on the part of the Congress to fulfil its part of the settlement. Need I tell you that the clause necessarily includes its converse? Even as it would be open to Government to set its machinery in motion, it is open to us also to resort to our infallible weapon as soon as we find that there is a deliberate breach.

But the present delays need not agitate or irritate you. For there is no occasion for it. A Satyagrahi has infinite patience, abundant faith in others, ample hope.

And now a word of warning. The settlement is obviously provisional. But it necessitates a change in our method of work. Whilst civil disobedience and jail going, or direct action was the method to be followed before the settlement, the way of argument and negotiation takes its place. But let no one forget that the settlement is provisional and the negotiations may break down at any stage. Let us therefore keep our powder

ever dry and our armour ever bright. Failure should not
find us napping, but ready to mobilize at the first command. In the meanwhile let us carry on the process of
self-purification with greater vigour and greater faith, so
that we may grow in strength day by day.

Young India, 19-3-'31

122

THE CONGRESS

The Congress will be upon us in a few days from now.
The broken-up organizations will hardly have been put
together by that time. The delegates, half of whom will
be ex-prisoners, will hardly have had time to collect themselves. And yet, it will meet with a greater prestige than
ever before, and with a consciousness of its new strength
born of a knowledge of suffering undergone by tens of
thousands of men, women and children, and perhaps un-
parallelled in history in the sense that the sufferers
suffered without retaliation.

But it would be wrong to brood over the sufferings,
to exaggerate them, or to be puffed up with pride. True
suffering does not know itself and never calculates. It
brings its own joy which surpasses all other joys. We
shall, therefore, be guilty of suicide if we live upon the
capital amassed during the past twelve months. Whilst
we must try always to avoid occasions for needless suffering, we must ever be ready for them. Somehow or other,
those who will walk along the right path cannot avoid
suffering notwithstanding the attempt to avoid it. It is the
privilege of the patriot, the reformer and, still greater, of
the Satyagrahi.

The settlement, provisional though it is, has come
through God's grace. During the negotiations there were
times when breakdown seemed a certainty. Beyond
doubt, the suffering would have been ten times multiplied
if a breakdown had taken place. And yet, I would have

been obliged to ask the nation to go through it, had an honourable peace proved impossible. But I am not sure that it will be possible to reach the goal without further, wider and deeper suffering. The measure of our purification seems hardly equal to the prize to be won. We have not yet consciously, and on a national scale, got rid of the curse of untouchability, we have not shed distrust of one another. Great though the awakening has been among the rich, they have not yet made common cause with the poor ; their life bears no resemblance to that of the poor. Though much progress has been made in the case of drink and drugs, much more yet remains to be done ; the progress made is still uncertain. The drunkard has yielded to pressure of public opinion. He has not yet definitely given up the habit. He knows the evil but has not been taught to shun it as poison. The word *taught* has been used advisedly. The workers have confined their attention to the drink and drug shops, they have not made a serious attempt to touch the heart of the addict. We have not shed the desire for foreign cloth and fineries, nor have the cloth merchants fully realized the magnitude of the wrong they have done to the nation by their trade. Many of them still parade the doctrine of individual freedom. These and several other evils that can be easily recalled show how much still remains to be done in the matter of self-purification. And so, it is little wonder if we do not find the atmosphere of *Purna Swaraj* pervading us. How far, therefore, the method of consultation and conference will succeed, it is difficult to forecast. This much is certain that argument is not what will carry conviction. The British conviction will be in exact proportion to the strength we have developed. And since the nation has decided that we will acquire strength only through self-purification, if we have not attained the wisdom during these good months of grace to rid ourselves of the evils I have enumerated, then we must go through a fiercer fire of suffering than ever before. Let us, therefore, approach the Congress with a humbled spirit and with a will bent on removing every form of weakness from our midst. We must not give undue weight to conferences and the like. The past twelve months have made it clear for us that Swaraj will come when it does, from within, by internal effort, not as a free gift from above or by simple argument.

Young India, 19-3-'31

123

LET US REPENT

" But the hatred which was created and which has been shown in words and actions has been so intolerable that it must set one to think whether release of such mighty forces of hatred all round the country is advisable. From morning till late night one heard through talks, songs, through slogans and felt such mighty torrents of hatred that it was sickening to find such a degradation in large masses of people. I use the word *degradation* with full responsibility. It appeared that speaking lies was a matter of full licence and liberty. To attack Government officers, police officers, men who disagreed, for something which was entirely untrue, for something which never happened, was a daily common event seen on the roads and everywhere. More than words can express the cruelties and the injustice inflicted on the traders of British goods especially, and some other foreign goods, were wide, intolerable, and unbearable. To request a man not to deal in one article and to request another not to purchase an article is one thing, but to *force* a man by all possible means, by abusing him, by obstructing him, by making his life miserable in every way is another thing, and there, I must admit, non-violence has miserably failed. I am certain in my mind that the hatred created and the cruelties inflicted were far from non-violence and against all principles and teachings of Mahatmaji. It was a common practice to obstruct and inflict with all kinds of tactics to make persons' lives miserable whenever one disagreed with the general movement. In every province there were different types of activities and it appears that either one had to accept such dictation of somebody or one had to go through whatever was inflicted upon him by any small or large band of children, ladies or full grown up men. According to them, to differ in any way was pro-British, pro-Government or unfaithfulness to the country, and today one can see clearly mental victims of these forces of hatred in several houses.

" But the danger is still greater. The taste of blood viz.

breaking laws, has been so attractive that one finds today this blessed Satyagraha on the lips of every one. As soon as you differ anywhere, be it in a school, in a house, in a group, in a circle of friends, in business, in an office, you find immediately threat of Satyagraha pointed out to you at every time. Between employer and employee, landlord and tenant, parents and children, teachers and pupils, brothers and friends, everywhere this pointed bayonet of Satyagraha seems to be ready for use. To break laws and rules of society or of the State seems to be so easy and handy. If a college professor suggests discipline, if a municipal officer recommends extra tax, if children are requested not to make noise, if hawkers are told to remove obstructions on roads, if changes or transfers are being arranged, if anything is done which does not suit anybody else, there is this dagger of Satyagraha pointed at you. Discrimination where to use and how to use seems to have been entirely lost in the whole nation, and this is a danger-signal for any nation or country. It is exactly like an aeroplane, which is being used generally to fly from one country to another speedily and is also used for throwing bombs. It is exactly like matches, which give light, and are also used for burning a house. One can clearly see this danger-signal in the Satyagraha weapon also. Satyagraha can be used to advantage but it can also be misused to entire destruction. I feel that unless those who proclaim Satyagraha as the best weapon to the wide world, did feel their responsibility in this matter, they would soon find the tables turned not only against themselves but on the whole country. If I can humbly suggest, I feel that some of the rigidly trained leaders, free from hatred, should now do nothing else, but pass some years of their lives in each province and each city and village to make people understand what real Satyagraha or true non-violence means, how it can be brought into operation and when it ought to be brought into operation. I would humbly suggest a regular school of non-violence in every province, where high-minded souls who thoroughly understand this subject scientifically and religiously ought to be teachers to the students of politics who in return should be kept as all-time workers to go round the country, give this message and teach what it is in reality. This can be the only safeguard for saving the country in my opinion."

Jamshed Mehta, the Lord Mayor of Karachi, is a patriot of the purest type. But for his identification with the Congress to the extent he was capable of and but for his having placed at the disposal of the Reception Committee all the resources of his Municipality, the wonderful Congress city would not have been brought into being in the incredibly short space of twenty-five days. His sympahy for the Satyagrahis when the campaign was going on is well known. Any criticism from one like him must, therefore, arrest attention. The quotation given above is an extract from Sjt. Jamshed Mehta's article in a Karachi Anglo-Gujarati weekly called *Parsi Sansar and Lokasevak*. The criticism I have copied follows a glowing tribute paid by him to the Satyagrahis who bore sufferings without retaliation. But we have no reason to be puffed up with pride over certificates of merit. In so far as we observed non-violence we only did our duty.

It is then the warning of this true friend of humanity and his country that we must treasure and profit by. What he has said of Karachi is likely to be true more or less of other places.

Non-violence to be a potent force must begin with the mind. Non-violence of the mere body without the co-operation of the mind is non-violence of the weak or the cowardly and has therefore no potency. It is, as Jamshedji says truly, a degrading performance. If we bear malice and hatred in our bosoms and pretend not to retaliate, it must recoil upon us and lead to our destruction. For abstention from mere bodily non-violence, i.e., not to be injurious, it is at least necessary not to entertain hatred if we cannot generate active love. All the songs and speeches betokening hatred must be taboo.

It is equally true to say that indiscriminate resistance to authority must lead to lawlessness, unbridled licence and consequent self-destruction.

If Jamshedji's criticism was not more than balanced by his appreciation, that is to say, if the sum total of real non-violence had not overbalanced the unreal, India would not have gone forward as it has done. But better even than the Karachi Lord Mayor's appreciation is the undoubted fact that the villagers have instinctively observed non-violence in a manner never before thought of. It is their non-violence that has conduced to the growth of national consciousness.

The mysterious effect of non-violence is not to be

measured by its visible effect. But we dare not rest content so long as the poison of hatred is allowed to permeate society. This struggle is a stupendous effort at conversion. We aim at nothing less than the conversion of the English. It can never be done by harbouring ill-will and still pretending to follow non-violence. Let those therefore who want to follow the path of non-violence and yet harbour ill-will retrace their steps and repent of the wrong they have done to themselves and the country.

Young India, 2-4-'31

124

POWER OF AHIMSA

A correspondent writes a Gujarati letter of which the following is a translation :

" For all that one can see, the support that world opinion has given to India in her present struggle has been most halting and feeble. Is it not surprising, in the face of this, to find Gandhiji claiming that we have received the fullest support from world-opinion ? An unarmed race struggling to win back its own from a most ruthless imperialistic power on earth armed to the teeth can only be compared to a poor, helpless woman defending herself against a ruffian in the face of heavy odds. Imagine this woman being brutally struck with *lathis* again and again by the heartless ruffian. Would it not make the blood of any human being boil with indignation ? Yet do we find signs of such moral indignation in the world today with regard to what was done to India ? And does not the absence of this moral indignation bespeak an indifferently developed sense of humanity in the world ? And if we admit that the question arises, can the weapon of *ahimsa* be at all effective in a world that is so devoid of humanity ? Why cannot Gandhiji see that the world has failed to rise at the sight of unarmed India's blood to that pitch of moral indignation which is essential to the success of truth and *ahimsa* ? "

If I have anywhere referred to India having received the fullest support from world opinion, it should be set down as an unconscious exaggeration. I should like to be shown such a statement of mine if I have made one. For myself I have absolutely no idea of having made any such statement.

The correspondent, by comparing the condition of unarmed India pitted against the British military power to that of a defenceless woman thrown at the tender mercy of a ruffian, has done an injustice to the strength as well of non-violence as of woman. Had not man in his blind selfishness crushed woman's soul as he has done or had she not succumbed to the 'enjoyments' she would have given the world an exhibition of the infinite strength that is latent in her. What she showed in the last fight was but a broken and imperfect glimpse of it. The world shall see it in all its wonder and glory when woman has secured an equal opportunity for herself with man and fully developed her powers of mutual aid and combination.

And it is wrong to say that a person is unarmed in the sense of being weak who has *ahimsa* as his weapon. The correspondent is evidently a stranger to the real use or the immeasurable power of *ahimsa*. He has used it, if at all, only mechanically and as an expedience for want of a better. Had he been saturated with the spirit of *ahimsa*, he would have known that it can tame the wildest beast, certainly the wildest man.

If, therefore, the world's blood did not boil over the brutalities of the past year, it was not because the world was brutal or heartless but because our non-violence, widespread though it was, good enough though it was for the purpose intended, was not the non-violence of the strong and the knowing. It did not spring from a living faith. It was but a policy, a temporary expedient. Though we did not retaliate, we had harboured anger, our speech was not free from violence, our thoughts still less so. We generally refrained from violent action, because we were under discipline. The world marvelled even at this limited exhibition of non-violence and gave us, without any propaganda, the support and sympathy that we deserved and needed. The rest is a matter of the rule of three. If we had the support that we received for the limited and mechanical non-violence we were able to practise during the recent struggle, how much more support should we command when we have risen to the full height of *ahimsa*? Then the world's blood will certainly boil. I know we are still far away from that divine event. We realized our weakness at Kanpur, Banaras, Mirzapur. When we are saturated with *ahimsa* we shall not be non-violent in our fight with the bureaucracy and violent among ourselves. When we have a living faith in non-violence, it will grow from day to day till it fills the whole world. It will be the mightiest propaganda that the world will have witnessed. I live in the belief that we will realize the vital *ahimsa*.

Young India, 7-5-'31

125

GOONDAISM WITHIN THE CONGRESS

The Congress has become a vast democratic body. It reached a high water-mark during the past twelve months. Without being technically on the register millions took possession of it and added lustre to it. But *goondaism* also entered the Congress to a much larger extent than hitherto. It was inevitable. The ordinary rules prescribed for the selection of volunteers were practically set aside during the last stages of the struggle. The result has been that in some places *goondaism* has made itself felt. Some Congressmen have even been threatened with disaster if they will not give the money demanded of them. Of course, professional *goondas* may also take advantage of the atmosphere and ply their trade.

The wonder is that the cases I have in mind are so very few compared to what they might have been, regard being had to the great mass awakening. My conviction is that this happy state is due to the Congress creed of non-violence, even though we have but crudely followed it. But there has been sufficient expression of *goondaism* to warn us to take time by the forelock and adopt preventive and precautionary measures.

The measures that suggest themselves to me are naturally and certainly a scientific and more intelligent and disciplined application of non-violence. In the first place, if we had a firmer faith in non-violence than we have shown, not one man or woman who did not strictly conform to the rules regarding the admission of volunteers would have been taken. It would be no answer to say that in that case there would have been no volunteers during the final stage and therefore there would have been a perfect failure. My experience teaches me to the contrary. It is possible to fight a non-violent battle even with one Satyagrahi. But it, i.e. a non-violent battle, cannot be fought with a million non-Satyagrahis. And I would welcome even an utter failure with non-violence unimpaired rather than depart from it by a hair's breadth to achieve a doubtful success. Without adopting a non-compromising attitude so far as non-violence is concerned, I can see nothing but disaster in the end. For, at the critical moment we may be found wanting, weighed in the scales of non-violence, and may be found hopelessly unprepared to meet the forces of disorder that might suddenly be arrayed against us.

But having made the mistake of indiscriminate recruiting how are we to repair the mischief in a non-violent way ? Non-violence means courage of the highest order and, therefore, readiness to suffer. There should, therefore, be no yielding to bullying, bluff or worse, even though it may mean the loss of a few precious lives. Writers of threatening letters should be made to realize that their threats will not be listened to. But at the same time their disease must be diagnosed and properly treated. Even the *goondas* are part of us and therefore they must be handled gently and sympathetically. People generally do not take to *goondaism* for the love of it. It is a symptom of a deeper-seated disease in the body politic. The same law should govern our relations with internal *goondaism* that we apply in our relations with the *goondaism* in the system of Government. And if we have felt that we have the ability to deal with that highly organized *goondaism*

in a non-violent manner how much more should we feel
the ability to deal with the internal *goondaism* by the same
method ?

It follows that we may not seek police assistance to
deal with the disease although it is open during the truce,
to any Congressman to seek it precisely in the same manner as any other citizen. The way I have suggested is the
way of reform, conversion, love. Seeking police assistance
is the way of punishment, fear, want of affection if not
actual disaffection. The two methods therefore cannot run
together. The way of reform appears at some stage or other
to be difficult but it is in reality the easiest.

Young India, 7-5-'31

126

CONQUEST OVER BODY

It is a fundamental principle of Satyagraha that the
tyrant whom the Satyagrahi seeks to resist has power
over his body and material possessions but he can have
no power over the soul. The soul can remain uncon-
quered and unnconquerable even when the body is
imprisoned. The whole science of Satyagraha was born
from a knowledge of this fundamental truth. In the purest
form of Satyagraha there should be no need for conveyan-
ces, carriage fare or even of doing *Hijrat*. And in case
Hijrat has to be performed it will be done by journeying on
foot. The *Hijratis* would have to be satisfied with whatever
hard fare falls to their lot and keep smiling when even
that fails. When we have developed this ' be careful for
nothing ' attitude, we shall be saved from many a bothera-
tion and trouble and freedom will dance attendance upon
us. Nor should one suppose that a ' careful for nothing '
person shall have always to be starving. God that provides
the little ant its speck of food and to the elephant his
daily one maund bolus will not neglect to provide man
with his daily meal. Nature's creatures do not worry

or fret about tomorrow but simply wait on tomorrow for the daily sustenance. Only man in his overweening pride and egotism imagines himself to be the lord and master of the earth, and goes on piling up for himself goods that perish. Nature tries every day by its rude shocks to wean him from his pride but he refuses to shed it. Satyagraha is a specific for bringing home to one the lesson of humility. We have travelled so much distance during the last year, we have gone through so much suffering and had so many rich experiences that we ought to have sufficient faith in us to be able to feel that if we throw ourselves upon God's mercy untroubled by doubt or fear, it would be well with us.

Young India, 21-5-'31

SECTION SEVENTH : INDIAN STATES SATYAGRAHA

[Rajkot was one of the States of Kathiawad, ruled by a Prince. Its people had, like those in other States of India, demanded Constitutional Reform, but their efforts met with repression buttressed by British authority. Gandhiji, whose childhood was spent in that State, had many personal links with the Ruler. He therefore went to Rajkot to bring about a peaceful settlement, especially to see that the agreement concluded by the Ruler with the people's leaders was kept. Towards this end, Gandhiji undertook a fast in Rajkot in 1939, and then appealed to the Viceroy, who intervened and brought about arbitration. The award was in Gandhiji's favour, but the latter felt that his fast was tainted by an element of coercion, and therefore denied himself the benefits of the award.   — Ed.]

127

SUSPEND CIVIL DISOBEDIENCE

In Satyagraha there is no such thing as disappointment or heartburning. The struggle always goes on in some shape or other till the goal is reached. A Satyagrahi is indifferent whether it is civil disobedience or some other phase of the struggle to which he is called. Nor does he mind if, in the middle of the civil disobedience march, he is called upon to halt and do something else. He must have faith that it is all for the best. My own experience hitherto has been that each suspension has found the people better equipped for the fight and for control over forces of violence. Therefore, in advising suspension, I dismiss from my mind the fear that it may lead to desertion and disbelief. If it does, I should not feel sorry, for it would be to me a sign that the deserters did not know what Satyagraha was and the movement was better without those who did not know what they were doing.

Harijan, 1-4-'39

RAJKOT SATYAGRAHA

In the course of conversation Gandhiji again put Rajkot Satyagraha under the lens : " I think the initial mistake was made when all Kathiawadis were permitted to join Rajkot Satyagraha. That step introduced an element of weakness in the fight. Thereby we put our reliance on numbers, whereas a Satyagrahi relies solely upon God who is the help of the helpless. A Satyagrahi always says to himself, ' He in whose name Satyagraha was launched, will also see it through.' If the people of Rajkot had thought in these terms, there would have been no temptation to organize big processions or mass demonstrations and probably there would have been no atrocities such as Rajkot has had to experience. A genuine Satyagrahi proceeds by setting the opponent at his ease. His action never creates panic in the breast of the ' enemy '. Supposing as a result of rigid enforcement of the rules of Satyagrahis Rajkot Satyagraha had been confined to a few hundred or even a few score true Satyagrahis and they had carried on their Satyagraha in the right spirit till their last breath, theirs would have served as a heroic example."

Harijan, 20-5-'39

ABOUT THE RAJKOT AWARD

[In the Rajkot dispute over which Gandhiji fasted, the Viceroy had to intervene and give his award, on Gandhiji appealing to him. Gandhiji, however, regarded this move of his as unworthy of a true Satyagrahi and repented in the following words :]

The very possession of this Award has made me a coward, and I am afraid if I were to retain it, it would make cowards of you too. A Satyagrahi does not depend for his strength on external means. His strength comes from within, from his reliance on God. God becomes his shield when he throws down all his earthly weapons. But if he were to hide a firearm in his pocket, his inner strength would go and he would cease to feel invulnerable. The Award was very like a firearm in the pocket of a votary of *ahimsa* like me. It stood between me and my God. It shamed me and made a coward of me. I have thrown it away as Christian did his load of sin, and I am feeling again free and invulnerable and one with my Maker.

Harijan, 3-6-'39

130

SUSPENSION OF CIVIL DISOBEDIENCE

In the afternoon the talks with the Travancore friends were resumed. They were afraid that indefinite suspension of civil disobedience would bring in depression from which it would be difficult for the people to recover. Gandhiji regarded this as a very disquieting symptom. It showed that what people had so far been practising was not genuine Satyagraha. The inwardness was lacking. They must start again from the very beginning. "Suspension should never bring despondency and weakness in a

Satyagraha struggle. Even though people may be ready and non-violence ensured, and suspension is ordered through a miscalculation of the general, it cannot jeopardize the future of the movement. Satyagraha means readiness to suffer and a faith that the more innocent and pure the suffering the more potent will it be in its effect. Helplessness is thus ruled out in Satyagraha. Suspension of civil disobedience, if it resulted in an accentuation of repression would itself become Satyagraha in its ideal form.

" Today the opponent is afraid of your numbers. You cannot expect him to show a change of heart while he is filled with panic. He senses in your action a spirit of retaliation which irritates him the more. It thus becomes a species of violence.

" Your struggle hereafter may have to be restricted to a few men only, but their Satyagraha will tell. While we are playing with non-violence we are only giving a chance to the powers that be in Travancore to organize the brute in man. This must not be."

He developed the theme further in his discussion with the Jaipur workers who came next : " Provoking *lathi* charges or receiving *lathi* blows on your body in a spirit of bravado is not Satyagraha. True Satyagraha consists in the readiness to face blows if they come in the course of performing one's duty.

" Today the whole atmosphere in the country is reeking of violence as was evidenced at Tripuri. Under violence I include corruption, falsehood, hypocrisy, deceit and the like. If our Satyagraha is to survive this atmosphere, we *ahimsaites* shall have to be more strict with ourselves. Let only the purest and the most innocent go to jail. It does not matter if they have to remain immured behind the prison bars for a whole lifetime. Their sacrifice will fill the prison with a sweet fragrance and its influence will even travel outside and subtly transform the entire atmosphere. They will never long for their release nor doubt that their sacrifice is being ' wasted '. They will realize that a consecrated resolve is more potent in its action than mere physical action can ever be. The discipline that they will be acquiring in prison will help the non-violent organization of the people outside and instil fearlessness among them.

" So much for those who are in prison, what about those outside ? They must engage in constructive work as the embodiment of the active principle of *ahimsa*. If it does not appeal to them, it will only betray their lack of faith in *ahimsa*.

" The other thing is internal. They must cultivate a living faith in God — an attitude of utter reliance on Him to the exclusion of all external aids. A single Satyagrahi imbued with such faith will inspire the whole people by his example and may induce a heart change even in the opponent who, freed from fear, will the more readily appreciate his simple faith and respect it."

Harijan, 3-6-'39

131

ITS IMPLICATIONS

The positive implication of the Rajkot chapter in my life is the discovery that the non-violence claimed for the movement since 1920, marvellous though it was, was not unadulterated. The results though brilliant would have been far richer if our non-violence had been complete. A non-violent action accompanied by non-violence in thought and word should never produce enduring violent reaction upon the opponent. But I have observed that the movement in the States has produced violent reaction on the Princes and their advisers. They are filled with distrust of the Congress. They do not want what they call interference from it. In some cases the very name *Congress* is anathema. This should not have been the case.

The value of the discovery lies in its reaction upon me. I have definitely stiffened in my demands upon would-be Satyagrahis. If my stiffness reduces the number to an insignificant figure, I should not mind. If Satyagraha is a universal principle of universal application, I must find an effective method of action even through a handful. And when I say I see the new light only dimly, I mean that I have not yet found with certainty how a handful can act effectively. It may be, as has happened throughout my life, that I shall know the next step only after the first has been taken. I have faith that when the time for action has arrived, the plan will be found ready.

But the impatient critic will say, ' The time has always been there for action ; only you have been found unready ! ' I cannot plead guilty. I know to the contrary. I have been for some years saying that there is no warrant for resumption of Satyagraha.

The reasons are plain.

The Congress has ceased to be an effective vehicle for launching nation-wide Satyagraha. It has become unwieldy, it has corruption in it, there is indiscipline among Congressmen, and rival groups have come into being which would radically change the Congress programme, if they could secure a majority. That they have failed hitherto to secure it is no comfort to me. The majority has no living faith in its own programme. In any case Satyagraha through a majority is not a feasible proposition. The whole weight of the Congress should be behind any nation-wide Satyagraha.

Then there is the ever-growing communal tension. Final Satyagraha is inconceivable without an honourable peace between the several communities composing the Indian nation.

Lastly, there is the provincial autonomy. I adhere to my belief that we have not done any thing like justice to the task undertaken by the Congress in connection with it. It must be confessed that the Governors have on the whole played the game. There has been very little interference on their part with the ministerial actions. But the interference, sometimes irritating, has come from Congressmen and Congress organizations. Popular violence there should not have been whilst the Congressmen were in office. Much of the ministerial energy has been devoted to dealing with the demands and opposition of Congressmen. If the ministers are unpopular, they can and should be dismissed. Instead they have been allowed to function without the active co-operation of many Congressmen.

It will be contrary to every canon of Satyagraha to launch upon the extreme step till every other is exhausted. Such haste will itself constitute violence.

It may be said in reply with some justification that if all the conditions I have mentioned are insisted upon civil disobedience may be well-nigh impossible. Is that a valid objection? Every measure carries with it conditions for its adoption. Satyagraha is no exception. But I feel within me that some active form of Satyagraha, not necessarily civil disobedience, must be available in order to end an impossible situation. India is facing an impossible situation. There must be either effective non-violent action or violence and anarchy within a measurable distance of time. I must examine this position on a future occasion.

Harijan, 24-6-'39

132

NON-VIOLENCE *v.* VIOLENCE

I must resume the argument about the implications of the Rajkot step, where I left it the week before.

In theory, if there is sufficient non-violence developed in any single person, he should be able to discover the means of combating violence, no matter how widespread or severe, within his jurisdiction. I have repeatedly admitted my imperfections. I am no example of perfect *ahimsa.* I am evolving. Such *ahimsa* as has been developed in me has been found enough to cope with situations that have hitherto arisen. But today I feel helpless in the face of the surrounding violence. There was a penetrating article in the *Statesman* on my Rajkot statement. The editor had therein contended that the English had never taken our

movement to be true Satyagraha, but being practical
people they had allowed the myth to continue though they
had known it to be a violent revolt. It was none the less
so because the rebels had no arms. I have quoted the
substance from memory. When I read the article, I felt
the force of the argument. Though I had intended the
movement to be pure non-violent resistance, as I look
back upon the happenings of those days, there was undoubtedly violence among the resisters. I must own that
had I been perfectly tuned to the music of *ahimsa*, I would
have sensed the slightest departure from it and my sensitiveness would have rebelled against any discord in it.

It seems to me that the united action of the Hindus
and the Muslims blinded me to the violence that was
lurking in the breasts of many. The English who are
trained diplomats and administrators are accustomed to
the line of least resistance, and when they found that it
was more profitable to conciliate a big organization than
to crush it by extensive frightfulness, they yielded to the
extent that they thought was necessary. It is, however,
my conviction that our resistance was predominantly non-
violent in action and will be accepted as such by the future
historian. As a seeker of truth and non-violence, however,
I must not be satisfied with mere action if it is not from
the heart. I must declare from the house-tops that the
non-violence of those days fell far short of the non-violence
as I have so often defined.

Non-violent action without the co-operation of the
heart and the head cannot produce the intended result.
The failure of our imperfect *ahimsa* is visible to the naked
eye. Look at the feud that is going on between Hindus
and Muslims. Each is arming for the fight with the other.
The violence that we had harboured in our breasts during
the non-co-operation days is now recoiling upon ourselves.
The violent energy that was generated among the masses,
but was kept under check in the pursuit of a common
objective, has now been let loose and is being used among
and against ourselves.

The same phenomenon is discernible, though in a less

crude manner, in the dissension among Congressmen themselves and the use of forcible methods that the Congress ministers are obliged to adopt in running the administrations under their charge.

This narrative clearly shows that the atmosphere is surcharged with violence. I hope it also shows that non-violent mass movement is an impossibility unless the atmosphere is radically changed. To blind one's eyes to the events happening around us is to court disaster. It has been suggested to me that I should declare mass civil disobedience and all internal strife will cease, Hindus and Muslims will compose their differences, Congressmen will forget mutual jealousies and fights for power. My reading of the situation is wholly different. If any mass movement is undertaken at the present moment in the name of non-violence, it will resolve itself into violence largely unorganized and organized in some cases. It will bring discredit on the Congress, spell disaster for the Congress struggle for independence and bring ruin to many a home. This may be a wholly untrue picture born of my weakness. If so, unless I shed that weakness, I cannot lead a movement which requires great strength and resolution.

Harijan, 8-7-'39

SECTION EIGHTH : INDIVIDUAL SATYAGRAHA AGAINST WAR

[When Britain involved India in World War II in 1939 without so much as consulting her, public opinion in the country was enraged, especially as Britain was unwilling to promise independence to India, and it was therefore felt that the War was being fought only to maintain the British Empire and not for the freedom of suppressed nations. Accordingly, the people were anxious to proclaim civil disobedience against the Government. Gandhiji did his best to restrain them, as he did not think it proper to embarrass the British when they were facing a crisis, and also because he did not feel that our people were sufficiently non-violent. But when after a whole year of such restraint, the people appeared to feel stifled, he permitted what was called individual Satyagraha to assert freedom of speech, and gave the right to individuals chosen by himself for their character, public work and belief in non-violence to offer civil disobedience by preaching against war and courting imprisonment. This limited kind of Satyagraha went on during 1940 and 1941. When the Cripps Mission sent out by the British in 1942 failed to bring about a settlement, Gandhiji started his Quit India slogan. This was followed by his imprisonment and that of his followers. As the *Harijan* was under a Government ban from November 1940, his instructions to his followers regarding Satyagraha came to an end. Gandhiji was permitted to publish the *Harijan* again only in February, 1946. — Ed.]

133

NO SUPPRESSION

A Bengal friend came to me during the week and said that though Bengal was ready for battle the Working Committee and especially I were suppressing it and thus damaging the nation's cause. This is a serious charge. The Working Committee can take care of itself. So far as I know, it has suppressed no province and no person. But I can say as the sole authority on Satyagraha that I have never suppressed any body or organization. Satyagraha does not admit of such suppression. Thus though I have been ignorantly accused of suppressing the people of Rajkot, I never suppressed them. They were at liberty, as they are now, to civilly resist authority. Even one person could do so if he had the conviction. If he is wrong, he can only harm himself, not his opponent. Hence it is that I have called Satyagraha the most harmless, if also the most potent, remedy against wrongs.

What, however, I did in the case of Rajkot was to use the authority the Satyagrahis of Rajkot had given me, to suspend civil resistance. It was open to them to reject my advice — it could hardly be dignified by the name of command. If they had, and if they had got responsible government, they would have received my congratulations.

Some readers may remember that the Working Committee had refused to sanction civil resistance in Chirala Perala but had left the Chirala people to declare it at their own risk. Likewise it is open to Bengal, as also to any other province, on its own initiative and at its own risk, to offer civil resistance. What it cannot have is my approval or support. And if the Bengal Provincial Congress Committee wholly repudiates the authority of the Working Committee, it can, with all the greater force and propriety, do as it likes. If it succeeds, it will cover itself with glory, overthrow the present leadership, and rule the Congress organization as it will deserve to. I have prescribed the conditions of successful civil resistance. But if the Bengal Provincial Congress Committee thinks that the Muslim masses are with the Congress, if it thinks that both Hindus and Muslims are ready for the fight, if it thinks that neither non-violence nor the *charkha* is necessary or that non-violence has no connection with the *charkha*, and if it fails to declare war, it will then be untrue to itself and to the country. What I have said applies to every province and part of India. But as the most experienced Satyagrahi I must be allowed to utter a note of warning to all concerned that whoever declares civil resistance without the proper training and a full appreciation of the conditions of Satyagraha is likely to bring disaster to the cause he espouses.

Harijan, 20-1-'40

134

EVERY CONGRESS COMMITTEE
A SATYAGRAHA COMMITTEE

In the coming struggle, if it must come, no half-hearted loyalty will answer the purpose. Imagine a general marching to battle with doubting, ill-prepared soldiers. He will surely march to defeat. I will not consciously make any such fatal experiment. This is not meant to frighten Congressmen. If they have the will, they will not find my instructions difficult to follow. Correspondents tell me that, though they have no faith in me or the *charkha*, they ply the latter for the sake of discipline. I do not understand this language. Can a general fight on the strength of soldiers who, he knows, have no faith in him ? The plain meaning of this language is that the correspondents believe in mass action but do not believe in the connection I see between it and the *charkha*, etc., if the action is to be non-violent. They believe in my hold on the masses, but they do not believe in the things which I believe have given me that hold. They merely want to exploit me and will grudgingly pay the price which my ignorance or obstinacy (according to them) demands. I do not call this discipline. True discipline gives enthusiastic obedience to instructions even though they do not satisfy reason. A volunteer exercises his reason when he chooses his general, but after having made the choice, he does not waste his time and energy in scanning every instruction and testing it on the anvil of his reason before following it. His is " not to reason why ".

Now for my instructions :

Every Congress Committee should become a Satyagraha Committee and register such Congressmen who believe in the cultivation of the spirit of goodwill towards all, who have no untouchability in them in any shape or form, who would spin regularly, and who habitually use *khadi* to the exclusion of all other cloth. I would expect those who thus register their names with their Committees to devote the whole of their spare time to the constructive programme. If the response is sincere, these Satyagraha Committees would become busy spinning depots. They will work in conjunction with and under the guidance of the A. I. S. A. branches in a businesslike manner so that there remain, in the jurisdiction of the Committees, no Congressmen who have not adopted *khadi* for exclusive use. I shall expect businesslike reports to be sent from provincial headquarters to the A. I. C. C. as to the progress of the work of the Satyagraha Committees. Seeing that this registration is to be purely voluntary, the reports would mention the numbers both of those who give their names for registration and those who do not.

The registered Satyagrahis will keep a diary of the work that they do from day to day. Their work, besides their own spinning, will consist in visiting the primary members and inducing them to use *khadi*, spin and register themselves. Whether they do so or not, contact should be maintained with them.

There should be visits paid to Harijan homes and their difficulties removed so far as possible.

Needless to say that names should be registered only of those who are willing and able to suffer imprisonment.

No financial assistance is to be expected by Satyagrahi prisoners whether for themselves or their dependants.

So much for the active Satyagrahis. But there is a much larger class of men and women who, though they will not spin or court or suffer imprisonment, believe in the two cardinal principles of Satyagraha and welcome and wish well to the struggle. These I will call passive Satyagrahis. They will help equally with the active ones, if they will not interfere with the course of the struggle by themselves courting imprisonment or aiding or precipitating strikes of labourers or students. Those who out of overzeal or for any other cause will act contrary to these instructions will harm the struggle and may even compel me to suspend it. When the forces of violence are let loose all over the world and when nations reputed to be most

civilized cannot think of any force other than that of arms
for the settlement of their disputes, I hope that it will be
possible to say of India that she fought and won the battle
of freedom by purely peaceful means.

I am quite clear in my mind that, given the co-operation of politically-minded India, the attainment of India's
freedom is perfectly possible through unmixed non-
violence. The world does not believe our pretension of
non-violence. Let alone the world, I, the self-styled general, have repeatedly admitted that we have violence in
our hearts, that we are often violent to one another in
our mutual dealings. I must confess that I will not be able
to fight so long as we have violence in our midst. But I
will fight if the proposed register is honest and if those
who courageously keep out will not disturb the even course
of the struggle.

Harijan, 30-3-'40

135

THE CHARKHA AND SATYAGRAHA

One of the speakers (at the open Congress Session)
said that he had no quarrel with the *charkha,* but he
wanted the *charkha* to be divorced from Satyagraha. Well
I tell you, as I have been telling you these 20 years, that
there is a vital connection between Satyagraha and the
charkha, and the more I find that belief challenged the
more I am confirmed in it. Otherwise I am no fool to persist
in turning the *charkha,* day in and day out, at home and
even on trains, in the teeth of medical advice. I want you
too to be turning the *charkha* with the same faith. And
unless you do it and unless you habitually use *khadi* you
will deceive me and deceive the world.

I know that you will not fight unless you have me
with you, but then you must know that I am here and I
would fight only as a representative of those dumb millions
for whom I live and for whom I want to die. My loyalty

to them is greater than any other loyalty, and it is for them that I would not give up the *charkha* even if you were to forsake me or kill me. For I know that, if I were to relax the conditions of the *charkha*, I should bring ruin upon those dumb millions for whom I have to answer before God. If, therefore, you do not believe in the *charkha* in the sense I believe in it, I implore you to leave me. The *charkha* is an outward symbol of truth and non-violence, and unless you have them in your hearts you will not take to the *charkha* either. Remember, therefore, that you have to fulfil both the internal and external conditions. If you fulfil the internal condition, you will cease to hate your opponent, you will not seek or work for his destruction, but pray to God to have mercy on him. Do not, therefore, concentrate on showing the misdeeds of the Government, for we have to convert and befriend those who run it. And after all no one is wicked by nature. And if others are wicked, are we the less so ? That attitude is inherent in Satyagraha, and if you do not subscribe to it, even then I would ask you to leave me. For without a belief in my programme and without an acceptance of my condition you will ruin me, ruin yourself and ruin the cause.

Harijan, 30-3-'40

136

CIVIL DISOBEDIENCE

Civil disobedience, if it is really civil, must appear so even to the opponent. He must feel that the resistance is not intended to do him any harm. At the present moment the average Englishman thinks that non-violence is merely a cloak. The Muslim Leaguers think that civil disobedience is aimed at them more than at the British. I protest with all the strength at my command that, so far as I am concerned, I have no desire whatsoever to embarrass the British, especially at a time when it is a question of life and death with them. All I want the Congress to do through civil disobedience is to deny the British Government the moral influence which Congress co-operation would give. The material resources of India and her man power are already being exploited by the British Government by reason of their control of the whole of this sub-continent.

If by civil disobedience the Congress has no desire to embarrass the British people, it has still less to embarrass the Muslim League. And I can say this on behalf of the Congress with far greater assurance than I can with regard to the British. Working in the midst of suspicion and terrible misrepresentation on the one hand and the prevailing lawlessness outside and inside the Congress on the other, I have to think a thousand times before embarking on civil disobedience.

So far as I can see, at present mass civil disobedience is most unlikely. The choice lies between individual civil disobedience on a large scale, very restricted, or confined only to me. In every case there must be the backing of the whole of the official Congress organization and the millions who, though not on the Congress register, have always supported the organization with their mute but most effective co-operation.

I have repeatedly shown in these columns that the

most effective and visible co-operation which all Congressmen and the mute millions can show is by not interfering with the course civil disobedience may take and by themselves spinning and using *khadi* to the exclusion of all other cloth. If it is allowed that there is a meaning in people wearing primroses on Primrose Day, surely there is much more in a people using a particular kind of cloth and giving a particular kind of labour to the cause they hold dear. From their compliance with the *khadi* test I shall infer that they have shed untouchability, and that they have nothing but brotherly feeling towards all without distinction of race, colour or creed. Those who will do this are as much Satyagrahis as those who will be singled out for civil disobedience.

Harijan, 27-4-'40

137

NOT YET

Many Congressmen are playing at non-violence. They think in terms of civil disobedience anyhow, meaning the filling of jails. This is a childish interpretation of the great force that civil disobedience is. I must continue to repeat, even though it may cause nausea, that prison-going without the backing of honest constructive effort and goodwill in the heart for the wrong-doer is violence and therefore forbidden in Satyagraha. Force generated by non-violence is infinitely greater than the force of all the arms invented by man's ingenuity. Non-violence, therefore, is the decisive factor in civil disobedience. I have been told that people cannot be non-violent overnight. I have never contended they can. But I have held that by proper training they can be, if they have the will. Active non-violence is necessary for those who will offer civil disobedience, but the will and proper training are enough for the people to co-operate with those who are chosen for civil disobedience. The constructive work prescribed by the

Congress is the proper training. Those, therefore, who wish to see India realize her destiny through non-violence should devote every ounce of their energy towards the fulfilment of the constructive programme in right earnest without any thought of civil disobedience.

Harijan, 1-6-'40

138

TO THE READER

You must have seen through my Press notice that the publication of *Harijan* and the other two weeklies * has been suspended. In it, I had expressed the hope that the suspension might be only for a week. But I see that the hope had no real foundation. I shall miss my weekly talks with you, as I expect you too will miss them. The value of those talks consisted in their being a faithful record of my deepest thoughts. Such expression is impossible in a cramped atmosphere. As I have no desire to offer civil disobedience, I cannot write freely. As the author of Satyagraha I cannot, consistently with my professions, suppress the vital part of myself for the sake of being able to write on permissible subjects such as the constructive programme. It would be like dealing with the trunk without the head. The whole of the constructive programme is to me an expression of non-violence. I would be denying myself if I could not preach non-violence. For that would be the meaning of submission to the latest Ordinance. The suspension must, therefore, continue while the gagging lasts. It constitutes a Satyagrahi's respectful protest against the gag. Is not Satyagraha giving an ell when an inch is asked for by the wrong-doer, is it not giving the cloak also when only the coat is demanded ? It may be asked why this reversal of the ordinary process ? The ordinary process is based on violence. If my life were

---

* *Harijansevak* and *Harijanbandhu* — Hindi and Gujarati editions of the English *Harijan*.

regulated by violence in the last resort, I would refuse to give an inch lest an ell might be asked for. I would be a fool if I did otherwise. But if my life is regulated by non-violence, I should be prepared to and actually give an ell when an inch is asked for. By so doing I produce on the usurper a strange and even pleasurable sensation. He would also be confounded and would not know what to do with me. So much for the ' enemy '. I, having made up my mind to surrender every non-essential, gain greater strength than ever before to die for the defence and pre-servation of what I hold to be essential. I was therefore wrongly accused by my critics of having advised cowardly surrender to Nazism by Englishmen when I suggested that they should lay down external arms, let the Nazis over-run Britain if they dare, but develop internal strength to refuse to sell themselves to the Nazis. Full surrender of non-essentials is a condition precedent to accession of in-ternal strength to defend the essential by dying.

But I am not writing this to convert the English to my view. I am writing this to suggest to you that my surrender to the framers of the gaging Ordinance is an object-lesson to you, the Reader, in Satyagraha. If you will quietly work out in your own life the implications of the lesson, you will then not need the weekly aid from the written word in *Harijan*. Even without your weekly *Harijan* you will know how I shall myself work out the full implications of giving an ell when an inch is wanted. A correspondent pleads with me that on no account should I suspend *Harijan*, for he says his non-violence is sustained by the weekly food he gets therefrom. If he has really done so, then this self-imposed restraint should teach him more than a vapid continuation of the weekly *Harijan*.

Harijan. 10-11-'40

I. FAST AS AN ELEMENT IN SATYAGRAHA

139

FASTING AS PENANCE

Once when I was in Johannesburg I received tidings of the moral fall of two of the inmates of the Ashram. News of an apparent failure or reverse in the Satyagraha struggle would not have shocked me, but this news came upon me like a thunderbolt. The same day I took the train for Phoenix. Mr Kallenbach insisted on accompanying me. He had noticed the state I was in. He would not brook the thought of my going alone, for he happened to be the bearer of the tidings which had so upset me.

During the journey my duty seemed clear to me. I felt that the guardian or teacher was responsible, to some extent at least, for the lapse of his ward or pupil. So my responsibility regarding the incident in question became clear to me as daylight. My wife had already warned me in the matter, but being of a trusting nature, I had ignored her caution. I felt that the only way the guilty parties could be made to realize my distress, and the depth of their own fall would be for me to do some penance. So I imposed upon myself a fast for seven days and a vow to have only one meal a day for a period of four months and a half. Mr Kallenbach tried to dissuade me, but in vain. He finally conceded the propriety of the penance, and insisted on joining me. I could not resist his transparent affection.

I felt greatly relieved, for the decision meant a heavy load off my mind. The anger against the guilty parties subsided and gave place to the purest pity for them. Thus considerably eased, I reached Phoenix. I made further investigation and acquainted myself with some more details I needed to know.

My penance pained everybody, but it cleared the atmosphere. Everyone came to realize what a terrible thing it was to be sinful, and the bond that bound me to the boys and girls became stronger and truer.

A circumstance arising out of this incident compelled me, a little while after, to go into a fast for fourteen days, the results of which exceeded even my expectations.

It is not my purpose to make out from these incidents that it is the duty of a teacher to resort to fasting whenever there is a delinquency on the part of his pupils. I hold, however, that some occasions do call for this drastic remedy. But it presupposes clearness of vision and spiritual fitness. Where there is no true love between the teacher and the pupil, where the pupil's delinquency has not touched the very being of the teacher and where the pupil has no respect for the teacher, fasting is out of place and may even be harmful. Though there is thus room for doubting the propriety of fasts in such cases, there is no question about the teacher's responsibility for the errors of his pupil.

Autobiography, pt. IV, chap. XXXVI

140

THE SATYAGRAHA WAY WITH CHILDREN

[Gandhiji went on a seven-day fast owing to some error in the conduct of his Ashram children. In this connection he wrote :]

I discovered errors among the boys and somewhat among the girls. I know that hardly a school or any other institution is free from the errors I am referring to. I am anxious to see the Ashram free from errors which are sapping the manhood of the nation and undermining the character of the youth. It was not permissible to punish the boys. Experience gained in two schools under my control has taught me that punishment does not purify, if anything it hardens children. In such cases in South Africa I have resorted to fasts with, in my opinion, the best of results. I have resorted to the same process here and let me say of a milder type. The basis of the action is mutual love. I know that I possess the love of the boys and the girls. I know too that if the giving up of my life can make them spotless, it would be my supreme joy to give it. Therefore, I could do no less to bring the youngsters to a sense of their error. So far the results seem to be promising.

What, however, if I cannot perceive the fruit? I can but do the will of God as I feel it. The result is in His disposing. This suffering for things great and small is the keynote of Satyagraha.

But why should not the teachers perform the penance? They cannot, so long as I remain the chief. If they had fasted with me all work would have come to a standstill. As with big institutions so with small ones. As the king must share the sins of his subjects even as he arrogates to himself all their virtues, so must I, a tiny chosen king in the little Ashram, atone for the sins of the least among the children of the Ashram, if I may proudly claim the presence in it of many noble characters. If I am to identify myself with the grief of the least in India, aye, if I have the power, the least in the world, let me identify myself with the sins of the little ones who are under my care. And so doing in all humility I hope some day to see God — Truth — face to face.

Young India, 3-12-'25

SATYAGRAHA — TRUE AND FALSE

There are many forms of Satyagraha, of which fasting may or may not be one, according to the circumstances of the case. A friend has put the following poser :

" A man wants to recover money another owes him. He cannot do so by going to law as he is a non-co-operator, and the debtor in the intoxication of the power of his wealth pays him no heed, and refuses even to accept arbitration. If in these circumstances, the creditor sits *dhurna* at the debtor's door, would it not be Satyagraha ? The fasting creditor seeks to injure no one by his fasting. Ever since the golden age of Rama we have been following this method. But I am told you regard this as intimidation. If you do, will you kindly explain ? "

I know the correspondent. He has written from the purest motive. But I have no doubt that he is mistaken in his interpretation of Satyagraha. Satyagraha can never be resorted to for personal gain. If fasting with a view to recovering money is to be encouraged, there would be no end of scoundrels blackmailing people by resorting to the means. I know that many such people are to be met with in the country. It is not right to argue that those who rightly resort to fasting need not be condemned because it is abused in a few cases. Any and every one may not draw his own distinction between fasting — Satyagraha — true and false. What one regards as true Satyagraha may very likely be otherwise. Satyagraha, therefore, cannot be resorted to for personal gain, but only for the good of others. A Satyagrahi should always be ready to undergo suffering and pecuniary loss. That there would not be wanting dishonest people to reap an undue advantage from the boycott of Law Courts practised by good people was a contingency not unexpected at the inception of non-co-operation. It was then thought that the beauty of non-co-operation lay just in taking those risks.

But Satyagraha in the form of fasting cannot be undertaken as against an opponent. Fasting can be resorted to only against one's nearest and dearest, and that solely for his or her good.

In a country like India, where the spirit of charity or pity is not lacking, it would be nothing short of an outrage to resort to fasting for recovering money. I know people who have given away money, quite against their will, but out of a false sense of pity. The Satyagrahi has, therefore, to proceed warily in a land like ours. It is likely that some men may succeed in recovering money due to them, by resorting to fasting; but instead of calling it a triumph of Satyagraha, I would call it a triumph of *duragraha* or violence. The triumph of Satyagraha consists in meeting death in the insistence on truth. A Satyagrahi is always unattached to the attainment of the object of Satyagraha; one seeking to recover money cannot be so unattached. I am, therefore, clear that fasting for the sake of personal gain is nothing short of intimidation and the result of ignorance.

Young India, 30-9-'26

142

FAST AS AN ELEMENT IN SATYAGRAHA

Suffering even unto death and, therefore, even through a perpetual fast is the last weapon of a Satyagrahi. That is the last duty which it is open to him to perform. Therefore, fast is a part of my being as, I hold, it has been, to a large or small extent, of every seeker of Truth. I am making an experiment in *ahimsa* on a scale perhaps unknown in history. That I may be wholly wrong is quite possible, but quite irrelevant to the present purpose. So long as I am not conscious of the error, but, on the contrary, am sure, as far as it is humanly possible to be, of being in the right, I must go on with my pursuit to the farthest end. And in this manner, but in no other, a fast or a series of fasts are always a possibility in my life. I have undergone many before now since childhood. There should be no alarm felt if they are undertaken for public causes. Nor must any one exploit them in anticipation. When they come, they will produce their own effect and result, whether anybody wills or no. But it is wrong to speculate over the contingency.

I, therefore, implore the public to dismiss from their minds, and be unaffected by the remote possibility of another fast by me in this campaign against untouchability and to accept my assurance that, if such a fast does come, it will have come in obedience to the call of Truth which is God. I will not be a traitor to God to please the whole world.

Harijan, 18-2-'33

143

FAST AS PRAYER

[After his fast for the Harijan cause in May, 1933, Gandhiji wrote :]

The fast was an uninterrupted twenty-one days' prayer whose effect I can feel even now. I know now more fully than ever that there is no prayer without fasting, be the latter ever so little. And this fasting relates not merely to the palate, but all the senses and organs. Complete absorption in prayer must mean complete exclusion of physical activities till prayer possesses the whole of our being and we rise superior to, and are completely detached from, all physical functions. That state can only be reached after continual and voluntary crucifixion of the flesh. Thus all fasting, if it is a spiritual act, is an intense prayer or a preparation for it. It is a yearning of the soul to merge in the divine essence. My last fast was intended to be such a preparation. How far I have succeeded, how far I am in tune with the Infinite, I do not know. But I do know that the fast has made the passion for such a state intenser than ever.

Harijan, 8-7-'33

144

IS FAST COERCION?

[In reply to Rev. Stanley Jones, Gandhiji said :]

If it is agreed that my fast sprang from love, then it was coercion, only if love of parents for their children or of the latter for the former, or love of husband for wife and wife for husband, or, to take a sweeping illustration, love of Jesus for those who own Him as their all, is coercion. It is the implicit and sacred belief of millions of Christians that love of Jesus keeps them from falling and that it does so against themselves. His love bends the reason and the emotion of thousands of His votaries to His love. I know that, in my childhood, love of my parents kept me from sinning, and, even after fifty years of age, love of my children and friends kept me positively from going to perdition, which I would have done most assuredly but for the definite and overwhelming influence of that love. And, if all this love could be regarded as coercion, then the love that prompted my fast and, therefore, my fast, was coercion, but it was that in no other sense. Fasting is a great institution in Hinduism, as perhaps in no other religion, and, though it has been abused by people not entitled to fast, it has, on the whole, done the greatest good to Hinduism. I believe that there is no prayer without fasting and there is no real fast without prayer. My fast was the prayer of a soul in agony.

Harijan, 11-2-'33

FAST AS THE LAST RESORT

Sacrifice of self even unto death is the final weapon in the hands of a non-violent person. It is not given to man to do more. I, therefore, suggest to this co-worker and all the others that in this religious battle against untouchability they must be prepared joyously even to " fast unto death ", if such an urgent call comes to them. If they feel that they are party to the September pledge given unsolicited to the Harijans and if they cannot make good the pledge in spite of ordinary effort, how else, being non-violent, will they propose to deliver the goods except by laying down their lives ?

The *shastras* tell us that, when people in distress prayed to God for relief and He seemed to have hardened His heart, they declared a ' fast unto death ' till God listened to their prayer. Religious history tells us of those who survived their fast, because God listened to them, but it tells us nothing of those who silently and heroically perished in the attempt to win the answer from a deaf God. I am certain that many have died in that heroic manner, but without their faith in God and non-violence being in the slightest degree diminished. God does not always answer prayers in the manner we want Him to. For Him life and death are one, and who is able to deny that all that is pure and good in the world persists because of the silent death of thousands of unknown heroes and heroines !

Harijan, 4-3-'33

FAST AS SELF-SURRENDER

Although the Sanatanists swear at me for the fast, and Hindu co-workers may deplore it, they know that fasting is an integral part of even the present-day Hinduism. They cannot long affect to be horrified at it. Hindu religious literature is replete with instances of fasting, and thousands of Hindus fast even today on the slightest pretext. It is the one thing that does the least harm. There is no doubt that, like everything that is good, fasts are abused. That is inevitable. One cannot forbear to do good, because sometimes evil is done under its cover.

My real difficulty is with my Christian Protestant friends, of whom I have so many and whose friendship I value beyond measure. Let me confess to them that, though from my very first contact with them I have known their dislike for fasts, I have never been able to understand it.

Mortification of the flesh has been held all the world over as a condition of spiritual progress. There is no prayer without fasting, taking fasting in its widest sense. A complete fast is a complete and literal denial of self. It is the truest prayer. "Take my life, and let it be consecrated, Lord, to Thee," is not, should not be, a mere lip or figurative expression. It has to be a wreckless and joyous giving without the least reservation. Abstention from food and even water is but the mere beginning, the least part of the surrender.

It is only proper that friends should know my fundamental position. I have a profound belief in the method of the fast, both private and public. It may come again any day without any warning even to me. If it comes, I shall welcome it as a great privilege and a joy.

Harijan, 15-4-'33

REQUIREMENTS FOR SATYAGRAHA FAST

But the mere fast of the body is nothing without the will behind it. It must be a genuine confession of the inner fast, an irrepressible longing to express truth and nothing but truth. Therefore, those only are privileged to fast for the cause of truth, who have worked for it and who have love in them even for opponents, who are free from animal passion and who have abjured earthly possessions and ambitions. No one, therefore, may undertake, without previous preparation and discipline the fast I have foreshadowed.

Harijan, 6-5-'33

148

COERCIVE FASTS

If the expression 'coercive effect' can be lawfully used for my fasts, then in that sense, all fasts can be proved to have that effect to a greater or less extent. The fact is that all spiritual fasts always influence those who come within the zone of their influence. That is why spiritual fasting is described as *tapas*. And all *tapas* invariably exerts purifying influence on those in whose behalf it is undertaken.

Of course, it is not to be denied that fasts can be really coercive. Such are fasts to attain a selfish object. A fast undertaken to wring money from a person or for fulfilling some such personal end would amount to the exercise of coercion or undue influence. I would unhesitatingly advocate resistance of such undue influence. I have myself successfully resisted it in the fasts that have been undertaken or threatened against me. And if it is argued that the dividing line between a selfish and an unselfish end is often very thin, I would urge that a person who regards the end of a fast to be selfish or otherwise base should resolutely refuse to yield to it, even though the refusal may result in the death of the fasting person. If people will cultivate the habit of disregarding fasts which in their opinion are taken for unworthy ends, such fasts will be robbed of the taint of coercion and undue influence. Like all human institutions, fasting can be both legitimately and illegitimately used. But as a great weapon in the armoury of Satyagraha, it cannot be given up because of its possible abuse. Satyagraha has been designed as an effective substitute for violence. This use is in its infancy and, therefore, not yet perfected. But as the author of modern Satyagraha I cannot give up any of its manifold uses without forfeiting my claim to handle it in the spirit of a humble seeker.

Harijan, 6-5-'33

149

FASTING

Fasting is a potent weapon in the Satyagraha armoury. It cannot be taken by every one. Mere physical capacity to take it is no qualification for it. It is of no use without a living faith in God. It should never be a mechanical effort nor a mere imitation. It must come from the depth of one's soul. It is therefore always rare. I seem to be made for it. It is noteworthy that not one of my colleagues on the political field has felt the call to fast. And I am thankful to be able to say that they have never resented my fasts. Nor have fellow-members of the Ashram felt the call except on rare occasions. They have even accepted the restriction that they may not take penitential fasts without my permission, no matter how urgent the inner call may seem to be.

Thus fasting, though a very potent weapon, has necessarily very strict limitations and is to be taken only by those who have undergone previous training. And, judged by my standard, the majority of fasts do not at all come under the category of Satyagraha fasts and are, as they are popularly called, hunger-strikes undertaken without previous preparation and adequate thought. If the process is repeated too often, these hunger-strikes will lose what little efficacy they may possess and will become objects of ridicule.

Harijan, 18-3-'39

150

FASTING IN SATYAGRAHA

Nowadays quite a number of fasts are undertaken in the name of Satyagraha. Many of the known fasts have been meaningless, many may be said to have been impure. Fasting is a fiery weapon. It has its own science. No one, as far as I am aware, has a perfect knowledge of it. Unscientific experimentation with it is bound to be harmful to the one who fasts, and it may even harm the cause espoused. No one who has not earned the right to do so should, therefore, use this weapon. A fast may only be undertaken by him who is associated with the person against whom he fasts. The latter must be directly connected with the purpose for which the fast is being undertaken. Bhagat Fulsinghji's recent fast was such a one. He was closely connected with the people of Moth village; he had served the Harijans of the place too. The wrong that was being enacted was done by the villagers to the Harijans. When every means of obtaining justice had failed there was no option left for a man like Fulsinghji except to resort to fasting. He did and succeeded. Success or failure depends entirely on the will of God and is not relevant to the issue under discussion.

All my public fasts have been of this category. Out of all of them perhaps there is most to be learnt from the Rajkot one. It has been roundly condemned by many people. Originally it was pure and necessary. The blemish crept in when I asked the Viceroy to intervene. Had I not done so, I am convinced that its result would have been brilliant. Even as it was, the result was a victory for the cause. Because God wanted to open my eyes, he took the bread out of my mouth, so to speak. The Rajkot fast is thus a useful study for the Satyagrahi. In regard to its necessity there is no doubt, assuming that the principles for fasting which I have laid down are accepted. The important thing to note about it is how a pure undertaking can become tainted owing to lack of watchfulness on the part of the doer. There can be no room for selfishness, anger, lack of faith, or impatience in a pure fast. It is no exaggeration to admit that all these defects crept into my Rajkot fast. My selfishness lay in the fact that inasmuch as its being given up depended on certain conditions being fulfilled by the late Thakoresaheb, I had in me the selfish desire for the realization of the fruit of my labour. If there had been no anger in me, I would not have looked to the Viceroy for assistance. My love should have deterred me from doing so. For if he was really as a son to me, why should I have complained about him to his overlord? I betrayed want of faith in that I thought the Thakoresaheb would not be melted by my love and I was impatient to break the fast. All these shortcomings were bound to make my fast impure. It would be irrelevant here to ponder over the many results of the Rajkot fast, and I therefore refrain from doing so. But we have learnt how infinitely watchful and prayerful he who fasts has to be and how even a little carelessness can damage a good cause. It is now apparent that in addition to truth and non-violence a Satyagrahi should have the confidence that, God will grant him the necessary strength and that, if there is the slightest impurity in the fast, he will not hesitate to renounce it at once. Infinite patience, firm resolve, single-mindedness of purpose, perfect calm, and no anger must of necessity be there. But since it is impossible for a person to develop all these qualities all at once, no one who has not devoted himself to following the laws of *ahimsa* should undertake a Satyagrahi fast.

I should like readers to note that I have not here dealt with fasts undertaken for bodily or spiritual purification. Nature-cure doctors should be consulted for the former. The greatest of sinners can undertake the latter. And for this type of fast we possess a veritable mine of literature. Fasts for spiritual purification have really been forgotten in our day. If they are ever undertaken, they are either purely imitative or merely for the sake of tradition, and we cannot therefore derive the benefit from them that we should. Those who want to go in for a Satyagrahi fast should certainly possess some personal experience of fasts for spiritual purification. Fasts for ridding the body of impurities are also beneficial. In the end, of course, there is only one basis for the whole ideal of fasting, and that is purification.

Harijan, 13-10-'40

151

FASTING IN THE AIR

I have had the temerity to claim that fasting is an infallible weapon in the armoury of Satyagraha. I have used it myself, being the author of Satyagraha. Any one whose fast is related to Satyagraha should seek my permission and obtain it in writing before embarking on it. If this advice is followed, there is no need for framing rules, at any rate, in my lifetime.

One general principle, however, I would like to enunciate. A Satyagrahi should fast only as a last resort when all other avenues of redress have been explored and have failed. There is no room for imitation in fasts. He who has no inner strength should not dream of it, and never with attachment to success. But if a Satyagrahi once undertakes a fast from conviction, he must stick to his resolve whether there is a chance of his action bearing fruit or not. This does not mean that fasting cannot or does not bear fruit. He who fasts in the exectation of fruit generally fails. And even if he does not seemingly fail, loses all the inner joy which a true fast holds.

Whether one should take fruit juices or not depends on one's physical powers of endurance. But no more fruit juice than is absolutely necessary for the body should be taken. He probably has the greatest inner strength who takes only water.

It is wrong to fast for selfish ends, e.g., for increase in one's own salary. Under certain circumstances it is permissible to fast for an increase in wages on behalf of one's group.

Ridiculous fasts spread like plague and are harmful. But when fasting becomes a duty it cannot be given up. Therefore, I do fast when I consider it to be necessary and cannot abstain from it on any score. What I do myself I cannot prevent others from doing under similar circumstances. It is common knowledge that the best of good things are often abused. We see this happening every day.

Harijan, 21-4-'46

152

TO THE WOMEN OF INDIA

The impatience of some sisters to join the good fight is to me a healthy sign. It has led to the discovery that however attractive the campaign against the Salt tax may be, for them to confine themselves to it would be to change a pound for a penny. They will be lost in the crowd, there will be in it no suffering for which they are thirsting.

In this non-violent warfare, their contribution should be much greater than men's. To call woman the weaker sex is a libel; it is man's injustice to woman. If by strength is meant brute strength, then indeed is woman less brute than man. If by strength, is meant moral power, then woman is immeasurably man's superior. Has she not greater intuition, is she not more self-sacrificing, has she not greater powers of endurance, has she not greater courage? Without her man could not be. If non-violence is the law of our being, the future is with woman.

I have nursed this thought now for years. When the women of the Ashram insisted on being taken along with men something within me told me that they were destined to do greater work in this struggle than merely breaking salt laws.

I feel that I have now found that work. The picketing of liquor shops and foreign cloth shops by men, though it succeeded beyond expectations up to a point for a time in 1921, failed because violence crept in. If a real impression is to be created, picketing must be resumed. If it remains peaceful to the end, it will be the quickest way of educating the people concerned. It must never be a matter of coercion but conversion, moral suasion. Who can make a more effective appeal to the heart than woman?

Prohibition of intoxicating liquors and drugs and boycott of foreign cloth have ultimately to be by law. But the law will not come till pressure from below is felt in no uncertain manner.

That both are vitally necessary for the nation, nobody will dispute. Drink and drugs sap the moral well-being of those who are given to the habit. Foreign cloth undermines the economic foundations of the nation and throws millions out of employment. The distress in each case is felt in the home and therefore by the women. Only those who have drunkards as their husbands know what havoc the drink devil works in homes that once were orderly and peace-giving. Millions of women in our hamlets know what unemployment means. Today the Charkha Sangha covers over one hundred thousand women against less than 10,000 men.

Let the women of India take up these two activities, specialize in them, they would contribute more than men to national freedom. They would have access of power and self-confidence to which they have hitherto been strangers.

Their appeal to the merchants and buyers of foreign cloth and to the liquor dealers and addicts to the habit cannot but melt their hearts. At any rate the women can never be suspected of doing or intending violence to these four classes. Nor can Government long remain supine to an agitation so peaceful and so resistless.

The charm will lie in the agitation being initiated and controlled exclusively by women. They may take and should get as much assistance as they need from men, but the men should be in strict subordination to them.

In this agitation thousands of women literate and illiterate can take part.

Highly educated women have in this appeal of mine an opportunity of actively identifying themselves with the massess and helping them both morally and materially.

They will find when they study the subject of foreign cloth boycott that it is impossible save through *khadi*. Mill-owners will themselves admit that mills cannot manufacture in the near future enough cloth for Indian requirements. Given a proper atmosphere, *khadi* can be manufactured in our villages, in our countless homes. Let it be the privilege of the women of India to produce this atmosphere by devoting every available minute to the spinning of yarn. The question of production of *khadi* is surely a question of spinning enough yarn. During the past ten days of the march under pressure of circumstances I have discovered the potency of the *takli* which I had not realized before. It is truly a wonder worker. In mere playfulness my companions have without interrupting any other activity spun enough yarn to weave 4 square yards per day of *khadi* of 12 counts. *Khadi* as a war measure is not to be beaten. The moral results of the two reforms are obviously great. The political result will be no less great. Prohibition of intoxicating drinks and drugs means the loss of twenty-five crores of revenue. Boycott of foreign cloth means the saving by India's millions of at least sixty crores. Both these achievements would monetarily be superior to the repeal of the Salt tax. It is impossible to evaluate the moral results of the two reforms.

"But there is no excitement and no adventure in liquor and foreign cloth picketing," some sisters may retort. Well, if they will put their whole heart into this agitation they will find more than enough excitement and adventure. Before they have done with the agitation, they might even find themselves in prison. It is not improbable that they may be insulted and even injured bodily. To suffer such insult and injury would be their pride. Such suffering if it comes to them will hasten the end.

If the women of India will listen and respond to my appeal, they must act quickly. If the all-India work cannot be undertaken at once, let those provinces which can organize themselves do so. Their example will be quickly followed by the other provinces.

Young India, 10-4-'30

153

WOMEN IN CONFERENCE

The conference of women on Sunday last at Dandi became a Congress as I had wanted it to be. Thanks to the Government prohibition against the Baroda territory cars plying between Navasari and Dandi, many had walked the full 12 miles to Dandi. The following resolutions were unanimously adopted :

1. This conference of the women of Gujarat assembled at Dandi on 13th April 1930 having heard Gandhiji, resolves that the women assembled will picket liquor and toddy shops of Gujarat and appeal to the shop-keepers and the shop-goers to desist from plying their trade or drinking intoxicating liquors as the case may be, and will similarly picket foreign cloth shops and appeal to the dealers and the buyers to desist from the practice of dealing in or buying foreign cloth as the case may be.

2. This conference is of opinion that boycott of foreign cloth is possible only through *khadi* and therefore the women assembled resolve henceforth to use *khadi* only and will so far as possible spin regularly and will learn all the previous processes and preach the message of *khadi* among their neighbours, teach them the processes up to spinning and encourage them to spin regularly.

3. This conference appoints the following Executive Committee * with power to draw up a constitution and to amend it from time to time and add to their number.

4. This conference hopes that women all over Gujarat and the other provinces will take up the movement initiated at this conference.

I regard this extension of the Swaraj movement as of the highest importance. I need not reiterate the argument already advanced in these pages. Mithubehn has already commenced operations. She is not the woman to let the grass grow under her feet. The idea is for twenty to twenty-five women to go in one batch and plant themselves near each liquor shop and come in personal contact with every visitor to the liquor or toddy shops, and wean them from the habit. They will also appeal to the shop-keepers

---

* The names were to be published later.

to give up the immoral traffic and earn their livelihood through better means.

Foreign cloth shops are to be treated in the same way as liquor shops as soon as there are enough trained women volunteers. Though the same committee will carry on the two boycotts it will necessarily have two branches. It will be open to any woman to offer her services for only one branch of work, nor is it necessary that every worker should belong to the Congress. Only this must be clearly understood, that the work is part of the Congress programme and has tremendous political results if it has also equally great moral and economic consequences.

Those who will belong to the foreign cloth boycott branch should realize that without the constructive work of *khadi* production the mere boycott will be a mischievous activity. Its very success without the production of *khadi* will prove the ruin of the national movement for independence. For the millions will take it up in simple faith. But they will curse us if they discover that they have no cloth to wear or the cloth they can get is too dear for their purse. The formula therefore is : Discard foreign cloth and make your own *khadi* and wear it. Already there is a dearth of *khadi*. Most of the *khadi* workers are in the salt campaign. Therefore the production has suffered a temporary check.

But there need never be any dearth of cloth the moment the country gets disabused of the superstition that it must buy cloth to cover its nakedness. It would be on a par with some one saying that we must starve if we cannot get Manchester or Delhi biscuits. Even as we cook our food and eat it so can we, if we but will it, make our own cloth and wear it. We did it only a hundred years ago and we can relearn the trick now. All the vital processes are almost too simple to learn. At this supreme crisis, this turning point in the nation's history, we must not hesitate and nurse idleness. I do not need to restate the argument about our mills. Even if every mill were genuinely Swadeshi and even if all became patriotic, they could not supply all our wants. Whichever way we look at it, whether we like it or not, we cannot escape *khadi* if we are to achieve independence through non-violent means and if we are to achieve the boycott of foreign cloth on which we began concentration in 1920.

Young India, 17-4-'30

154

MEN'S PART

[The following is a free rendering of extracts from my speech delivered before men just after the women's conference at Dandi on 13th instant. — M. K. G.]

I have just finished the women's conference. You will like to know what part we men may take in the women's movement. In the first place, we men may not meddle with the women's picketing of liquor and foreign cloth shops. If we do, we are likely to make a hash of it as we did in 1921. We can assist them in a variety of ways. The two classes of picketing have been designed to provide them with a special and exclusive field of activity. We can help by making the acquaintance of liquor and toddy dealers and interviewing them personally and asking them to give up the traffic now that the nation is going through the throes of a new birth. One can help also by showing greater and more delicate respect towards our women. Such general levelling up of the atmosphere will act upon the liquor dealer and also the foreign cloth dealer and buyer and the drinker, as neither will then be able to resist the appeal made to the heart by the gentle sex. In my opinion, these are virtues in which *women* excel men. *Ahimsa* is pre-eminently such a virtue. Woman exercises it naturally and intuitively when man reaches it through a laborious analytical process. Women left to themselves are likely quicker to reach the goal than if we men were to meddle with their picketing though we may help them with advice and guidance whenever they need them. Dr Sumant Mehta and Sjt. Kanjibhai have already undertaken that task.

But there is the constructive activity of the women, i.e. manufacture . of *khadi*. This is an activity which requires the assistance of every man, woman and child. We must all learn how to pick cotton, gin it, card it and spin it. These are all easy processes easily learnt if we have the will. It is no more difficult to learn than it is to cook or swim. Believe me there will be no boycott of foreign cloth, if we do not learn to manufacture *khadi* in our homes. The problem of *khadi* manufacture is the problem of every one becoming his or her own spinner. This natural and universal distribution of one simple process solves the whole of the problem of cloth supply. We have enough weavers in the land, we have not enough spinners. And when we have yarn spun from day to day by millions of hands, we men must approach the weavers and get them to weave it. This requires some organizing in the beginning. But it will be done as soon as we have made up our minds, as we have about the Salt tax.

So much for what we may and ought to do. Now for what we may never do. I have complaints from correspondents in Bombay that the forcible seizing of foreign caps from other people's heads has begun as happened in 1921. I do not know to what extent this is true. But whatever the extent, it must not be repeated. We may not use compulsion even in the matter of doing a good thing. Any compulsion will ruin the cause. I feel that we are within reach of the goal. But all the marvellous work done during this week of self-purification will be undone if the movement is vitiated by the introduction of compulsion. This is a movement of conversion, not of compulsion, even of the tyrant. We can offer Satyagraha against those whom we know as our friends or associates when they will not do a good thing or when they break promises. If you have the strength and the purity, you can offer Satyagraha, say by fasting, against your associates when they do not listen to a good thing. If I had the strength and the purity I should do so today against the nation. I confess I have not developed it to the extent required. It is not a mechanical art. Something within you impels you to it and then no one on earth can prevent you. I have no such impelling force as yet. If *you* have it, you can do it. I did it in 1921 when Bombay went mad. I did it in 1917 when the mill hands who had made a promise in the name of God were about to break it in a moment of weakness. In each case the act was spontaneous and its effect was electrical.

But this was a process of conversion. The exercise of compulsion by our men simply unnerves me and unfits me for service. This time whatever happens, the struggle has to go on. There is no turning back. But that is one thing and my capacity for service is another. I can promise not to suspend the movement but I have no capacity for promising not to die or collapse through sickness or weakness during the struggle. I admit that I am utterly weak in the face of any violence on our part and when I hear of any such thing, a doctor examining my pulse would at once detect a ruffle in the heart beat. It really takes a few moments, a waiting on God for help before I regain the normal beat of the heart. I cannot help this weakness of mine. Rather do I nurse it. This sensitiveness keeps me fit for service and true guidance, and keeps me humble and ever reliant on God. He only knows when I may become so upset and disconcerted by some violent act of ours as to declare a perpetual or temporary fast. It is the last weapon of a Satyagrahi against loved ones. If India continually takes resolutions in the name of God about non-violence, *khadi*, untouchability, communal unity and what not and as often denies God by breaking them, — India that has in her infatuation for me made me a *Mahatma*, — I do not know when God within may provoke me to offer the final Satyagraha against her who has loved me not wisely but too well. May the occasion never arise ; but if it does, may God give me the strength and the purity to undertake that final sacrifice.

155

NOTES

The Frontier Provinces

When I marched to Dandi, friends in the Frontier Provinces had offered to send some volunteers to help me. I sent them thanks in appreciation of their offer but did not avail myself of it. How nice perhaps it would have been if they had not actively participated in the movement. Those who not being sure of perfect non-violence being observed, do not take an active part in the struggle, are most assuredly helping it. Those who wanting to serve take part in it and violence results, as happened at Peshawar, are as assuredly harming the movement. That the people in Peshawar meant well I have no doubt. They are perhaps more impatient (if such a thing were possible) than I am to win freedom. But nobody can get freedom today in this land except through non-violence. We cannot get India's freedom through the way of violence ; we are within reach of it, if we would but keep up non-violence to the end. The way lies not through the burning of armoured cars and taking the lives of administrators of the Government machinery ; it lies through disciplined organized self-suffering. I deeply regret the occurrences in Peshawar. Brave lives have been thrown away without the cause itself being served.

Boycott and Picketing

There is a great deal of bartering among us. The position taken up by foreign cloth merchants is but a symptom of that spirit. They want to give up foreign cloth trade only if they can do so without suffering any loss. But patriotism does not admit of barter. People are expected like Dattatreya to face death, like Kachhalia in South Africa to face compulsory insolvency, like the late Gopabandhu Das and others, not known to fame, to face poverty, and like the widow of Viththalbhai of Ambheti to suffer the death of nearest and dearest ones. Therefore the reluctance of foreign cloth merchants to suffer losses, in my opinion, betrays want of real patriotism.

But the Delhi merchants contend that the local Congress Committee has bound itself to stop picketing under certain conditions. If that be so, the promise has to be fulfilled at any cost. If the word of a Congressman or a Congress organization cannot be relied upon, we shall ultimately lose the battle. Satyagraha means insistence on truth. Breach of promise is a base surrender of truth. I have therefore advised the parties that if they cannot agree as to the text of the promise, if any, to refer the matter to arbitration.

I understand, too, that in Delhi, they have resorted to mixed picketing. I have suggested that it should be confined only to women. It does not matter if picketing is suspended for want of sufficient women pickets. Every occasion for violence must be avoided. Men can produce, by careful propaganda and production of *khadi,* an irresistible atmosphere for the boycott. But picketing whereever it is done must be confined to women.

Young India, 1-5-'30

156

HOW TO DO THE PICKETING

1. At least ten women are required for picketing a liquor or foreign cloth shop. They must choose a leader from among themselves.

2. They should all first go in a deputation to the dealer and appeal to him to desist from carrying on the traffic and present him with leaflets setting forth facts and figures regarding drink or foreign cloth as the case may be. Needless to say the leaflets should be in the language understood by the dealer.

3. If the dealer refuses to suspend traffic, the volunteers should guard the shop leaving the passage free and make a personal appeal to the would-be purchasers.

4. The volunteers should carry banners or light boards bearing warnings in bold letters against buying foreign cloth or indulging in intoxicating drinks, as the case may be.

5. Volunteers should be as far as possible in uniforms.

6. Volunteers should at frequent intervals sing suitable *bhajans* bearing on the subject.

7. Volunteers should prevent compulsion or interference by men.

8. On no account should vulgarity, abuse, threat or unbecoming language be used.

9. The appeal must always be to the head and the heart, never to fear of force.

10. Men should on no account congregate near the place of picketing nor block the traffic. But they should carry on propaganda generally through the area against foreign cloth and drink. They should help and organize processions of women to parade through the area carrying the message of temperance and *khadi* and the necessity of boycott of drink and foreign cloth.

11. There should be at the back of these picketing units a network of organizations for spreading the message of the *takli* and the *charkha* and thinking out new leaflets and new lines of propaganda.

12. There should be an absolutely accurate and systematic account of all receipts and expenditure. This should be periodically audited. This again should be done by men under the supervision of women. The whole scheme pre-supposes on the part of men a genuine respect for women and sincere desire for their rise.

Young India, 24-4-'30

157

SOME PICKETING RULES

In picketing foreign cloth or intoxicating drinks and drugs, let it be remembered, that the aim is to convert the addict or the buyer. Our object is moral and economic reform. The political consequence is but a bye-product. If Lancashire ceased to send us its cloth and the Government ceased to use the *abkari* revenue for any purpose save that of weaning the drunkard or opium-eater from his vice, we should still be engaged in picketing work and allied propaganda. The following rules, therefore, must be read in that light :

1. In picketing shops your attention must be rivetted on the buyer.

2. You should never be rude to the buyer or the seller.

3. You may not attract crowds or form cordons.

4. Yours must be a silent effort.

5. You must seek to win over the buyer or the seller by your gentleness, not by the awe of numbers.

6. You may not obstruct traffic.

7. You may not cry *hai hai* or use other expressions of shame.

8. You should know every buyer and his address and occupation and penetrate his or her home and heart. This presupposes continuity of same picketers.

9. You should try to understand the difficulties of buyers and sellers, and where you cannot remove them you should report them to your superiors.

10. If you are picketing foreign cloth, you should have some *khadi* or at least a sample book with prices and should know the nearest *khadi* shop to which you could take the buyer. If the buyer does not wish to buy *khadi* and insists on mill cloth, you should direct the buyer to an indigenous mill-cloth seller.

11. You should have relevant literature upon your person for distribution among the buyers.

12. You should join or organize processions, lectures with or without magic lantern, *bhajan* parties etc.

13. You should keep an accurate diary of your day's work.

14. If you find your effort failing do not be disheartened but rely upon the universal law of cause and effect and be assured that no good thought, word or deed goes fruitless. To think well, to speak well is ours, reward is in the hands of God.

Young India, 19-3-'31

158

A STERN REPROOF

[To certain foreign-cloth dealers who presented Gandhiji with a purse and an address in Navasari Gandhiji administered the following reproof :]

This function appears to me to be to a great extent out of place and uncalled for. The association of merchants, dealers as they are in foreign cloth, ought not to have thought of presenting the address to me or the Sardar. The presentation, if it must be made, ought to be accompanied by a pledge that they would never in future have anything to do with foreign cloth and also the intimation that they have either burnt their present stock or sealed it. How can we, whose daily prayer is for the entire extinction of this trade, accept an address and a purse from dealers in it ? I would, therefore, plead with the friends to take back their purse and their address. The address affords no information about the association and reads as though it was a citizens' address. That smacks somewhat of a bogus translation, as I said to the Sardar. Satyagraha eschews all make-believe. I have no relish for the title of the *Mahatma* given me by the people, if only because I am unworthy of it but I have given myself a title of which I am proud. I call myself a Satyagrahi, and so I must live up to it. I cannot but utter the bitter truth, whenever there is an occasion for it. The acceptance of the purse and the address would be a bitter dose for me, as its presentation should be for you too. But, if I cannot convince you, I must ask you to take both of them back. I have had occasions in my life when I have practised Satyagraha against my brother and my wife, and today's occasion can be no exception. I would have to return the address and the purse, as I would return a title from a government with which I non-co-operate or a gift from a liquor seller. I want you to understand that I would compromise myself to the cause if I agreed to accept your address. I would, however, spare you a sudden shock, hold the address and the purse in trust for you. You can ponder over what I have said and decide whether you will present them on my terms or take them back because you will not give up foreign-cloth trade.

Young India, 19-3-'31

159

PICKETING

My critics are shocked over my recent remarks on picketing. They think that in describing as a species of violence the formation of a living wall of pickets in order to prevent the entry of persons into picketed places, I have contradicted my sayings and doings during the civil disobedience campaign. If such is really the case, my recent writing must be held as cancelling my comparatively remote sayings and doings. Though my body is deteriorating through age, no such law of deterioration, I hope, operates against wisdom which I trust is not only not deteriorating but even growing. Whether it is or not, my mind is clear on the opinion I have given on picketing. If it does not appeal to Congressmen, they may reject it, and if they do, they will violate the laws of peaceful picketing. But there is no discrepancy between my past practice and the present statement. When civil disobedience was first organized by me in South Africa, my companions discussed with me the question of picketing. The registration office had to be picketed in Johannesburg, and the suggestion made was that we should form there a living wall of pickets. I at once rejected the idea as violent. And pickets were posted in marked positions in a big public square so that no one could elude the eagle eyes of the pickets and yet every one could go to the registration office, if he liked, without touching any one. Reliance was put upon the force of public opprobrium which would be evoked by the publication of the names of the ' blacklegs '. This method was copied by me here when liquor shops were to be picketed. The work was specially entrusted to the women as better representatives of non-violence than men. Thus there was no question of the formation of a living wall. Many unauthorized things were no doubt done during those days as they are now. But I cannot recall a single instance in which I countenanced the kind of picketing condemned by the article that has come in for sharp criticism. And is there really any difficulty about regarding a living wall of pickets as naked violence ? What is the difference between force used against a man wanting to do a particular thing, and force exercised by interposing yourself between him and the deed ? When, during the non-co-operation days, the students in Banaras blocked the passage to the University gates I had to send a peremptory message and, if my recollection serves me right, I strongly condemned their action in the columns of *Young India*. Of course, I have no argument against those who hold different views from mine regarding violence and non-violence.

Harijan, 27-8-'38

WHEN IS PICKETING PEACEFUL ?

A correspondent writes :

"I find that here in Bombay this weapon of 'peaceful picketing' is being misused on the ground that peaceful picketing, with whatsoever just or unjust object it may be resorted to, is no offence. The aggrieved party against whom such picketing is aimed at. fails to get any protection either from the police or law. For instance, A happens to be a shop-keeper. B an employee of A, having no legal claim against A, threatens A with picketing his shop in case A does not accede to B's demands and actually, with the help of C and D posing as 'leaders', starts picketing A's shop and misleads A's customers, with a view to dissuading them from patronizing A's shop. Would such picketing, even though there be no actual physical force used, be termed 'peaceful' ? "

I cannot speak about the legality of such picketing, but I can say that such picketing cannot be called peaceful, i.e. non-violent. All picketing without indubitably just cause is violent even though no physical force is used. Picketing without such cause becomes a nuisance and interferes with the exercise of private right. Generally no picketing should be resorted to by individuals unless it is promoted by a responsible organization. Picketing like civil disobedience has its well-defined limits without a strict observance of which it becomes illegitimate and reprehensible.

Harijan, 2-12-'39

PICKETING AND LOVE

A writer in the public Press indignantly asks : " How can I reconcile picketing with my doctrine of love ? Is not picketing a form of violence or undue pressure ? " It can be that certainly. It has been that in several cases, I am sorry to say. But it has been also an act of love, I know. Several sisters and young lads have gone on picketing purely out of love. Nobody has accused me of hatred against Marwadis. Nobody can possibly accuse Sheth Jamnalalji of hatred against his own caste-men and fellow merchants. And yet both he and I are countenancing picketing of Marwadi foreign-cloth shops. When a daughter stands guard over her erring father, she does it purely out of love. The fact is, that there are certain acts that are common to all classes of men. And when they are not in themselves objectionable, the motive alone decides their quality.

Young India, 22-9-'21

162

STUDENTS' NOBLE SATYAGRAHA

In referring to the universality of Satyagraha I have time and again observed in these columns that it is capable of application in the social no less than in the political field. It may equally be employed against Government, society, or one's own family, father, mother, husband or wife, as the case may be. For it is the beauty of this spiritual weapon that when it is completely free from the taint of *himsa* and its use is actuated purely and solely by love it may be used with absolute impunity, in any connection and in any circumstance whatever. A concrete instance of its use against a social evil was furnished by the brave and spirited students of Dharmaj (in Kheda District) a few days back. The facts as gleaned from the various communications about the incident received by me were as follows :

A gentleman of Dharmaj, some days back, gave a caste dinner in connection with the twelfth-day ceremony of the death of his mother. It was preceded by a keen controversy about the subject among the young men of the place who shared with a number of other local inhabitants their strong dislike of this custom. They felt that on this occasion something must be done. Accordingly, most of them took all or some of the following three vows :

1.   Not to join their elders at the dinner or otherwise partake of the food served on that occasion.

2.   To fast on the day of the dinner as an emphatic protest against this practice.

3.   To bear patiently and cheerfully any harsh treatment that might be accorded to them by their elders for taking this step.

In pursuance of this decision quite a large number of students, including some children of tender age, fasted on the day on which the dinner was given and took upon themselves the wrath of their so-called elders. Nor was the step free from the dangers of serious pecuniary consequences to the students. The 'elders' threatened to stop the allowances of their boys and even to withdraw any financial aid that they were giving to local institutions, but the boys stood firm. As many as two hundred and eighty-five students thus refused to take part in the caste dinner and most of them fasted.

I tender my congratulations to these boys and hope that everywhere students will take a prominent part in effecting social reform. They hold in their pocket, as it were, the key to social reform and the protection of their religion just as they have in their possession the key to Swaraj — though they may not be aware of it owing to their negligence or carelessness. But I hope that the example set by the students of Dharmaj will awaken them to a sense of their power. In my opinion, the true *shraddha* of the deceased lady was performed by these young men fasting on that day, while those who gave the dinner wasted good money and set a bad example to the poor. The rich, moneyed class ought to use their God-given wealth for philanthropic purposes. They should understand that the poor cannot afford to give caste dinners on wedding or on funeral ceremonies. These bad practices have proved to be the ruin of many a poor man. If the money that was spent in Dharmaj on the caste dinner had been used for helping poor students, or poor widows, or for *khadi*, or cow-protection, or the amelioration of the 'untouchables', it would have borne fruit and brought peace to the departed soul. But as it is, the dinner has already been forgotten. It has profited nobody and it has caused pain to the students and the sensible section of the Dharmaj public.

Let no one imagine that the Satyagraha has gone in vain because it did not succeed in preventing the dinner in question from taking place. The students themselves knew that there was little possibility of their Satyagraha producing any immediate tangible result. But we may safely take it that if they do not let their vigilance go to sleep no *shethia* will again dare to give a post-mortem dinner. A chronic and long-standing social evil cannot be swept away at a stroke ; it always requires patience and perseverence.

When will the ' elders ' of our society learn to recognize the signs of the times ? How long will they be slaves to custom instead of using it as a means for the amelioration of society and the country ? How long will they keep their children divorced from a practical application of the knowledge which they are helping them to acquire ? When will they rescue their sense of right and wrong from its present state of trance and wake up and be *mahajans* in the true sense of the word ?

Young India, 1-3-'28

163
LIMITS OF SATYAGRAHA

A correspondent impatient to stop the marriages of aged men with young girls writes :

" This evil requires drastic remedies. Twenty-five young men of character should form themselves into a band of Satyagrahis, proceed to the place of the marriage eight or ten days before the event and plead with both the parties, with the heads of the caste organization, and with all concerned. They should parade the streets with suitable placards condemning such marriages and produce an atmosphere of opposition to the proposed marriage. They should persuade the people of the town or village to declare a peaceful boycott against the parties to the marriage, and court arrest or whatever other punishment that comes to them.

" Thus the Satyagrahi band would soon become a power in the locality, and these marriages would be a thing of the past."

The suggestion looks attractive, but I am afraid it cannot be of use on more than one occasion. Where lust and cupidity join hands the slaughter of the innocents becomes almost impossible to avoid. As soon as lustful old candidates for brides and the greedy parents get scent of the invasion of the Satyagrahi band, they will evade the band by performing the wedding secretly, and they will find enough priests and wedding guests to help them in the ceremony. The readers of *Navajivan* may be aware of an incident that happened some time ago. The old man in that case feigned contrition, and successfully threw dust into the eyes of all by a hollow public apology. The reformers were delighted, but before they had finished congratulating themselves the old man managed to get secretly married. What happened in one case may happen in many cases. We should, therefore, devise other means to grapple with the evil. I have an idea that it may be easier to reach the greedy father of the bride than the slave of his lust. There is a great necessity for cultivating public opinion in the matter. The parents who readily sell away their girls, out of cupidity, should be sought out and pleaded with, and caste organizations should be persuaded to pass resolutions condemning such marriages. Evidently such reforms cannot be carried out all at once by the same band in large areas. Their field must needs be circumscribed. A Satyagrahi band in Cape Comorin will not be able to prevent a monstrous marriage in Kashmir. The reformers will have, therefore, to recognize their limitations. We may not attempt the impossible.

Love and *ahimsa* are matchless in their effect. But in their play there is no fuss, show, noise or placards. They presuppose self-confidence which in its turn presupposes self-purification. Men of stainless character and self-purification will easily inspire confidence and automatically purify the atmosphere around them. I have long believed that social reform is a tougher business than political reform. The atmosphere is ready for the latter, people are interested in it, and there is an impression abroad that it is possible without self-purification. On the other hand, people have little interest in social reform, the result of agitation does not appear to be striking and there is little room for congratulations and addresses. The social reformers will have therefore to plod on for some time, hold themselves in peace, and be satisfied with apparently small results.

I may here throw out a practical suggestion. The most effective means of creating an atmosphere against the marriages of aged persons with young girls is to create public opinion against the actual marriage and to set in motion a peaceful social boycott against the aged bridegroom and the greedy father of the bride.

If a successful boycott can be carried out even in one single instance, parents will hesitate to sell their daughters and old men will hesitate to run after young brides.

It will not be easy to wean lustful old men from their lust. They may be, therefore, induced to marry old widows, if they must marry. In Europe old men easily seek out old widows.

In conclusion, we must be clear about our objective in opposing these marriages. It cannot be our object to wean old men from their lust ; if it is we will have first to deal with lustful young men. But that is a tall order. Our objective can be only to save young girls from the clutches of lustful old men and the cupidity of their parents. The reformer must, therefore, address himself to carrying on a crusade against the sale of brides. It is the bride's parents who have to be reached. Let the Satyagrahi, therefore, chalk out the field of his activities, have a census of all girls of a marriageable age living in that area, let him get into touch with their parents, and awaken them to a sense of their duty towards their daughters.

Let not the reformer go outside these limits if he wants to achieve success. The scheme proposed in the correspondent's letter easily transgresses these limits.

Young India, 6-9-'28

SATYAGRAHA AGAINST THE COLOUR BAR BILL

[With reference to the Colour Bar Bill which was due to be passed in South Africa, Gandhiji wrote :]

What are then our countrymen in South Africa to do ? There is nothing in the world like self-help. The world helps those who help themselves. Self-help in this case, as perhaps in every other, means self-suffering ; self-suffering means Satyagraha. When their honour is at stake, when their rights are being taken away, when their livelihood is threatened, they have the right and it becomes their duty to offer Satyagraha. They offered it during 1907 and 1914 and won the support even of the Government of India, indeed the recognition of the Europeans and the Government of South Africa. They can do likewise again if they have the will and the courage to suffer for the common good.

That time is not yet. They must, as they are doing, exhaust every diplomatic remedy. They must await the result of the negotiations the Government of India are carrying on with the Union Government. And when they have explored and tried every other available channel and failed to find a way out, the case for Satyagraha is complete. Then it would be cowardice to flinch. And victory is a certainty. No power on earth can make a person do a thing against his will. Satyagraha is a direct result of the recognition of this great Law and is independent of numbers participating in it.

Young India, 18-2-'26

THE JEWS

The German persecution of the Jews seems to have no parallel in history. Can the Jews resist this organized and shameless persecution? Is there a way to preserve their self-respect, and not to feel helpless, neglected and forlorn? I submit there is. No person who has faith in a living God need feel helpless or forlorn. Jehovah of the Jews is a God more personal than the God of the Christians, the Mussalmans or the Hindus, though, as a matter of fact, in essence, He is common to all and one without a second and beyond description. But as the Jews attribute personality to God and believe that He rules every action of theirs, they ought not to feel helpless. If I were a Jew and were born in Germany and earned my livelihood there, I would claim Germany as my home even as the tallest gentile German may, and challenge him to shoot me or cast me in the dungeon; I would refuse to be expelled or to submit to discriminating treatment. And for doing this, I should not wait for the fellow Jews to join me in civil resistance but would have confidence that in the end the rest are bound to follow my example. If one Jew or all the Jews were to accept the prescription here offered, he or they cannot be worse off than now. And suffering voluntarily undergone will bring them an inner strength and joy which no number of resolutions of sympathy passed in the world outside Germany can. Indeed even if Britain, France and America were to declare hostilities against Germany, they can bring no inner joy, no inner strength. The calculated violence of Hitler may even result in a general massacre of the Jews by way of his first answer to the declaration of such hostilities. But if the Jewish mind could be prepared for voluntary suffering, even the massacre I have imagined could be turned into a day of thanksgiving and joy that Jehovah had wrought deliverance of the race even at the hands of the tyrant. For to the God-fearing, death has no terror. It is a joyful sleep to be followed by a waking that would be all the more refreshing for the long sleep.

It is hardly necessary for me to point out that it is easier for the Jews than for the Czechs to follow my prescription. And they have in the Indian Satyagraha campaign in South Africa an exact parallel. There the Indians occupied precisely the same place that the Jews occupy in Germany. The persecution had also a religious tinge. President Kruger used to say that the white Christians were the chosen of God and Indians were inferior beings created to serve the whites. A fundamental clause in the Transvaal Constitution was that there should be no equality between the whites and coloured races including Asiatics. There too the Indians were consigned to ghettoes described as locations. The other disabilities were almost of the same type as those of the Jews in Germany. The Indians, a mere handful, resorted to Satyagraha without any backing from the world outside or the Indian Government. Indeed the British officials tried to dissuade the Satyagrahis from their contemplated step. World opinion and the Indian Government came to their aid after eight years of fighting. And that too was by way of diplomatic pressure not of a threat of war.

But the Jews of Germany can offer Satyagraha under infinitely better auspices than the Indians of South Africa. The Jews are a compact, homogeneous community in Germany. They are far more gifted than the Indians of South Africa. And they have organized world opinion behind them. I am convinced that if someone with courage and vision can arise among them to lead them in non-violent action, the winter of their despair can in the twinkling of an eye be turned into the summer of hope. And what has today become a degrading man-hunt can be turned into a calm and determined stand offered by unarmed men and women possessing the strength of suffering given to them by Jehovah. It will be then a truly religious resistance offered against the godless fury of dehumanized man. The German Jews will score a lasting victory over

the German gentiles in the sense that they will have converted the latter to an appreciation of human dignity.
They will have rendered service to fellow-Germans and
proved their title to be the real Germans as against those
who are today dragging, however unknowingly, the German name into the mire.

Harijan, 26-11-'38

166

THE SATYAGRAHA WAY WITH CRIME

A villager was brought to him with injuries on his
body, received at the hands of thieves who had taken
away ornaments etc. from his house. There were three
ways, Gandhiji told the villagers of Uruli, of dealing with
the case. The first was the stereotyped orthodox way of
reporting to the police. Very often, it only provided the
police a further opportunity for corruption and brought
no relief to the victim. The second way, which was followed by the general run of the village people, was to
passively acquiesce in it. This was reprehensible as it
was rooted in cowardice. Crime would flourish, while
cowardice remained. What was more, by such acquiescence we ourselves became party to the crime. The
third way, which Gandhiji commended, was that of pure
Satyagraha. It required that we should regard even
thieves and criminals as our brothers and sisters, and
crime as a disease of which the latter were the victims
and needed to be cured. Instead of bearing ill-will towards
a thief or a criminal and trying to get him punished they
should try to get under his skin, understand the cause that
had led him into crime and try to remedy it. They should,
for instance, teach him a vocation and provide him with
the means to make an honest living and thereby transform
his life. They should realize that a thief or a criminal
was not a different being from themselves. Indeed, if they
turned the searchlight inward and closely looked into their

own souls, they would find that the difference between them was only one of degree. The rich, moneyed man who made his riches by exploitation or other questionable means, was no less guilty of robbery than the thief who picked a pocket or broke into a house and committed theft. Only the former took refuge behind the facade of respectability and escaped the penalty of law. Strictly speaking, remarked Gandhiji, all amassing or hoarding of wealth, above and beyond one's legitimate requirements was theft. There would be no occasion for thefts and, therefore, no thieves, if there was a wise regulation of riches and absolute social justice prevailed. In the Swaraj of his conception, there would be no thieves and no criminals, or else it would be Swaraj only in name. The criminal was only an indication of the social malady and since nature cure, as he envisaged it, included the triple cure for body, mind and soul, they must not be satisfied with merely banishing physical illness from Uruli, their work must include the healing of the mind and soul, too, so that there would be perfect social peace in their midst.

The Way of Satyagraha

If they followed the nature-cure way of dealing with the criminal, which, as he had already explained, was the way of Satyagraha, they could not sit still in the face of crime. Only a perfect being could afford to lose himself within himself and withdraw completely from the cares and responsibilities of the world. But who could claim that perfection ? " On the high sea a sudden calm is always regarded by experienced pilots and mariners with concern. Absolute calm is not the law of the ocean. It is the same with the ocean of life. More often than not, it portends rough weather. A Satyagrahi would, therefore, neither retaliate nor would he submit to the criminal, but seek to cure him by curing himself. He will not try to ride two horses at a time, viz. to pretend to follow the law of Satyagraha, while at the same time, seek police aid. He must forswear the latter, in order to follow the former. If the criminal himself chooses to hand himself over to the police, it would be a different matter. You cannot expect to touch his heart and win his confidence, if at the same time you are prepared to go to the police and inform against him. That would be gross betrayal of trust. A reformer cannot afford to be an informer." And by way of illustration, he mentioned several instances of how he had refused to give information to the police, about persons who had been guilty of violence and came and confessed to him. No police officer could compel a Satyagrahi to give evidence against a person who had confessed to him. A Satyagrahi would never be guilty of a betrayal of trust. He wanted the people of Uruli to adopt the method of Satyagraha for dealing with crime and criminals. They should contact the criminals in their homes, win their confidence and trust by loving and selfless service, wean them from evil and unclean habits and help to rehabilitate them by teaching them honest ways of living.

Harijan, 11-8-'46

167

SOCIALISM AND SATYAGRAHA

Truth and *ahimsa* must incarnate in socialism. In order that they can, the votary must have a living faith in God. Mere mechanical adherence to truth and *ahimsa*, is likely to break down at the critical moment. Hence have I said that truth is God. This God is a living Force. Our life is of that Force. That Force resides in, but is not the body. He who denies the existence of that great Force, denies to himself the use of that inexhaustible Power and thus remains impotent. He is like a rudderless ship which, tossed about here and there, perishes without making any headway. The socialism of such takes them nowhere, what to say of the society in which they live.

The fact is that it has always been a matter of strenuous research to know this great Force and its hidden possibilities.

My claim is that in the pursuit of that search lies the discovery of Satyagraha. It is not, however, claimed that all the laws of Satyagraha have been laid down or found. This I do say, fearlessly and firmly, that every worthy object can be achieved by the use of Satyagraha. It is the highest and infallible means, the greatest force. Socialism will not be reached by any other means. Satyagraha can rid society of all evils, political, economic and moral.

Harijan, 20-7-'47

168

SOME QUESTIONS

With reference to the imminent civil disobedience some pertinent questions have been put by friends as well as critics. These need answering.

Q. Surely you are not so impatient as to start your campaign without letting the authorities know your plans and giving them an opportunity of meeting you and arresting you ?

A. Those who know my past should know that I hold it to be contrary to Satyagraha to do anything secretly or impatiently. My plans will be certainly sent to the Viceroy before I take any definite step. A Satyagrahi has no secrets to keep from his opponent or so-called enemy.

Q. Did you not say even at Lahore that the country was not prepared for civil disobedience, especially, no-tax campaign on a mass scale ?

A. I am not even now sure that it is. But it has become clear to me as never before that the unpreparedness in the sense that a non-violent atmosphere is wanting will as time goes by, very likely increase as it has been increasing all these years. Young men are impatient. I know definitely many stayed their violent designs because in 1921 the Congress had decided to offer civil disobedience. That school has been more active than before because of my repeated declarations that the country was not prepared for civil disobedience. I feel then that if non-violence is an active force, as I know it is, it should work even in the face of the most violent atmosphere. One difficulty in the way was that the Congress claiming to represent the whole nation could not very well offer civil disobedience and disown

354

responsibility for violence especially by Congressmen. I have procured discharge from that limitation by taking over the responsibility for launching on civil disobedience. I represent no one but myself and at the most those whom I may enrol for the campaign. And I propose at present to confine myself only to those who are amenable to the Ashram discipline and have actually undergone it for some time. It is true that I may not shirk responsibility indirectly for any violence that may break out on the part of the nation and in the course of the campaign. But such responsibility will always be there and can be only a degree more than the responsibility I share with the British rulers in their sins against the nation in so far as I give my co-operation however reluctantly and ever so slightly. For instance I give my co-operation by paying taxes direct or indirect. The very salt I eat compels my voluntary co-operation. Moreover it has dawned on me never so plainly as now that if my non-violence has suffered the greatest incarnation of violence which the British Imperialistic rule is, it must suffer the crude and ineffective violence of the impatient patriots who know not that by their ineffectiveness they are but helping that imperialistic rule and enabling it to consolidate the very thing they seek to destroy. I see now as clearly as daylight that my non-violence working as it has done against the British misrule has shaken it somewhat. Even so will it shake the counter-violence of the patriot if taking courage in both my hands I set my non-violence actively in motion, i.e., civil disobedience. I reduce the risk of the outbreak of counter-violence to a minimum by taking sole charge of the campaign. After all is said and done, however, I feel the truth of the description given to my proposal by the *Times of India*. It is indeed 'the last throw of a gambler'. I have been a 'gambler' all my life. In my passion for finding the truth and in relentlessly following out my faith in non-violence, I have counted no stake too great. In doing so I have erred, if at all, in the company of the most distinguished scientist of any age and any clime.

Q. But what about your much vaunted faith in Hindu-Muslim unity ? Of what value will even independence be without that unity ?

A. My faith in that unity is as bright as ever. I do not want independence at the cost even of the weakest minority, let alone the powerful Mussalman and the no less powerful Sikh. The Lahore Congress resolution on unity finally sums up all its previous effort in that behalf. The Congress rules out all solutions proposed on a communal basis. But if it is ever compelled to consider such a solution it will consider only that, which will give (not merely justice) but satisfaction to all the parties concerned. To be true to its word, therefore, the Congress cannot accept any scheme of independence that does not give satisfaction, so far as communal rights are concerned, to the parties concerned. The campaign that is about to be launched is calculated to generate power for the whole nation to be independent. But it will not be in fact till all the parties have combined. To postpone civil disobedience which has nothing to do with communalism till the latter is set at rest will be to move in a vicious circle and defeat the very end that all must have in view. What I am hoping is that the Congress being free from the communal incubus will tend it, if it remains true to the nation as a whole, to become the strongest centre party jealously guarding the rights of the weakest members. Such a Congress will have only servants of the nation, not office-seekers. Till independence is achieved or till unity is reached it will have nothing to do with any office or favours from the Government of the day in competition with the minorities. Happily the Congress has now nothing to do with the legislatures which have perhaps more than anything else increased communal bitterness. It is no doubt unfortunate that at the present moment the Congress contains largely only the Hindu element. But if the Congress Hindus cease to think communally and will take no advantage that cannot be shared to the full with all the other communities, it will presently disarm all suspicion and will attract to itself the noblest among

Mussalmans, Sikhs, Parsis, Christians, Jews and all those who are of India. But whether the Congress ever approaches this ideal or not, my course is, as it always has been, perfectly clear. This unity among all is no new love with me. I have treasured it, acted up to it from my youth upward. When I went to London as a mere lad in 1889 I believed in it as passionately as I do now. When I went to South Africa in 1893 I worked it out in every detail of my life. Love so deep seated as it is in me will not be sacrificed even for the realm of the whole world. Indeed this campaign should take the attention of the nation off the communal problem and rivet it on the things that are common to all Indians, no matter to what religion or sect they may belong.

Q. Then you will raise, if you can, a force ultimately hostile to the British ?

A. Never. My love for non-violence is superior to every other thing mundane or supramundane. It is equalled only by my love for Truth which is to me synonymous with non-violence through which and which alone I can see and reach Truth. My scheme of life, if it draws no distinction between different religionists in India, it also draws none between different races. For me " man is a man for a' that." I embark upon the campaign as much out of my love for the Englishman as for the Indian. By self-suffering I seek to convert him, never to destroy him.

Q. But may not all this be your hallucination that can never come to pass in this matter-of-fact world of ours ?

A. It may well be that. It is not a charge wholly unfamiliar to me. My hallucinations in the past have served me well. This last is not expected to fail me. If it does, it will but harm me and those who may come or put themselves under its influence. If my hallucination is potent to the authorities, my body is always at their disposal. If owing to my threatened action any Englishman's life is put in greater danger than it is now, the arm of English authority is long enough and strong enough to overtake any outbreak that may occur between Kashmir

and Cape Comorin or Karachi and Dibrugarh. Lastly,
no campaign need take place, if all the politicians and
editors instead of addressing themselves to me will address
themselves to the authorities and ask them to undo the
continuing wrongs some of which I have inadequately
described in these pages.

Young India, 20-2-'30

169

ON NON-VIOLENCE

Questions in Paris and Geneva

" In the method we are adopting in India, fraud,
lying, deceit and all the ugly brood of violence and
untruth have absolutely no room. Everything is done
openly and above board, for truth hates secrecy. The
more open you are the more truthful you are likely to be.
There is no such thing as defeat or despair in the dictionary
of a man who bases his life on truth and non-violence.
And yet the method of non-violence is not in any shape
or form a passive or inactive method. It is essentially
an active movement, much more active than the one in-
volving the use of sanguinary weapons. Truth and non-
violence are perhaps the activest forces you have in the
world. A man who wields sanguinary weapons and is
intent upon destroying those whom he considers his
enemies, does at least require some rest and has to lay
down his arms for a while in every twenty-four hours.
He is, therefore, essentially inactive, for a certain part
of the day. Not so the votary of truth and non-violence,
for the simple reason that they are not external weapons.
They reside in the human breast and they are actively
working their way whether you are awake or whether you
are asleep, whether you are walking leisurely or playing
an active game. The panoplied warrior of truth and non-
violence is ever and incessantly active."

" How then can one be effectively non-violent ? By
simply refusing to take up arms ? "

" I would say that merely to refuse military service is not enough. To refuse to render military service when the particular time arrives is to do the thing after all the time for combating the evil is practically gone. Military service is only a symptom of the disease which is deeper. I suggest to you that those who are not on the register of military service are equally participating in the crime if they support the State otherwise. He or she who supports a State organized in the military way — whether directly or indirectly — participates in the sin. Each man old or young takes part in the sin by contributing to the maintenance of the State by paying taxes. That is why I said to myself during the war that so long as I ate wheat supported by the army whilst I was doing everything short of being a soldier, it was best for me to enlist in the army and be shot ; otherwise I should retire to the mountains and eat food grown by nature. Therefore, all those who want to stop military service can do so by withdrawing all co-operation. Refusal of military service is much more superficial than non-co-operation with the whole system which supports the State. But then one's opposition becomes so swift and so effective that you run the risk of not only being marched to jail, but of being thrown into the streets."

" Then may not one accept the non-military services of the State ? "

" Now," said Gandhiji, " you have touched the tenderest spot in human nature. I was faced with the very question as author of the non-co-operation movement. I said to myself, there is no State either run by Nero or Mussolini which has not good points about it, but we have to reject the whole, once we decide to non-co-operate with the system. There are in our country grand public roads, and palatial educational institutions, said I to myself, but they are part of a system which crushes the nation. I should not have anything to do with them. They are like the fabled snake with a brilliant jewel on its head, but which has fangs full of poison. So I came to the conclusion that the British rule in India had crushed the spirit of the nation and stunted its growth, and so I decided to deny myself all the privileges — services, courts, titles. The policy would vary with different countries but sacrifice and self-denial are essential."

"But is there not a big difference between an independent nation and a subject nation ? India may have a fundamental quarrel with an alien Government, but how can the Swiss quarrel with their State ? "

"Difference there undoubtedly is," said Gandhiji. "As a member of a subject nation I could best help by shaking myself rid of my subjection. But here I am asked as to how best to get out of a military mentality. You are enjoying your amenities on condition that you render military service to the State. There you have to get the State rid of its military mentality."

In answer to a similar question at another meeting Gandhiji said : "Non-co-operation in military service and service in non-military matters are not compatible. 'Definitely' military service is an ill-chosen word. You are all the while giving military service by deputy because you are supporting a State which is based on military service. In Transvaal and other countries some are debarred from military service, but they have to pay money to the State. You will have to extend the scope of non-co-operation to your taxes."

"How could a disarmed neutral country allow other nations to be destroyed ? But for our army which was waiting ready at our frontier during the last war we should have been ruined."

"At the risk of being considered a visionary or a fool I must answer this question in the only manner I know. It would be cowardly of a neutral country to allow an army to devastate a neighbouring country. But there are two ways in common between soldiers of war and soldiers of non-violence, and if I had been a citizen of Switzerland and a President of the Federal State what I would have done would be to refuse passage to the invading army by refusing all supplies. Secondly, by re-enacting a Thermopylae in Switzerland, you would have presented a living wall of men and women and children and invited the invaders to walk over your corpses. You may say that such a thing is beyond human experience and endurance. I say that it is not so. It was quite possible. Last year in Gujarat women stood *lathi* charges unflinchingly and in Peshawar thousands stood hails of bullets without resorting to violence. Imagine these men and women staying in front of an army requiring a safe passage to another country. The army would be brutal enough to walk over them, you might say. I would then say you will still have done your duty by allowing yourself to be annihilated. An army that dares to pass over the corpses of innocent men and women would not be able to repeat that experiment. You may, if you wish, refuse to believe in such courage on the part of the masses of men and women, but then you would have to admit that non-violence is made of sterner stuff. It was never conceived as a weapon of the weak, but of the stoutest hearts."

" Is it open to a soldier to fire in the air and avoid violence ? "

" A soldier who having enlisted himself flattered himself that he was avoiding violence by shooting in the air did no credit to his courage or to his creed of non-violence. In my scheme of things such a man would be held to be guilty of untruth and cowardice both — cowardice in that in order to escape punishment he enlisted, and untruth in that he enlisted to serve as soldier and did not fire as expected. Such a thing discredits the cause of waging war against war. The War Resisters have to be like Caesar's wife — above suspicion. Their strength lies in absolute adherence to the morality of the question."

Young India, 31-12-'31

170

WHAT ARE BASIC ASSUMPTIONS

An esteemed correspondent, who has for years been following, as a student, the non-violent action of the Congress and who ultimately joined the Congress, expresses certain doubts with lucid argument. Whilst the argument is helpful to me it is unnecessary to reproduce it here. He lays down three basic assumptions and argues that India is hardly able to satisfy these assumptions under all circumstances.

The suggested basic assumptions are :

" 1. Complete unity of the people in their desire and demand for freedom ;

" 2. Complete appreciation and assimilation of the doctrine in all its implications by the people as a whole with consequent control over one's natural instincts for resort to violence either in revenge or as a measure of self-defence ; and (this is the most important of all).

" 3. Implicit belief that the sight of suffering on the part of multitudes of people will melt the heart of the aggressor and induce him to desist from his course of violence."

For the application of the remedy of non-violence complete unity is not an indispensable condition. If it was, the remedy would possess no special virtue. For complete unity will bring freedom for the asking. Have I not said repeatedly in the columns of *Young India* and these columns that even a few true Satyagrahis would suffice to bring us freedom? I have maintained that we would require a smaller army of Satyagrahis than that of soldiers trained in modern warfare, and the cost will be insignificant compared to the fabulous sums devoted by nations to armaments.

Nor is the second assumption necessary. Satyagraha by the vast mass of mankind will be impossible if they had all to assimilate the doctrine in all its implications. I cannot claim to have assimilated all its implications nor do I claim even to know them all. A soldier of an army does not know the whole of the military science ; so also does a Satyagrahi not know the whole science of Satyagraha. It is enough if he trusts his commander and honestly follows his instructions and is ready to suffer unto death without bearing malice against the so-called enemy.

The third assumption has to be satisfied. I should word it differently, but the result would be about the same.

My friend says there is no historical warrant for the third assumption. He cites Ashoka as a possible exception. For my purpose, however, Ashoka's instance is unnecessary. I admit that there is no historical instance to my knowledge. Hence it is that I have been obliged to claim uniqueness for the experiment. I have argued from the analogy of what we do in families or even clans. The humankind is one big family. And if the love expressed is intense enough it must apply to all mankind. If individuals have succeeded even with savages, why should not a group of individuals succeed with a group, say, of savages ? If we can succeed with the English, surely it is merely an extension of faith to believe that we are likely to succeed with less cultured or less liberally-minded nations. I hold that if we succeed with the English, with unadulterated non-violent effort, we must succeed with the others, or which is the same thing as saying that if we achieve freedom with non-violence, we shall defend it also with the same weapon. If we have not achieved that faith our non-violence is a mere expedient, it is alloy, not pure gold.

Harijan, 22-10-'38

171

BELIEF IN GOD

In his inaugural address before the annual conference
of the Gandhi Seva Sangh at Brindavan (Bihar), Gandhiji
had said that belief in God was one of the indispensable
qualifications of a Satyagrahi. One of the members asked
if some of the Socialists and Communists who did not
believe in God could not be Satyagrahis.

"I am afraid not. For a Satyagrahi has no other
stay but God, and he who has any other stay or depends
on any other help cannot offer Satyagraha. He may be
a passive resister, non-co-operator and so on, but not a
true Satyagrahi. It is open to you to argue that this excludes brave comrades, whereas it may include men who
profess a belief in God but who in their daily lives are
untrue to their profession. I am not talking of those who
are untrue to their profession, I am talking of those who
are prepared in the name of God to stake their all for
the sake of their principle. Don't ask me again why I am
enunciating this principle today and did not do so 20 years
ago. I can only say that I am no prophet, I am but an
erring mortal, progressing from blunder towards truth.
'What about the Buddhists and Jains, then?' someone
has asked. Well, I will say that if the Buddhists and
Jains raise this objection themselves, and say that they
would be disqualified if such a strict rule were observed,
I should say to them that I agree with them.

"But far be it from me to suggest that you should believe in the God that I believe in. Maybe your definition is
different from mine, but your belief in that God must be
your ultimate mainstay. It may be some Supreme Power
or some Being even indefinable, but belief in it is indispensable. To bear all kinds of tortures without a murmur
of resentment is impossible for a human being without
the strength that comes from God. Only in His strength
we are strong. And only those who can cast their cares

and their fears on that immeasurable Power have faith in God."

Other Conditions of Satyagraha

But someone may not be a *khadi*-wearer and yet his heart may be fired with patriotism. He may even have given up his legal practice and yet may not be a *khadi*-wearer. What about him ?

" Such a one may be an estimable man. But why should he do civil disobedience ? There are various ways of service. Millions need not be civil resisters. The field of constructive work is open to them. Some special rigid discipline is necessary for civil resisters. The privilege of resisting or disobeying a particular law or order accrues only to him who gives willing and unswerving obedience to the laws laid down for him. This may exclude men who may be otherwise far worthier than the common men who observe the Satyagrahi's code. Those others may perform worthier tasks, but not civil disobedience."

On another occasion speaking on the same topic and in the same strain he said : " You know that word *Himalayan blunder* which has now passed into the English language and is flung at me on all occasions. It was coined by me to translate a Gujarati word. I had to condemn my own blunder in placing civil disobedience before the people in Kheda and Ahmedabad in 1919. In Kheda the proportion of crime is greater than in any other district. These people with cries of *Mahatma Gandhiji ki jai* on their lips pulled out rails and derailed trains and, but for a lucky accident, would have killed hundreds of soldiers. The mill workmen in Ahmedabad did likewise. A false rumour was spread that Anasuyabehn was arrested or assaulted. They attacked police stations, seized an English sergeant, killed him and burnt him on the streets ; they burnt telegraph offices and did much other damage. I realized that I had committed a Himalayan blunder in placing civil disobedience before those who had never learnt the art of civil disobedience. The art comes instinctively to those who are by nature law-abiding. I was by nature law-abiding. In South Africa I was neither desirous of registering the births of my children nor of getting them vaccinated. But I obeyed the laws. Then I became a confirmed anti-vaccinationist. In jail it was no easy thing to defy the rule regarding vaccination. But they respected my conscientious objection, because they knew that I had systematically respected all the civil and moral laws of the State. It is from this obedience that the capacity for civil defiance springs, and therefore my civil disobedience sits well upon me."

There were still more questions. " There is one who believes in *ahimsa* and truth, satisfies other conditions, but is compelled by circumstances, say, to sell foreign cloth. Would he come under the ban ? "

" Of course. We cannot be too strict in this matter."

" And what is the scope of freedom from bad habits ? Is tobacco-smoking a bad habit ? Or *pan**-chewing ? "

" I may not fix the limit. It must be understood that all intoxicants warp or cloud a man's intellect, and he who allows his intellect to be warped or clouded cannot offer Satyagraha. But I will not be judge in this matter. *Ganja, bhang,* opium, etc. are recognized intoxicants and come under prohibition. Not so tobacco, though I cannot quite understand how men can bear to foul their mouths with smoking and tobacco-chewing."

" Is it permissible to offer Satyagraha in jail against inhuman treatment ? "

" It is, but inhuman treatment is a very difficult term to define and anything and everything may not come under it. A Satyagrahi goes prepared to put up with tortures, brutal treatments, even humiliations, but he may do nothing that outrage his sense of self-respect or honour. However, Satyagraha is not a weapon to be used lightly or easily and at the slightest provocation. It is better that he who is easily provoked does not go to jail."

Harijan, 3-6-'39

---

* A kind of leaf chewed by people with slacked lime and betel nut.

NOT GUILTY

Dr Lohia has sent me a long well-reasoned letter on the current controversy on the Congress resolution on Satyagraha. There is a portion in it which demands public discussion. Here it is :

> " You will not permit the slightest separation of the principle of Satyagraha from your own specific programme. Is it not possible to universalize the principle of Satyagraha, to make it the bed-rock of programmes other than your own ? Perhaps, it is not; but I have this argument against you that you have not permitted and encouraged any such experiment. The people today do not regard your own programme of ministerial action and constructive activities as wholly adequate ; they are experimenting with such programmes as those of peasant action. These newer programmes entail an amount of local and isolated action even during such times when there is no general Satyagraha. Will you stop these little Satyagrahas till you have found the formula for a general Satyagraha ? In such a course of action there is the danger of anarchy that arises out of suppression. Non-violent collective action is among the rarest and most precious gifts received by mankind in all history ; we may not, however, know how to treasure it and continue it."

Not only have I not prohibited separation of the principle of Satyagraha from my own specific programme, I have often invited new programmes. But hitherto I have not known a single case of any new programme. I have never suggested that there can never be any departure from or addition to my programme. What, however, I have said and would like to repeat here is that I cannot bless or encourage a new programme that makes no appeal to me. My programme I claim is a deduction from the Satyagraha of my conception. It is therefore likely that if there was any such vital activity favouring the growth of Satyagraha, it would not escape me.

I am painfully conscious of the fact that my programme has not made a general appeal to the Congress intelligentsia. I have already pointed out that the reason for the apathy of Congressmen is not to be sought in any inherent defect in the programme, but that it is due to the want of a living faith in *ahimsa*. What can be more patent than that we should have complete communal harmony, eradication of untouchability, sacrifice of the drink revenue by the closing of liquor shops, and the replacement of mill cloth by *khadi*? I suggest that non-violent Swaraj is impossible if Hindus, Muslims and others do not shed their mutual distrust and do not live as blood-brothers, if Hindus do not purify themselves by removing the curse of untouchability and thus establish intimate contact with those whom they have for ages put beyond the pale of society, if the wealthy men and women of India will not tax themselves so that the poor who are helpless victims of the drink and drug habit may have the temptation removed from them by the closing of drink and drug shops, and, lastly, if we all will not identify ourselves with the semi-starved millions by giving up the taste for mill cloth and revert to *khadi* produced by the many million hands in the cottages of India. In all that has been written against the constructive programme, I have not come across a single convincing argument against either its intrinsic merit or its merit in terms of non-violent Swaraj. I make bold to say that if all Congressmen concentrate themselves on this constructive programme, we shall soon have the requisite non-violent atmosphere throughout the length and breadth of the land for cent per cent Satyagraha.

Take the peasant action suggested by Dr Lohia as a possible new programme. I regret to have to say that in most cases the peasants are not being educated for non-violent action. They are being kept in a state of perpetual excitement and made to entertain hopes which can never be fulfilled without a violent conflict. The same may safely be said about labour. My own experience tells me that both the peasantry and labour can be organized for effective non-violent action, if Congressmen honestly work for it. But they cannot, if they have no faith in the ulti-mate success of non-violent action. All that is required is the proper education of the peasantry and labour. They need to be informed that if they are properly organized they have more wealth and resources through their labour than the capitalists through their money. Only capitalists have control over the money market, labour has not over its labour market, although if labour had been well served by its chosen leaders, it would have become conscious of the irresistible power that comes from proper instruction in non-violence. Instead, labour in many cases is being taught to rely on coercive methods to compel compliance with its demands. The kind of training that labour generally receives today leaves it in ignorance, and relies upon violence as the ultimate sanction. Thus it is not possible for me to regard the present peasant or labour activity as a new programme for the preparation of Satyagraha.

Indeed what I see around me is not preparation for a non-violent campaign but for an outbreak of violence, however unconscious or unintended it may be. If I was invited to hold myself responsible for this ending to the past twenty years' effort, I should have no hesitation in pleading guilty. Have I not said as much already in these columns? But my admission will not take us anywhere, unless it results in the retracing of our steps, the undoing of the wrong already done. This means having a reasoned faith in the non-violent method as the only means of gaining complete independence. When we have that faith, all bickerings within the Congress will cease, there will be no longer an ungainly scramble for power, and there will be mutual help instead of mutual mud-flinging. But it may be that Congressmen have come to believe that non-violence of my definition is played out or is not possible of attainment. In that case there should be a conference, formal or informal, between all Congress groups or a special meeting of the A. I. C. C. to consider the question whether time has not come to revise the policy of non-violence and the consequent constructive programme and to find out and frame a programme in consonance with and answering the present temper of Congressmen.

Harijan, 29-7-'39

173

QUESTION BOX

A Domestic Difficulty

Q. You have rightly said that no one who has not renounced untouchability in every shape and form can take part in Satyagraha. Supposing a Congressman's wife does not share his conviction in this regard and won't let him bring Harijans into his house, what should he do — coerce his wife into conformity with his views, renounce her, or renounce the Satyagraha struggle?

A. No occasion for coercing your wife. You should let her go her way and you should go yours. This would mean her having a separate kitchen for herself and, if she likes, also a separate room. Thus there is no question of renouncing the struggle.

The More Essential

Q. Which is the more essential requirement in your mind for starting civil disobedience — your inner urge which may make you fight even single-handed, or the fulfilment of your conditions by Congressmen? What will be the position if they are prepared and you have not felt the call?

A. There can be no inner urge if my conditions are not fulfilled. It is possible that there may be apparent fulfilment of conditions but there may be no inner response in me. In such a case I cannot declare civil disobedience; but it will be open to the Congress to repudiate me and declare civil disobedience independently of me.

Secrecy

Q. You should give your opinion clearly about secrecy. During the last struggle there was a great deal of secrecy to outwit the authorities.

A. I am quite clear that secrecy does no good to our cause. It certainly gave joy to those who were able successfully to outwit the police. Their cleverness was undoubted. But Satyagraha is more than cleverness. Secrecy takes away from its dignity. Satyagrahis have no reason to have secret books or secret funds. I am aware that my opinion has not found favour among many co-workers. But I have seen no reason to change it. I admit I was lukewarm before. Experience has taught me that I should have been firm.

Damage to Property

Q. You know that many Congressmen openly preached that there was no violence in damaging property, i.e. destroying rails, burning *thanas* when they are not occupied, cutting telegraph poles, burning post boxes, etc.

A. I have never been able to understand this reasoning. It is pure violence. Satyagraha is self-suffering and not inflicting suffering on others. There is surely often more violence in burning a man's property than doing him physical injury. Have not so-called Satyagrahis preferred imprisonment to fines or confiscation of their property? Well has one of my critics said that I have succeeded in teaching disruptive disobedience till at last it has come home to roost, but that I have signally failed in teaching people the very difficult art of non-violence. He has also said that in my haste I have put the cart before the horse and therefore all my talk of civil disobedience is folly if not worse. I am not able to give a satisfactory reply to this criticism. I am but a poor mortal. I believe in my experiment and in my uttermost sincerity. But it may be that the only fitting epitaph after my death will be " He tried but signally failed."

Harijan, 13-4-'40

174

QUESTION BOX

Spinning Regularly

Q. What do you mean by 'spinning regularly'? If one spins for a couple of hours during a month or for half an hour once or twice a week, would he be deemed to have satisfied the condition about spinning regularly?

A. 'Regularly' was put in the place of 'daily'. This was meant to provide for accidental or unavoidable omissions. Therefore, spinning every week or at stated intervals will not meet the case. A Satyagrahi will be expected to spin daily except for valid reasons such as sickness, travelling or the like.

Satyagraha Camps and Untouchability

Q. Satyagraha camps are being organized for the training of volunteers all over the country. But the principle with regard to the renunciation of untouchability in every shape and form is not being rigorously enforced. Don't you agree that it ought to be made an absolute rule in the camps that no one who regards the touch of Harijans as polluting and does not freely mix with them should be permitted to attend them?

A. I have no hesitation whatsoever in saying that he who has the slightest untouchability in him is wholly unfit for enrolment in the Satyagraha *sena*. I regard untouchability as the root cause of our downfall and of Hindu-Muslim discord. Untouchability is the curse of Hinduism and therefore of India. The taint is so pervasive that it haunts a man even after he has changed over to another faith.

Legal Practice and Satyagraha

Q. Knowing as you do how lying and deceit have become the stock-in-trade of the legal profession in this country, would you permit practising lawyers to enlist as active Satyagrahis?

A. I am unable to subscribe to your sweeping proposition. The fact that a lawyer wants to become a Satyagrahi presupposes on his part a certain standard of purification. No doubt there may be, to my knowledge there are, black sheep in the Congress. This is inevitable in any big organization. But it would be unbecoming of a Satyagrahi to condemn a man because he belongs to a certain profession.

Satyagraha and Obstructionism

Q. Is the policy of obstructionism compatible with Satyagraha? Can a Satyagrahi, who is supposed to stand for principles rather than party, adopt one attitude with regard to a measure when it is sponsored by his party, and another when the same measure is sponsored by the opposite party? Would you approve of this policy in Municipalities and District Boards as is being done by some Congressmen at present?

A. I have always opposed obstruction as being anti-Satyagraha. Congressmen, to be correct in their behaviour, should always give co-operation to their opponents when the latter are in a majority and adopt any wise measure. The object of Congressmen should never be attainment of power for power's sake. Indeed such discriminatory co-operation will enhance the prestige of the Congress and may even give it majority.

Harijan, 25-5-'40

FIVE QUESTIONS

1. Can Satyagrahis (i.e. those who have signed the Satyagraha pledge) offer defence when they are arrested ?

2. May a Satyagrahi make an effort to get better class treatment, i.e. ' A ' or ' B ' ?

3. Ought a Satyagrahi in jail to acquiesce in the conditions imposed upon him, or should he endeavour to secure what he regards more humane and satisfactory treatment ?

4. What is the minimum time for which a Satyagrahi ought to spin or what is the minimum quantity of yarn he should produce ?

5. Can a man sign the Satyagraha pledge immediately you declare civil disobedience and court arrest, or is there any definite period for which he should have remained a Satyagrahi to be eligible to take part in the civil disobedience campaign ?

Answers

1. There is no objection to offering defence, and in certain cases it would be a duty to do so as, say, in the Ajmer case.

2. In my opinion he should not make any attempt to alter the class. Personally I am against any classification.

3. He is entitled to make every legitimate effort for change to human conditions.

4. I think one hour per day should be the minimum and 300 rounds per hour is a reasonable speed. Men engaged in public work may spin less.

5. A man who intentionally refrains from signing a pledge in order to avoid fulfilment of conditions is a cheat and unworthy of being a Satyagrahi. But I can conceive an honest man just signing the pledge and straightaway going to jail. Even at the risk of losing prospective pledge-takers and those who have taken the pledge, I would say that there is no immediate prospect of my giving the call.

Harijan, 25-5-'40

THE SERMON ON THE MOUNT

Q. You often refer to the Sermon on the Mount. Do you believe in the verse, " If any man will take away thy coat, let him have thy cloak also " ? Does it not follow from the principle of non-violence ? If so, then do you advise the weak and poor tenant of a village to submit gladly to the violent encroachment of the zamindar on his ' *abadi* land ' or tenancy rights, which so often occurs in a village these days ?

A. Yes, I would unhesitatingly advise tenants to evacuate the land belonging to a tyrant. That would be like giving your cloak also when only the coat is demanded. To take what is required may be profitable ; to have more given to you is highly likely to be a burden. To overload a stomach is to court slow death. A zamindar wants his rent, he does not want his land. It would be a burden on him when he does not want it. When you give more to a robber than he needs, you spring a surprise on him, you give him a shock although agreeable. He has not been used to it. Historical instances are on record to show that such non-violent conduct has produced a wholesome effect upon evil-doers. These acts cannot be done mechanically ; they must come out of conviction and love or pity for the other man. Nor need you work out all the apparent implications of my answer. If you do, you will come across blind alleys. Suffice it to say that in the verse quoted by you Jesus put in a picturesque and telling manner the great doctrine of non-violent non-co-operation. Your non-co-operation with your opponent is violent when you give a blow for a blow, and is ineffective in the long run. Your non-co-operation is non-violent when you give your opponent all in the place of just what he needs. You have disarmed him once for all by your apparent co-operation, which in effect is complete non-co-operation.

Harijan, 13-7-'40

WHAT CAN A SOLITARY SATYAGRAHI DO ?

Q. There is one solitary Satyagrahi in one of our villages. The rest do not worry about violence or non-violence. What discipline is that single Satyagrahi to undergo ?

A. Yours is a good question. The solitary Satyagrahi has to examine himself. If he has universal love and if he fulfils the conditions implied in such a state, it must find its expression in his daily conduct. He would be bound with the poorest in the village by ties of service. He would constitute himself the scavenger, the nurse, the arbitrator of disputes, and the teacher of the children of the village. Every one, young and old, would know him ; though a householder he would be leading a life of restraint ; he would make no distinction between his and his neighbour's children ; he would own nothing but would hold what wealth he has in trust for others, and would, therefore, spend out of it just sufficient for his barest needs. His needs would, as far as possible, approximate those of the poor, he would harbour no untouchability, and would, therefore, inspire people of all castes and creeds to approach him with confidence.

Such is the ideal Satyagrahi. Our friend will always endeavour to come up to, wherever he falls short of, the ideal, fill in the gaps in his education, will not waste a single moment. His house will be a busy hive of useful activities centring round spinning. His , will be a well-ordered household.

Such a Satyagrahi will not find himself single-handed for long. The village will unconsciously follow him. But whether they do or not, at a time of emergency he will, single-handed, effectively deal with it or die in the attempt. But I firmly hold that he will have converted a number of others. I may add in this connection that I had come to Sevagram as a solitary Satyagrahi. Luckily or unluckily, I could not remain alone, several from outside came and settled with me. I do not know whether any inhabitant of the village proper can be counted as a Satyagrahi, but I do hope that some of them are unconsciously shaping themselves as such. Let me say that I do not fulfil all the tests I have laid down. But I should not have mentioned them, had I not been striving to put into practice all of them. My present ambition is certainly to make of Sevagram an ideal village. I know that the work is as difficult as to make of India an ideal country. But while it is possible for one man to fulfil his ambition with respect to a single village some day, one man's lifetime is too short to overtake the whole of India. But if one man can produce one ideal village, he will have provided a pattern not only for the whole country, but perhaps for the whole world. More than this a seeker may not aspire after.

Harijan, 4-8-'40

178

NON-VIOLENT NON-CO-OPERATION

Q. There is a report about some new scheme that you want to propound in one of your *Harijan* articles about non-violent non-co-operation if any invader came to India. Could you give us an idea ?

A. It is wrong. I have no plan in mind. If I had, I should give it to you. But I think nothing more need be added when I have said that there should be unadulterated non-violent non-co-operation, and if the whole of India responded and unanimously offered it, I should show that without shedding a single drop of blood Japanese arms — or any combination of arms — can be sterilized. That involves the determination of India not to give quarter on any point whatsoever and to be ready to risk loss of several milllion lives. But I would consider that cost very cheap and victory won at that cost glorious.

That India may not be ready to pay that price may be true. I hope it is not true, but some such price must be paid by any country that wants to retain its independence. After all, the sacrifice made by the Russians and the Chinese is enormous, and they are ready to risk all. The same could be said of the other countries also, whether aggressors or defenders. The cost is enormous. Therefore, in the non-violent technique I am asking India to risk no more than other countries are risking and which India would have to risk even if she offered armed resistance.

Harijan, 24-5-'42

179

SABOTAGE AND SECRECY

A friend put before Gandhiji some of his doubts. Was destruction of Government property violence ? " You say that nobody has a right to destroy any property not his own. If so, is not Government property mine ? I hold it is mine and I may destroy it."

" There is a double fallacy involved in your argument," replied Gandhiji. " In the first place, conceding that Government property is national property — which today it is not — I may not destroy it because I am dissatisfied with the Government. But even a national Government will be unable to carry on for a day if everybody claimed the right to destroy bridges, communications, roads, etc., because he disapproved of some of its activities. Moreover, the evil resides not in bridges, roads, etc., which are inanimate objects but in men. It is the latter who need to be tackled. The destruction of bridges, etc. by means of explosives does not touch this evil but only provokes a worse evil in the place of the one it seeks to end."

" I agree," rejoined the friend, " that the evil is within ourselves, not in the bridge which can be used for a good purpose as well as an evil one. I also agree that its blowing up provokes counter-violence of a worse type. But it may be necessary from a strategic point of view for the success of the movement and in order to prevent demoralization."

"It is an old argument," replied Gandhiji. "One used to hear it in the old days in defence of terrorism. Sabotage is a form of violence. People have realized the futility of physical violence but some people apparently think that it may be successfully practised in its modified form as sabotage. It is my conviction that the whole mass of people would not have risen to the height of courage and fearlessness that they have but for the working of full non-violence. How it works we do not yet fully know. But the fact remains that under non-violence we have progressed from strength to strength even through our apparent failures and setbacks. On the other hand terrorism resulted in demoralization. Haste leads to waste."

"We have found," rejoined the friend, "that a person who has had a schooling in violent activity comes nearer to true non-violence than one who has had no such experience."

"That can be true only in the sense that having tried violence again and again he has realized its futility. That is all. Would you maintain also that a person who has had a taste of vice is nearer to virtue than the one who has had none? For, that is what your argument amounts to."

The discussion then turned upon secrecy. The friend in question argued that whilst individual secrecy created a fear complex and was therefore an evil, organized secrecy might be useful. "It is no secrecy if the person concerned is boldly prepared to face the consequences of his action. He resorts to secrecy in order to achieve his object. He can refuse to take any part in subsequent interrogations during his trial. He need not make a false statement."

But Gandhiji was adamant. "No secret organization, however big, could do any good. Secrecy aims at building a wall of protection round you. *Ahimsa* disdains all such protection. It functions in the open and in the face of odds, the heaviest conceivable. We have to organize for action a vast people that have been crushed under the heel of unspeakable tyranny for centuries. They cannot be organized by any other than open truthful means. I have grown up from youth to 76 years in abhorrence of secrecy. There must be no watering down of the ideal. Unless we cling to the formula in its fulness, we shall not make any headway."

Harijan, 10-2-'46

180

SATYAGRAHA IN FACE OF HOOLIGANISM

A friend has gently posed the question as to what a Satyagrahi should do to prevent looting by *goondas*. If he had understood the secret of Satyagraha he would not have put it.

To lay down one's life, even alone, for what one considers to be right, is the very core of Satyagraha. More, no man can do. If a man is armed with a sword he might lop off a few hands but ultimately he must surrender to superior force or else die fighting. The sword of the Satyagrahi is love and the unshakable firmness that comes from it. He will regard as brothers the hundreds of *goondas* that confront him and instead of trying to kill them he will choose to die at their hands and thereby live.

This is straight and simple. But how can a solitary Satyagrahi succeed in the midst of a huge population? Hundreds of hooligans were let loose on the city of Bombay for arson and loot. A solitary Satyagrahi will be like a drop in the ocean. Thus argues the correspondent.

My reply is that a Satyagrahi may never run away from danger, irrespective of whether he is alone or in the company of many. He will have fully performed his duty if he dies fighting. The same holds good in armed warfare. It applies with greater force in Satyagraha. Moreover, the sacrifice of one will evoke the sacrifice of many and may possibly produce big results. There is always this possibility. But one must scrupulously avoid the temptation of a desire for results.

I believe that every man and woman should learn the art of self-defence in this age. This is done through arms in the West. Every adult man is conscripted for army training for a definite period. The training for Satyagraha is meant for all, irrespective of age or sex. The more important part of the training here is mental, not physical. There can be no compulsion in mental training. The surrounding atmosphere no doubt acts on the mind but that cannot justify compulsion.

It follows that shopkeepers, traders, mill-hands, labourers, farmers, clerks, in short, every one ought to consider it his or her duty to get the necessary training in Satyagraha.

Satyagraha is always superior to armed resistance. This can only be effectively proved by demonstration, not by argument. It is the weapon that adorns the strong. It can never adorn the weak. By weak is meant the weak in mind and spirit, not in body. That limitation is a quality to be prized and not a defect to be deplored.

One ought also to understand one of its other limitations. It can never be used to defend a wrong cause.

Satyagraha brigades can be organized in every village and in every block of buildings in the cities. Each brigade should be composed of those persons who are well-known to the organizers. In this respect Satyagraha differs from armed defence. For the latter the State impresses the service of everybody. For a Satyagraha brigade only those are eligible who believe in *ahimsa* and *satya*. Therefore, an intimate knowledge of the persons enlisted is necessary for the organizers.

Harijan, 17-3-'46

181

THE NON-VIOLENT SANCTION

Q. What is the place of Satyagraha in making the rich realize their duty towards the poor ?

A. The same as against the foreign power. Satyagraha is a law of universal application. Beginning with the family its use can be extended to every other circle. Supposing a land-owner exploits his tenants and mulcts them of the fruit of their toil by appropriating it to his own use. When they expostulate with him he does not listen and raises objections that he requires so much for his wife, so much for his children and so on. The tenants or those who have espoused their cause and have influence will make an appeal to his wife to expostulate with her husband. She would probably say that for herself she does not need his exploited money. The children will say likewise that they would earn for themselves what they need.

Supposing further that he listens to nobody or that his wife and children combine against the tenants, they will not submit. They will quit if asked to do so but they will make it clear that the land belongs to him who tills it. The owner cannot till all the land himself and he will have to give in to their just demands. It may, however, be that the tenants are replaced by others. Agitation short of violence will then continue till the replacing tenants see their error and make common cause with the evicted tenants. Thus Satyagraha is a process of educating public opinion, such that it covers all the elements of society and in the end makes itself irresistible. Violence interrupts the process and prolongs the real revolution of the whole social structure.

The conditions necessary for the success of Satyagraha are : (1) The Satyagrahi should not have any hatred in his heart against the opponent. (2) The issue must be true and substantial. (3) The Satyagrahi must be prepared to suffer till the end for his cause.

Harijan, 31-3-'46

182

MY FAITH IN NON-VIOLENCE

[From a talk after the evening prayer on board the ship at Suez on the way to London for the Round Table Conference.]

I have found that life persists in the midst of destruction and, therefore, there must be a higher law than that of destruction. Only under that law would a well-ordered society be intelligible and life worth living. And if that is the law of life, we have to work it out in daily life. Wherever there are jars, wherever you are confronted with an opponent, conquer him with love. In a crude manner I have worked it out in my life. That does not mean that all my difficulties are solved. I have found, however, that this law of love has answered as the law of destruction has never done. In India we have had an ocular demonstration of the operation of this law on the widest scale possible. I do not claim therefore that non-violence has necessarily penetrated the three hundred millions, but I do claim that it has penetrated deeper than any other message, and in an incredibly short time. We have not been all uniformly non-violent ; and with the vast majority, non-violence has been a matter of policy. Even so, I want you to find out if the country has not made phenomenal progress under the protecting power of non-violence.

It takes a fairly strenuous course of training to attain to a mental state of non-violence. In daily life it has to be a course of discipline though one may not like it, like for instance, the life of a soldier. But I agree that, unless there is a hearty co-operation of the mind, the mere outward observance will be simply a mask, harmful both to the man himself and to others. The perfect state is reached only when mind and body and speech are in proper co-ordination. But it is always a case of intense mental struggle. It is not that I am incapable of anger, for instance, but I succeed on almost all occasions to keep my feelings under control. Whatever may be the result, there is always in me a conscious struggle for following the law of non-violence deliberately and ceaselessly. Such a struggle leaves one stronger for it. Non-violence is a weapon of the strong. With the weak it might easily be hypocrisy. Fear and love are contradictory terms. Love is reckless in giving away, oblivious as to what it gets in return. Love wrestles with the world as with the self and ultimately gains a mastery over all other feelings. My daily experience, as of those who are working with me, is that every problem lends itself to solution if we are determined to make the law of truth and non-violence the law of life. For truth and non-violence are, to me, faces of the same coin.

The law of love will work, just as the law of gravitation will work, whether we accept it or not. Just as a scientist will work wonders out of various applications of the law of nature, even so a man who applies the law of love with scientific precision can work greater wonders. For the force of non-violence is infinitely more wonderful and subtle than the material forces of nature, like, for instance, electricity. The men who discovered for us the law of love were greater scientists than any of our modern scientists. Only our explorations have not gone far enough and so it is not possible for every one to see all its working. Such, at any rate, is the hallucination, if it is one, under which I am labouring. The more I work at this law the more I feel the delight in life, the delight in the scheme of this universe. It gives me a peace and a meaning of the mysteries of nature that I have no power to describe.

The Nation's Voice, part II, pp. 109-10

183

THE FUTURE

A friend writing from America propounds the following two questions :

"1. Granted that Saytagraha is capable of winning India's independence, what are the chances of its being accepted as a principle of State policy in a free India ? In other words, would a strong and independent India rely on Satyagraha as a method of self-preservation, or would it lapse back to seeking refuge in the age-old institution of war, however defensive its character ? To restate the question on the basis of a purely theoretic problem : Is Satyagraha likely to be accepted only in an up-hill battle, when the phenomenon of martyrdom is fully effective, or is it also to be the instrument of a sovereign authority which has neither the need nor the scope of behaving on the principle of martyrdom ?

"2. Suppose a free India adopts Saytagraha as an instrument of State policy how would she defend herself against probable aggression by another sovereign State ? To restate the question on the basis of a purely theoretic problem : What would be the Satyagrahic action-patterns to meet the invading army at the frontier ? What kind of resistance can be offered the opponent before a common area of action, such as the one now existing in India between the Indian nationalists and the British Government, is established ? Or should the Satyagrahis withhold their action until after the opponent has taken over the country ? "

The questions are admittedly theoretical. They are also premature for the reason that I have not mastered the whole technique of non-violence. The experiment is still in the making. It is not even in its advanced stage. The nature of the experiment requires one to be satisfied with one step at a time. The distant scene is not for him to see. Therefore, my answers can only be speculative.

In truth, as I have said before, now we are not having unadulterated non-violence even in our struggle to win independence.

As to the first question, I fear that the chances of non-violence being accepted as a principle of State policy are very slight, so far as I can see at present. If India does not accept non-violence as her policy after winning independence, the second question becomes superfluous.

But I may state my own individual view of the potency of non-violence. I believe that a State can be administered on a non-violent basis if the vast majority of the people are non-violent. So far as I know, India is the only country which has a possibility of being such a State. I am conducting my experiment in that faith. Supposing, therefore, that India attained independence through pure non-violence, India could retain it too by the same means. A non-violent man or society does not anticipate or provide for attacks from without. On the contrary, such a person or society firmly believes that nobody is going to disturb them. If the worst happens, there are two ways open to non-violence. To yield possession but non-co-operate with the aggressor. Thus, supposing that a modern edition of Nero descended upon India, the representatives of the State will let him in but tell him that he will get no assistance from the people. They will prefer death to submission. The second way would be non-violent resistance by the people who have been trained in the non-violent way. They would offer themselves unarmed as fodder for the aggressor's cannon. The underlying belief in either case is that even a Nero is not devoid of a heart. The unexpected spectacle of endless rows upon rows of men and women simply dying rather than surrender to the will of an aggressor must ultimately melt him and his soldiery. Practically speaking there will be probably no greater loss in men than if forcible resistance was offered ; there will be no expenditure in armaments and fortifications. The non-violent training received by the people will add inconceivably to their moral height. Such men and women will have shown personal bravery of a type far superior to that shown in armed warfare. In each case the bravery consists in dying, not in killing. Lastly, there is no such thing as defeat in non-violent resistance. That such a thing has not happened before is no answer to my speculation. I have drawn no impossible picture. History is replete with instances of individual non-violence of the type I have mentioned. There is no warrant for saying or thinking that a group of men and women cannot by sufficient training act non-violently as a group or nation. Indeed the sum total of the experience of mankind is that men somehow or other live on. From which fact I infer that it is the law of love that rules mankind. Had violence, i.e. hate, ruled us, we should have become extinct long ago. And yet the tragedy of it is that the so-called civilized men and nations conduct themselves as if the basis of society was violence. It gives me ineffable joy to make experiments proving that love is the supreme and only law of life. Much evidence to the contrary cannot shake my faith. Even the mixed non-violence of India has supported it. But if it is not enough to convince an unbeliever, it is enough to incline a friendly critic to view it with favour.

Harijan, 13-4-'40

INDEX

ACCOUNT KEEPING, its purification, 264, 335

Action, if not *yajna*, promotes bondage, 48

Ahimsa, 40-42, 91-92; and Truth are two sides of a coin, 42; cannot be subject to decision of majority, 221; hurt by evil thought, 78; its power, 285-87; never faileth, 220-22; only force of universal application, 78; positive active state of love, 161; who obeys, cannot marry, 43; with, guiding all would be well, 221; see Non-violence

A. I. C. C., at Ahmedabad passes Satyagraha resolution (1930) under Gandhiji's leadership, 239

Allegiance, oath of, to British Government is meaningless, 160

Anand, Swami, made Navajivan sound business proposition, 267

Anarchist, enemy of State and misanthrope, 60

Anasuyabehn, Gandhiji's comrade in Kheda, 205; her arrest inflamed labour, 27

Aney, his resignation, 258

Anti-untouchability movement, does not aim at inter-dining or inter-marrying, 185; meant to throw open all public wells, roads, schools, temples etc. to suppressed classes, 185

Arms, laying down of, risky step in non-co-operation, 151

Army, daring to pass over corpses of non-violent men once would not repeat the experiment, 361

Arrest, normal condition of a non-co-operator, 172

Asiatic Act of 1907 of Transvaal, 35

Attachment, freedom from, is God-realization, 42

Auditing, 264, 335

BANDE MATARAM, 62, 63

Banker, Shankarlal, Gandhiji's comrade in Kheda, 205

Bardoli Satyagraha (1922) its resolution of no-tax campaign, 209-10; its suspension, 186; its suspension is the wisest, 223

Bardoli Satyagraha (1928), is sign of the times, 218; is to be kept isolated, 215; its refusal to pay unjust assessment, 214; its spread can be limited by how much government wants to go, 216; its success should be consolidated by constructive work, 217; means only non-payment of a portion of tax unjustly imposed, 214; not directed for attaining Swaraj, 214; people should recognize that non-violent combination to vindicate Truth can be formed, 218; Sardar Vallabhbhai invited to take lead, 214; seeks an independent, judicial and open enquiry, 213; settlement, 217-18

Bavazeer, Imamsaheb, 266

Belief, in God is Satyagrahi's mainstay, 364; that suffering would melt heart is necessary for Satyagraha, 363

Bengal, seethes with violence because of government oppression, 259

Bengal Provincial Congress Committee, may start Satyagraha on its initiative, 301

Blacklegs, would be found in every struggle, 73

Blocking, of ways to temples etc. is compulsion, 201

cipline regarding prayer, spinning and diary, 236; intends to serve Britain even by non-co-operation, 227; invites prospective Satyagrahis to consult him, 71; is against classification in jails, 374; is arrested for Salt Satyagraha, 276-77; is authorized by Working Committee to start Salt Satyagraha, 220; is inundated with telegrams not to continue Satyagraha (1931), 278; is paralysed by blood spilt by non-co-operators, 61; issues instructions to individual Satyagrahis, 302; lays down rules for picketing, 334-37; on boycott and picketing of liquor and foreign cloth shops, 333-34; on boycott of British goods, 145-46; on *brahmacharya*, 95; on constructive programme, 100-01; on Dandi Women's Conference, 328-30; on Frontier Provinces violence, 333; on *hatha-yoga*, 93; on Hindu Muslim question, 250-51; on his picketing campaign in S. Africa, 339; on how to deal with a thief, 350; on how to resist foreign invasion by non-violence, 377-78; on Jews' persecution by Germans, 348-50; on Nandanar, 72; on Rajkot Award, 293; on Rajkot fast, 321-23; on relations between constructive programme and Satyagraha, 368; on Satyagraha against Colour Bar Bill, 347; on women's role in Satyagraha, 325-41; opines Indians are cautious and slow to move, 158; organizes Satyagraha in Kheda, 204-08; prescribes individual C.D. regarding Bengal detenus, 70; prohibited from going to Punjab, 9; protests he does not intend to embarrass either British or Muslim League, 306; proud of

Ashram having many noble characters, 312; raises Satyagrahi Corps in Bombay, 76; realizes his error in calling upon people to launch C. D. in 1920, 74; realizes progress of training in Satyagraha would not be rapid, 76; refuśes to give information to police about persons confessing their guilt to him, 352; refuses (1930) to return to Ashram without Swaraj, 246; says all Satyagraha laws are not still found, 353; says chances of non-violence being accepted as a State policy are very slight, 385-87; says he counted no stake too great in following non-violence, 355; says he is by nature law-abiding, 365-66; says he is evolving, 297; says he is neither a saint nor a politician, 108-12; says he is not incapable of anger, 384; says he might offer Satyagraha by fast if violence is repeated, 332; says he would begin Dharasana raid to divert government wrath in a clean manner, 275; says his non-violence has somewhat shaken British misrule, 355; says his task will be done if he and his Dandi comrades perish in Satyagraha (1930), 233; serves Britain blindly till 1919, 227; stiffens in his demands upon would-be Satyagrahis, 295; still to demonstrate Satyagraha to be assimilable *en masse*, 72; suggests *hijrat* to Bardoli people, 212; suggests Satyagraha in 1930 must continue in spite of violence, 222; suspends C. D. (1919), 25; suspends Rajkot Satyagraha, 301; takes survey of Salt Satyagraha, 258-64; urges concentration on Swadeshi as a step to C. D., 173; utters warning to those intending to launch